KIBBUTZ
BUCHENWALD

KIBBUTZ BUCHENWALD

Survivors and Pioneers

Judith Tydor Baumel

Rutgers University Press
NEW BRUNSWICK, NEW JERSEY

Library of Congress Cataloging-in-Publication Data

Baumel, Judith Tydor, 1959–
    [Kibuts Bukhenvald. English]
    Kubbutz Buchenwald : survivors and pioneers / Judith Tydor Baumel ;
based on a translation by Dena Ordan.
        p.   cm.
    Includes bibliographical references and index.
    ISBN 0-8135-2336-2 (cloth : alk. paper). — ISBN 0-8135-2337-0
(paper : alk. paper)
        1. Holocaust survivors—Germany—Societies, etc. 2. Labor
Zionists—Germany—Societies, etc. 3. Jews—Germany—History—1945–
4. Holocaust survivors—Israel. I. Title.
DS135.G332B3813   1997
940.53′18—dc20   96-18311
                                                                        CIP

British Cataloging-in-Publication information available

A version of this book was published in Hebrew in 1995 by Kibbutz Hameuehad
and Beit Lochamei Hagetaot in Tel Aviv.

This translation copyright © 1997 by Judith Tydor Baumel

Based on the translation by Dena Ordan

Manufactured in the United States of America

In memory of my father, Yechezkel Tydor

Contents

Preface

My "love affair" with Kibbutz Buchenwald dates from the summer of 1968, when I was nine years old. One hot August morning, when I was visiting Jerusalem with my parents, a man fell out of the sky and landed at my feet. Having dropped from what was actually the porch of a nearby building, he embraced my embarrassed father while shouting at the top of his voice, "It's Tydor! It's Tydor!" My mother, who had witnessed similar encounters on previous visits to Israel, nonchalantly watched the spectacle unfold. Seeing my open-eyed stare, she attempted to reassure me, saying, "Don't worry, it must be one of your father's boys from Buchenwald." A few minutes later, when we were all seated in a café on the busy thoroughfare, my father explained that the "angel from the sky" was not from the Buchenwald concentration camp, but from Kibbutz Buchenwald. Of the camp I had already heard; about the kibbutz, not as yet. As we sat, watching the hustle and bustle of the Israeli capital from the recesses of the café, I was introduced to another facet of my father's unusual biography and made my first acquaintance with a kibbutz that bore the name of a concentration camp. In between sips of Jaffa orange juice I learned of a different kind of struggle that my father and his friends from the Holocaust had undergone, not one of survival but of rebirth, as they began piecing together the threads of their former lives. The pivot around which these new lives revolved was Kibbutz Buchenwald, the Zionist training farm that they founded shortly after liberation, the first of its kind to be established in postwar Germany.

My conscious decision to write the story of Kibbutz Buchenwald was certainly not made on that occasion. Years passed before I met the kibbutz's founders and members, before I took an interest in the details of its founding, and more time went by before I conceived of Kibbutz Buchenwald as a research project and began to assemble data preparatory to writing a book. Undoubtedly, though, the initial spark was ignited on that hot morning in Jerusalem, when two men with blue numbers tattooed on their arms embraced in the street, their eyes brimming with tears.

Over a period of several years, I compiled documentary data on Kibbutz Buchenwald, and interviewed various individuals who had been involved with the kibbutz—founders, *chalutzim* (Zionist pioneers), American GIs, Jewish Brigade members, as well as representatives of *Yishuv* (pre-State Israel) institutions and the settlement movements. Although I had amassed a considerable amount of material during the 1980s, I put off the actual writing of this book until the summer of 1991. At that point, what had started as a leisurely research project ended up as a race against time. In the spring of 1992 my father became seriously ill, and the final chapters were written by his sickbed, in the hope that he would live to see them. Although I was privileged to have him read the book almost in its entirety, he succumbed to his illness in the spring of 1993, before the abridged Hebrew version of the book was published.

Many individuals believed in this book even before I myself was convinced of its existence. Yisrael Gutman and Yehudah Bauer of the Institute of Contemporary Jewry, at the Hebrew University, Jerusalem, and Dan Michman, chairman of the Institute of Holocaust Studies at Bar-Ilan University, provided unfailing support and encouragement. Four friends deserve special mention: Yechiam Weitz, with ironic humor that matches his depth of knowledge regarding the Israeli political scene, unlocked the secrets of Israeli politics in the forties and fifties for me; Yoav Gelber, military expert par excellence, helped me to delve into the inner workings of the Jewish Brigade and its interaction with the Jewish DPs (displaced persons); Aviva Halamish, with unique insight into the role of immigration in the Middle East, taught me much about illegal immigration to Palestine and about British government policy toward the DPs; and Eli Tzur, a unique scholar and unrivaled friend, generously devoted hours of his time to reviewing the history of the different kibbutz movements and, above all, provided unending support and encouragement throughout the various stages of research and writing. Many others saw me through the crises that accompany the writing of every book. Among them I must single out Shmuel Almog, Dana Arditi, Yehudah Ben-Avner, Chava Eshkoli, Ya'akov Goldstein, William Helmreich, Menachem Kaufman, Nehemiah Levtzion, Penina Meizlish, Avihu Ronen, Chaim Shatzker, Kenneth R. Stow, Zev Tzachor, Hannah Yablonka, Mira Yungman, and finally my dear friend and editor of the Hebrew edition, Zev Utitz. Some read parts of the book while it was in progress, and I thank them for their insightful comments. My heartfelt thanks to all.

It is a pleasant task to thank the directors of the archives and the librarians who assisted me in locating important and fascinating material. I must single out for special thanks Sarah Erez of the Hakibbutz Hameuchad Archive at Yad Tabenkin, Yisrael Chofesh of the Kibbutz Afikim Archive, and Akiva Eiger, director of the Kibbutz Netzer Sereni Archive. At Netzer Sereni, I found Avraham and Lola Ahuvia, and Pize and Hilda Simcha particularly helpful. Finally, the research and translation of this book were made possible through the generous assistance of the following awards, prizes, and foundations: the Memorial Foundation for Jewish Culture, the Blitzer Prize in memory of their daughter Shoshana who perished in the Holocaust, The Open University and Bar-Ilan University research prizes, and the H. and I. Brettler, S. and G. Hershdorfer, R. and S. Kantrowitz, and S. and M. Brettler grants.

Dena Ordan, faithful translator, editor, colleague, and friend, deserves the highest praise for her translation of the original Hebrew manuscript upon which the English book is based. To my colleagues at the University of Haifa and the Open University, my thanks for providing supportive scientific environments for composing this book. Finally to Martha Heller of Rutgers University Press, my unending thanks for the support, assistance, guidance, and above all, patience that she showed during the editing of this book. Many thanks also to Adaya Henis and to the staff of Rutgers University Press for their assistance and support.

All members of my family bore the trials and tribulations that accompanied this book's birth pangs. While they shared my excitement and scholarly enthusiasm, they also suffered from the absence of a wife, daughter, and mother who was glued to the word processor as this book took shape. However, above all, this book is dedicated to the memory of my late father, Yechezkel Tydor, a unique person who unfailingly encouraged my development as a researcher, author, daughter, and human being. It is privilege to have had such a parent. Without him this book would never have been born, and, more important, without him it is even doubtful whether Kibbutz Buchenwald would ever have been created.

Ramat Gan, 1996

KIBBUTZ
BUCHENWALD

PART ONE:

THE DREAM

". . . the words 'the remnant of Israel' or 'a remnant shall return' and all the prophecies regarding a sole survivor from a city have now acquired an entirely different connotation. Suddenly, they have become dreadful words for us. . . ."

—*Berl Katznelson: Mapai secretariat meeting,*
5 January 1944

INTRODUCTION

The Founders

IN THE SPRING AND SUMMER OF 1945, Germany was a strange mixture of contrasts—a place where the illogical, or even the impossible, could become a reality overnight. The "omnipotent" Nazis had been defeated; millions of forced laborers, "resettled" ethnic Germans, and prisoners of war traversed the country in an attempt to return to their homelands; tens of thousands of liberated Jews were slowly beginning to piece together the interrupted mosaic of their lives. Among this group were sixteen survivors of the Buchenwald concentration camp who on June 3, 1945, founded the first postwar kibbutz training farm (*hachsharah*) in liberated Germany. Scarcely two months had passed since the camp's liberation and less than four weeks since the war's end. What caused a handful of survivors to take their fate into their own hands within days of their liberation, at a time when the majority were barely making tentative steps toward rehabilitation, waiting passively in the camps for orders from the occupying forces? From what wellsprings did they draw the physical and emotional strength to being life anew as Zionist pioneers in a world that had turned upside down?[1]

Kibbutz Buchenwald is the story of a nightmare that became a dream and a dream that became a reality. Emerging from the depths of the liberated concentration camp, a group of sixteen gaunt and battered young men set out to fulfill a dream that they had carried throughout the war and that, in turn, had carried them through the cataclysm they were forced to endure. Forming the first Zionist pioneering training center in postwar Germany, the rapidly growing group of young Holocaust survivors took its first steps to become free Jews in their own country and became a symbol of hope and action among the masses of the she'erit hapletah—the surviving remnant of European Jewry.

Incorporating into the movement veteran Zionists and newcomers, orthodox and freethinking, and members of various Zionist political movements that were traditionally antagonistic to each other, this unique experiment in collective living took on a life of its own during its three years of existence on German soil. Between 1945 and 1948, over half a dozen groups of pioneers immigrated from the training farm in Germany to Palestine, with a third of them deciding to establish their own kibbutz in their new homeland. Others, unable to see themselves living in an agricultural communal setting after immigration, chose city life, either before or after the establishment of the State of Israel. Undaunted by political machinations and the reluctance of the kibbutz establishment in pre-State Israel to allow a group of Holocaust survivors to found a separate agricultural collective, members of Kibbutz Buchenwald eventually established their own settlement—later renamed Kibbutz Netzer Sereni—which exists until today. The story of these pioneers, both in Germany and in Palestine, and their physical, psychological, ideological, and political struggles, form the nucleus of this book.

Our examination of Kibbutz Buchenwald's history is divided into two sections. Part 1, "The Dream," examines the kibbutz from its creation until the departure of the founding group for Palestine in late summer 1945. The opening chapter describes the liberation period and introduces the kibbutz founders. Chapters 2 and 3 describe the kibbutz's early days and analyze its coming-of-age process during the months of July and August 1945. Part 2, "The Reality," traces the kibbutz's subsequent history in Palestine and Germany, from the autumn of 1945 until the mid-1950s. Chapter 4 describes the efforts of Kibbutz Buchenwald's members to integrate themselves into pioneering life in the Yishuv (pre-State Jewish community in Israel) while undergoing agricultural training on Kibbutz Afikim in northern Palestine. Chapter 5 continues the saga of Kibbutz Buchenwald in Germany until its dissolution in 1948, its training farms providing reinforcements for the group that was already acclimatizing in Palestine. Chapter 6 returns us to the Yishuv, where we accompany the members of Kibbutz Buchenwald until 1948, when they established their own independent settlement at Bir Salim, which eventually became the present-day Kibbutz Netzer Sereni. The chapter carries them into the mid-1950s, when the kibbutz began taking on its final form. The concluding chapter analyzes the story of Kibbutz Buchenwald in historical perspective, comparing it to other enterprises established by the Holocaust survivors who immigrated to Israel.

In addition to analyzing the specific history of Kibbutz Buchenwald by chronologically studying the development of its operative, instrumental, and integrative patterns, we will also examine the kibbutz in a larger context by placing it within several conceptual frameworks. In addition to examining Kibbutz Buchenwald's position within the broader concept of communes in general, we will observe it against the background of the European scene, asking where Kibbutz Buchenwald belongs within the larger context of the nature and activity of the *she'erit hapletah* (Holocaust survivors) in Europe. Furthermore, we will explore the link between the plight of postwar European Jewry and the solution of the Palestine problem. Finally, we will move to the Yishuv/Israeli scene, exploring how Kibbutz Buchenwald attempted to express its unique, nonpartisan identity as compared to other kibbutzim similarly initiated by European Holocaust survivors. These conceptual frameworks will provide the added perspective necessary to expand the saga of Kibbutz Buchenwald from an isolated episode in the history of the she'erit hapletah into a test case, a microcosm incorporating various elements that played a major role in the life of the survivors in Europe during the immediate postwar years.

CHAPTER ONE

From Death March
to Liberation

"Shalom aleykhem yidn: Ihr send frei."
(Yiddish for "Greetings, Jews:
You are free.")

JANUARY 1945: snow, wind, biting cold; the middle of one of the worst winters in years—but January 1945 also signaled the dawning of the long-hoped-for end of both the "Final Solution" and the war. This was the transitional period when Germany's impending defeat turned from abstract hope into concrete reality, becoming *"nunter vie varter"* ("nearer rather than farther") in the words of the Yiddish saying. Throughout the month of January, inmates of the Auschwitz-Birkenau concentration camp could make out the sound of nearby Russian artillery fire. For the umpteenth time since 1942, rumors flew: The Allies were near and liberation was imminent. As in the past, this dream rapidly dissipated. As the Russian forces drew near, the Germans implemented the last stage of the "Final Solution"—the "Death Marches." From dozens of camps in the East, hundreds of thousands of prisoners—including more than two hundred thousand Jews—were dragged across Europe in forced marches from one locale to another.[1]

These death marches were initiated at the orders of SS Reichsfuehrer Heinrich Himmler, who sought to transfer the prisoners, still a useful workforce, deeper into Germany and away from the Russian front.[2] No precise statistics are available regarding the number of prisoners who walked, or rode, hundreds of miles in open boxcars, in subzero temperatures. From Auschwitz alone, more than sixty-three thousand "starved prisoners [set out], trembling from the penetrating winter cold, clad in their thin striped pajamas, and shod with wooden shoes or rags."[3] These forced wanderings, which began in late January, were destined to last for months, well into May 1945. In the course of this four-month period, some two hundred fifty thousand prisoners died, due to exposure, starvation, and harsh treatment by the guards, mainly raw SS recruits who accompanied the prisoners on what was, for many, their final journey.

Among the tens of thousands of prisoners who marched through the gates of Auschwitz that snowy day were Arthur Poznansky and Yechezkel Tydor. Poznansky, a handsome young Jew in his late twenties, had been active in the Zionist Hechalutz pioneering movement in Germany prior to the war, serving as leader in the hachsharot at Haffelberg and Neuendorf in the early 1940s. Having arrived at Auschwitz in the last transport from Germany in 1943, Poznansky was almost immediately assigned to the Buna-Monowitz work camp (Auschwitz III). There, he organized the Zionist youth movement members into a group that he coordinated throughout his stay at the camp. During the death march of January 1945, Poznansky was separated from his youth group, which had been sent in the direction of Bergen-Belsen while he was heading toward Buchenwald.[4]

Yechezkel Tydor, who, together with Poznansky, marched from Buna to Buchenwald, had also organized a group of youths during the war years. Tydor, an observant Jew in his forties, was a Buchenwald "veteran" who had been transferred to Buna in late 1942. While in Buchenwald, he had attempted to mitigate the suffering of the camp's young inmates by organizing them and establishing a network of older prisoners to provide them with extra food and protection. He also made certain that the youths learned a trade, based on the assumption that this would enhance their chances of survival. In autumn 1942, he was transferred to Auschwitz; nonetheless, from time to time he received word from the group he had left behind in Buchenwald.

At the beginning of the death march, Tydor had no idea how many, if any, of his former circle had survived. In the bedlam surrounding the first twenty-four hours after they left Auschwitz, prisoners began attaching themselves to transports—groups of prisoners collected by the Nazis for transfer elsewhere—rumored to be leaving for a particular destination. Preferring to march to a known destination, rather than to risk the unknown, Tydor joined the party reputedly bound for Buchenwald. Poznansky, relying on his older comrade's judgement, chose to accompany Tydor and thousands of others in the march to Buchenwald. It quickly became apparent that they had made the right decision. Upon reaching Buchenwald, they were welcomed by the surviving members of Tydor's group; thus they immediately found themselves among friends.[5]

Among those greeting the newcomers to Buchenwald was Eliyahu Gruenbaum, Elik to his friends. Like Tydor a Buchenwald veteran, Gruenbaum had escaped the transports to Auschwitz in 1942 and thus he could remain in one camp for the duration of the war. Like Poznansky, Gruenbaum had been a chalutz before the war; as an active participant in

Tydor's Buchenwald aid network, Gruenbaum continued to look after youths from Zionist backgrounds throughout the war.[6]

These young protégés who joined Gruenbaum toward the war's end included the Gottlieb brothers—Avraham, Chaim Meir, and Shmuel—members of the left-wing Po'alei Zion (Zionist Workers) movement since the thirties. Their wartime vicissitudes were typical of much of Polish Jewry: wandering, slave labor, labor camps, and a forced trek to a concentration camp—in this case, Buchenwald. At Buchenwald, the trio met Elik. On February 5, 1945, Avraham began to keep the diary that would be his constant companion for the next eight months, through liberation, hachsharah, and immigration to Palestine. His first thoughts were: "I imagine that Buchenwald will be my last camp in this awful war. Moreover, I firmly believe that the war is nearing its end, and that we, the people of Buchenwald, will see an era of peace. Therefore, I have decided to take these pieces of paper and to write."[7]

In this diary, *As a Human Being in Buchenwald*, Avraham described camp life during the final months of the war:

> Every few days transports of inmates reach Buchenwald from different camps. How pitiful is the state of these new arrivals! The Auschwitz inmates, for example, were in transit for nine days, on foot and by open boxcar, with 130 people sandwiched in each car. Many froze to death. Others had frostbitten ears and fingers. Food was distributed only three times. And in what a fashion! Bread was flung into the crowded car—the lucky ones had their portion; the unlucky, none. They came to blows—consequently, their faces are bruised and torn. Many corpses were removed from the cars, and many are ill. The healthy are painfully thin. They have no flesh on their faces or bodies; they walk slowly on unsteady legs, and die, daily they die.[8]

Forced labor had come to a virtual halt in Buchenwald in February 1945 due to the disorganized administration and to the epidemics that swept through the camp. Avraham and his friends spent their days trying to organize food ("organize" was the term used in wartime and postwar Europe for "arranging or obtaining something"), taking short walks around the camp, and discussing the nature and goals of postwar Jewish society. Elik and his friends started a small commune patterned on the prewar kibbutz model, pooling food and resources and apportioning them according to individual need. "Time creeps," wrote Avraham on March 23.[9]

This was not true for long. During the month of March, the American Third Army was advancing toward Buchenwald, bringing with it a person destined to play a crucial role in the future of the Jewish inmates—a young Jewish American chaplain, Rabbi Herschel Schacter. Schacter, the youngest child of elderly parents, had volunteered to serve in the army in 1942. Upon reaching Europe in the autumn of 1944, Schacter found himself ministering to units numbering more than one hundred thousand soldiers. On March 29, the first day of Passover, these units crossed the Rhine into Germany and began a path that would take them to the Ohrdruf and Buchenwald concentration camps.[10]

In Buchenwald, the first day of Passover 1945 was characterized by chaos and confusion. Rumors flew, centering around the fear that the Germans were about to liquidate the camp. These rumors were confirmed on the bleak day of April 3, when hundreds of Jewish inmates were shipped off from Buchenwald to an unknown destination. The transports now became a daily occurrence, punctuated by the approaching American artillery fire, which could be clearly heard throughout the camp. Some prisoners placed large signs reading SOS, BUCHENWALD in the camp's empty lots, hoping that they would be spotted by American planes bombing the area. Others opted not to join the transports, choosing to hide until they could be liberated by the advancing Allied armies.[11] Avraham's diary clearly reflects the apprehensions of those remaining in the camp:

Fearful days. The threat of expulsion hangs over the Jews especially, and then over the remaining Buchenwald residents. [This fear] is like death. I hide— sleeping here and there. Or I do not sleep at all. I manage to escape the transports by running here, by fleeing there. I long to get through the final days of the war, to survive. I must taste freedom! These notes are hidden in my straw mattress for now, thrust deep into the straw. They too await liberation.[12]

Nightly, the camp inmates fell asleep to the sound of the approaching American artillery fire. On Wednesday morning, April 11, the remaining inmates were able to discern the sounds of machine-gun fire, a sure sign that the front was moving ever nearer. At dawn, many inmates decided to go into hiding until liberation. There, they waited the entire day until evening, after several chaotic hours when the inmates had taken over the camp. Yechezkel Tydor recalled the shouts heard in the camp at about four P.M., when the first American tanks arrived. Fearing that it was a cruel trick, prisoners nevertheless decided to take their chances rather than rot in their hiding places, and slowly they began to emerge, embracing one another. "From every corner of the camp we could hear the announcement over American loudspeakers— '*Ihr seid frei*'—you are free. This was the day of our liberation."[13]

Some forty years later, Rabbi Herschel Schacter recalled how the inmates were still "floating" when he first saw them at about five P.M. "They looked like walking corpses," he said. What drew his attention the most were the still-smoking chimneys that contained the remnants of the last camp victims. Schacter continued:

I got out of my army jeep and opened the crematorium door. At that moment, my heart broke. I stood there for maybe half an hour, or half a minute, I have no idea how long it was. When I turned away, I approached a soldier and asked whether any live Jews remained in the camp. Answering "Yes," he led me to one of the blocks. Upon entering, I saw pallets with people lying on lice-infested straw mattresses, people from another planet who stared at me wide-eyed. I shouted excitedly, "*Sholem aleykhem yidn: Ihr send frei. Ikh bin a Amerikaner ruv.*" ["Greetings, Jews: You are free. I am an American rabbi."] This was my first encounter with the survivors.[14]

The chaos that had prevailed for weeks prior to the arrival of the American forces was still apparent the following day, particularly in matters of food and administration. While attempting to restore a semblance of order to the camp, the U.S. Army quickly realized that it had to deal with a variety of national groups, each with different requests. Shortly after liberation, the inmates began to display outward signs of their various national identities. Patriotism began to rear its head, and various groups began to prepare their national flags in anticipation of liberation ceremonies and the return to their homelands. Indeed, the question of voluntary repatriation occupied more than a few inmates' thoughts almost from the moment of liberation. Here, too, differences appeared between various national groups. The former inmates from Western, Northern, and Southern Europe were pressing to return immediately to their long-liberated homelands, while the former prisoners from Eastern Europe often debated the wisdom of returning to Communist-occupied areas. Furthermore, the liberated inmates' desires did not center solely around repatriation. Many healthy prisoners made known their desire to go to nearby villages and slake their hunger for revenge on the local population, while others wished to leave the camp immediately in order to search for relatives and friends. Individual soldiers were approached for assistance in these matters, and requests for then-unavailable transportation were the rule rather than the exception.

Even before attempting to organize the camp, the American army had to satisfy the inmates' primary physical needs—food, medicine, and corpse removal. In addition to the newly discovered vast food resources that the Nazis had kept hidden while the inmates starved, K rations were issued. Kosher food was virtually unobtainable, but due to the proximity to Passover, Rabbi Schacter still had dozens of boxes of matzah, which he distributed among the liberated Jews. Indeed, it was food, which had occupied the minds and dreams of inmates for years, that was both the former prisoners' salvation and their damnation. In liberated camps throughout Germany and Austria, kindhearted American soldiers, who had no inkling of the potentially tragic results of their generosity, offered unlimited and unsuitable food to liberated concentration camp inmates whose shrunken digestive systems could barely cope with more than a slice of bread at a time. Hundreds of cans of army meat were opened and consumed; the fatty protein caused indescribable agony to those who had undergone prolonged starvation. One former inmate recalled how the veteran prisoners burned wood and ate the charred remains as a preventive against the life-threatening intestinal gases that erupted with the first bites of normal food. However, most were unaware of the results of eating too much too soon or were incapable of controlling a hunger that had not been satisfied for years. Thus, in Buchenwald and other camps, time and again, hundreds of inmates died of overeating shortly after liberation, having tasted the flavor of freedom for only a day, or even less.[15]

Liberation marked the first step in a rehabilitation process that would take months, and for some stages, years. Physically, the camp inmates had to recover from years of deprivation, disease, and starvation. Apart from the difficulty of reaccustoming themselves to normal amounts of food, the survivors were beset with a plethora of medical problems, many of which only manifested themselves long after liberation. Some came out of the camp with scarred lungs, weakened hearts, atrophying muscles, and unusable limbs. Others bore visible scars and limps that would remind them of their wartime torture for the remainder of their lives. A number had undergone medical experiments rendering them incapable of producing children. These physical ailments and handicaps often had their psychological effect, causing various degrees of mental disturbances, anxiety-related syndromes, and the like, which would affect survivors for years to come.

As if that alone were not sufficient, in the spring of 1945, a familiar enemy raised its head; a typhus epidemic claimed many victims. Camp hospitals were filled with hundreds of makeshift beds in which typhus victims were placed until they recovered or succumbed. Army medical personnel gave untrained healthy survivors hasty instructions on how to care for the delirious patients, who were burning up with fever. Yechezkel Tydor recalled how he caught the disease in May 1945, spending over a week unconscious in the liberated camp's hospital. When he came back to life, his eyes swept around the room and lighted upon a familiar figure seated at the edge of his sickbed. During the entire week, a young liberated inmate with whom he had developed a close relationship during the war had sat at his bedside, saying psalms for Tydor's recovery. The older survivor was one of the lucky ones; most of the older and weaker liberated inmates did not survive their illness.

On the psychological level, matters were no less complex. After years of imprisonment and slavery, the liberated inmates now had to readjust themselves gradually to freedom. Practical issues such as obtaining clothing, toilet supplies, and wristwatches were accompanied by a psychological sense of being like Rip van Winkle; the survivors had woken up to a world in which six years had passed, while for them, time had stood still. Apart from the technical aspect of returning to life, survivors had now to grapple with questions pertaining not only to their present existence but to their future: What awaited them outside the camp? Had any family members survived the war? Were they to remain destitute, or could any of their former possessions be found somewhere in their former homelands? Above all, a momentous question persistently tormented their minds: Where would the liberated Jews go following their recovery?

Rabbi Schacter was able to provide a partial solution to this nagging question. During the initial days after liberation, this dynamic young officer met with some of the Jews in the camp in an attempt to persuade to concentrate their energies on recovery, leaving their concerns about the future temporarily in abeyance. Schacter's presence and devotion left a strong impression on his audience, including Avraham Gottlieb, who wrote in his diary of the handsome American soldier who has been wandering about the camp showing interest in the Jews. "He converses with us and makes speeches (in Yiddish)," wrote the young survivor. "He assures us that all American Jewry is behind us; their thoughts are with us, they rejoice that we have survived to the end of the war and empathize with our losses. As yet, he cannot inform us what will happen to us, where we will go. But we mustn't worry, he says, for someone is looking after us. We should be content for the moment with having achieved freedom."[16]

Schacter was a man not only of words, but of deeds. On Friday, April 20, a week after liberation, the rabbi, aided by religious camp inmates, organized a festive Friday evening service. This was the first public prayer service in the camp history, one that gave vent to religious as well as national feelings. While others had prepared flags, sung national anthems, and initiated national gatherings, Jews had, as yet, no opportunity to express an ethnic or national identity. Still in a state of shock, most Jews had found it difficult to direct attention to their unique status among the sea of released inmates. Thus, the Friday night prayer service enabled them to give concrete expression to their Jewishness.

The prayer service, which was held in the "exercise hall" (formerly a large punishment hut), the only building capable of holding more than a thousand people, quickly turned into a huge demonstration of Jewish identity. Tydor recalled the festive atmosphere pervading the hall, the hut packed with Jewish survivors, and the improvised platform from which Rabbi Schacter led the prayers:

It is impossible to describe the excitement on the part of observant and nonobservant Jews alike, who were able, for the first time since the war, to openly and fully identify as Jews. Many of us felt that this event symbolized the start of a new life. Where would this new life take us? It was too soon to think about that. For the moment, it sufficed to gather as Jews and to utter sincerely the words of the prayer *Lechah Dodi* [welcoming the Sabbath as a queen]: "Too long have you dwelt in the vale of tears. He will have compassion upon you."[17]

On this note of renewal and hope for the future, the Jews of Buchenwald concluded their first week as free men.

American Army Policy in Occupied Germany

Kibbutz Buchenwald was born within a specific historical context. The daring organizational initiative taken by a few survivors immediately after liberation was molded by a number of factors influencing not only the kibbutz but the she'erit hapletah in its entirety. The first factor was American army policy in occupied Germany during the spring and summer of 1945. Initially, this policy sought to regulate the lives of those concentration camp survivors liberated in Germany by the Allied forces. Concentrated mainly in the American zone, by spring 1945 the Jews among this group numbered some thirty thousand men and women. By the year's end, they had been joined by a second group—some ten thousand survivors from Eastern Europe, whose disenchanting exposure to postwar Polish anti-Semitism had dissuaded them from seeking rehabilitation in Poland. In 1946, a third group swelled the ranks of the survivors in Germany—tens of thousands of Jews exiled to the USSR during the war, who had returned to Poland with the waves of repatriation. These three groups—camp survivors, partisans, and the so-called Asiatics—differed in nature, composition, and behavior. Together, they comprised the turbulent human mosaic of the she'erit hapletah in Germany.[18]

As early as November 1943, representatives of the Allied governments grappled with the question of who would bear the responsibility for the survivors after liberation. At that time, they decided to create a central agency to deal with DPs in Europe—UNRRA, the United Nations Relief and Rehabilitation Administration. Reality, however, did not mirror expectation, and care of the DPs passed through several hands until UNRRA personnel finally appeared on the scene in the autumn of 1945. The multiplicity of agencies and the frequent transfer of authority hampered the formulation of a consistent DP policy. Consequently, during the spring and summer of 1945, the fate of the DPs in a particular region was usually determined by a single individual—the military officer in charge of the Displaced Persons Section of the civil administration in that zone.[19]

An additional problem facing American military personnel was the lack of clear instructions as to the special needs of the liberated Jewish prisoners. Before embarking on a European tour of duty, American military officers received detailed briefings regarding the treatment of enemy populations and liberated prisoners. Particular attention was devoted to the treatment of Soviet citizens liberated on German territory. However, few if any instructions were given regarding the treatment of surviving Jews, regardless of origin. Even after reaching Europe and beginning to sense that the Jewish DPs required different treatment than the non-Jewish ones because of their particular experiences and problems of repatriation, the commanding officers had nowhere to turn for official army directives addressing the situation. In the words of one army colonel in the American Eighth Army, responsible for overseeing the civil administration of the occupied Weimar region in which Buchenwald was situated, "They told me what to do with the Germans, what to do with the Poles, what to do with the Frenchmen. They even told me what to do with the Russians. But no one told me what to do with the Jews."[20]

Consequently, the prevalent attitude among members of the American military government in Germany toward the liberated Jews was at best, one of inaction and at worst, one of alienation. A prevalent approach combined "official" policy with a lack of preparation and plain ignorance. The claim that no instructions had been issued regarding "what to do with the Jews" reflects General Dwight D. Eisenhower's insistence that the Jews were a religious group, and not a distinct national or ethnic group. Accordingly, despite the distinct evidence that the problems of Jewish survivors—particularly those from Eastern Europe—strongly differed from those of other liberated prisoners, the commanders were not briefed on the particular problems of the Jewish DPs. Nor can it be denied that only a minority of these commanders knew anything about Germany, and even fewer still actually spoke German, thus effectively barring them from communicating with local residents and Jewish survivors alike. Matters did not improve with time. Within six months after the war, the original officer staff had accumulated enough seniority to request transfer back to the United States. Their replacements were generally young officers lacking military experience as well as the requisite sensitivity to handle severe social problems.

The most serious issue differentiating the Jewish DPs from the mass of displaced persons in Germany was that of repatriation. In spite of the official negligence of the unique Jewish plight, even the American high command was aware of the difficulties inherent in repatriating the Jews. An Allied army memorandum issued on April 16 declared that no DP was to be forcibly repatriated to his country of origin unless he had committed war crimes or was a Soviet citizen.[21] Nevertheless, many American commanders neglected to inform the Jews of the option to remain in the locale of liberation. This stemmed from their unfamiliarity with the memo's particulars, as well as from the inability to grasp why Eastern European Jews might wish to be recognized as a distinct nationality. The rapid repatriation of various nationals liberated in the concentration camp of Buchenwald was a major factor affecting the establishment of the kibbutz of the same name.

In addition to repatriation difficulties, the Jewish DPs' singular fate was further emphasized by the establishment of central DP centers in Germany and Austria. One of the underlying principles of American army policy during the spring of 1945 was the understanding that the liberated DPs had to be provided with some form of framework as soon as possible, even if it lacked the basic amenities necessary for a comfortable existence. Consequently, as early as the summer of 1945, the homeless DPs were assembled in centers established near or on the grounds of the liberated concentration camps. Conditions in these centers were deplorable: Up to four people shared a single bed; food rations were reminiscent of concentration camp portions; sanitary conditions were poor, and above all, Jewish DPs were forced to live side by side in uncomfortably close quarters with non-Jewish DPs, who often were exceedingly anti-Semitic. Only after Special U.S. Envoy Earl Harrison submitted a harrowing report to President Harry S. Truman in August 1945, regarding the conditions in these camps, did the American administration take steps to ameliorate the situation. Furthermore, only then did the American military commanders finally receive special instructions pertaining to the unique lot of the Jewish DPs. It took a unique commanding officer to understand and accept the exceptional situation of the Jewish DPs, and to be able to provide suitable solutions to their unparalleled problems.

THE JEWISH RESPONSE TO ALLIED ARMY POLICY

A second factor affecting the fate of Jews in occupied Germany in general, and shaping the future of Kibbutz Buchenwald in particular, was the Jewish response to Allied army policy. Unlike the members of other religious groups and nationalities, the liberated Jews had not experienced an immediate sense of relief immediately after their liberation by the Allied forces. The reality they were forced to confront, which included homelessness, anti-Semitism, and inter-Allied politics, was both complex and disheartening. Nevertheless, in view of the fact that most Allied commanders were incapable of comprehending the Jewish survivors' unprecedented lot, by and large, a good number of the Jewish DPs realized early that they would have to fend for themselves. After regaining their physical strength, the liberated Jews took active steps to regulate their lives in the DP camps. First, they rapidly established central administrative committees to organize their living conditions and present their demands to the camp administrators. These committees, which organized Jewish life in the camps, emerged when the survivors realized that they would need official representatives to negotiate with the occupying forces, and they formed the cornerstone of Jewish postwar organization in liberated Germany.

In addition to creating administrative and organizational frameworks, the Jewish DPs adopted a strong Zionist stance, demanding free immigration to Palestine and the establishment of a Jewish national homeland. Zionism often became their burning ideology, more out of a hatred of the Diaspora in general and of Europe in particular—a phenomenon characterizing many survivors—than out of love of the Zionist ideal. Both the organizational concept and the Zionist phenomenon were expressions of the survivors' fervent desire to control their own lives and determine their own future. Thus, as an internal she'erit hapletah leadership rapidly emerged, it was characterized by individuals who already had organizational experience and clearly formulated ideologies before they were caught up in the maelstrom of the Holocaust. Among them were the founders of Kibbutz Buchenwald.[22]

Issues of ideology aside, the survivors were also faced with immediate practical problems, one of which was their pressing material needs. Like others in postwar Germany, many survivors met basic needs through profiteering on the black market; some eventually turned a stopgap measure into a temporary profession. Supplies provided by the U.S. military forces could be sold or bartered for necessities not provided, or "luxuries," as they were called, that would make the existence in the DP camps bearable. Indeed, as in most occupied areas after devastating wars, the black market was one of the few institutions bridging the gaps between almost all sectors of society— Germans, Jews, American GIs, and Eastern European DPs. The early emergence of a black market in the liberated Buchenwald camp caused several older survivors to worry about the moral pollution of their young charges and thus was an immediate impetus for the creation of a pioneering Zionist framework outside of the camp's environs. These three tools of survival— central committees, Zionism, and black market trade—allowed the liberated Jews to cope with the surrealistic conditions of postwar Germany.

BRITISH POLICY ON PALESTINE

British immigration policy toward Palestine during the latter half of 1945 was a third factor shaping the fate of the DPs in Germany, and specifically that of the founders and members of Kibbutz Buchenwald. Toward the end of the war, policy makers in Britain had suggested gradually revoking the 1939 White Paper (the British document limiting immigration to Palestine to a total of seventy-five thousand within five years), in order to enunciate a new policy vis-a-vis the DP problem and the question of Palestine's future. In mid-July 1943, the Cabinet began to implement its new policy by deciding to permit immigration to Palestine to continue past the March 31, 1944, deadline set in the White Paper, until the full original quota of seventy-five thousand immigrants was reached. Only then would the immigration issue be reexamined. In December 1945, when the quota was finally reached, the Cabinet resolved to permit fifteen hundred individuals to enter Palestine monthly, until a decision would be made regarding the future of the British Mandate in Palestine.[23]

The condition of the DPs motivated two bodies in particular to exert pressure upon Great Britain to alter its immigration policy. The first was the Jewish Agency for Palestine, the official Jewish representative to the British government, responsible for matters of immigration to Palestine and internal Jewish administration in that area. Upon receiving initial information about the survivors, the Jewish Agency reopened the question of "certificates" (entry permits) to Palestine. Following internal discussion, the Jewish Agency leaders forwarded a request to the British government to allow one hundred thousand survivors to immigrate immediately. Simultaneously, the United States entered the picture when President Harry S. Truman appealed to Prime Minister Winston Churchill to lift all restrictions on immigration to Palestine. The British government's answer was delayed by the fall of Churchill's government, and in late August, Truman appealed to the new prime minister, Clement Atlee, to allow one hundred thousand European Jewish DPs to enter the British Mandate's borders. Truman's urgent request was largely prompted by the conclusions of the Harrison Report regarding the state of Jewish DPs in Germany.[24]

The British government now faced a quandary. On one hand, Britain had no interest in arousing Arab anger by changing its Palestine immigration policy. On the other hand, it could not ignore American pressure in the long run. Therefore, while the government denied the American request, it suggested the establishment of a joint Anglo-American committee that would examine the conditions of Jews in Europe, assess the absorption capacity of Palestine, and explore the possibility of absorption by other countries, including the United States and the British Commonwealth nations. Britain now desired to transform the United States from a critic into a full-fledged responsible partner, so it invited direct U.S. involvement in examining the broader issue of Palestine's future. On November 13, 1945, Foreign Secretary Ernest Bevin made an announcement to this effect in Parliament. Although Bevin reiterated what had been the official British line since the thirties—that the DP (then refugee) problem must be solved in the countries of origin, not in Palestine—his speech marked a turning point in British policy. Within the context of the proposed committee, Britain had finally agreed to recognize both a political and a practical link between the plight of European Jewry and the solution of the Palestine problem.[25]

Nevertheless, British government limitations on immigration to Palestine continued until the eventual establishment of the State of Israel in May 1948. Consequently, of the tens of thousands of survivors who attempted to make their way through the Mediterranean by clandestine routes, more than five thousand were caught en route and sent to British detention camps in Cyprus. Among the illegal immigrants, or *ma'apilim*, as they were known, were almost all of the members of Kibbutz Buchenwald who left Europe after the autumn of 1945.

ZIONIST GOALS AND DP POLICY

Zionist policy goals in the immediate postwar period were the fourth factor affecting the development of Kibbutz Buchenwald. Sparked by the encounter with Polish refugees who reached Teheran in the spring of 1942, the Yishuv leaders began debating how they would deal with the survivors. This initial confrontation not only shook the Yishuv's leadership; it raised fundamental questions regarding the nature of those who might survive the war and their future role in Zionist plans. At the war's end, when theory became reality and Yishuv leaders faced practical decisions, the debate over how to treat the survivors entered a new phase, in terms of both depth and intensity.[26]

Two factors significantly affected Zionist policy vis-à-vis the DPs: their image in the eyes of the Yishuv's leadership, and their perceived role in Zionist political calculations. A number of the Yishuv's top leaders, including David Ben-Gurion, head of the Yishuv labor party and later prime minister of Israel, viewed the survivors as an extremely problematic base for Palestine. Before the war, most potential immigrants to Palestine were granted entry certificates only if they were pioneers or could prove themselves able to contribute positively to the Yishuv. As a multifaceted population, the postwar survivor-immigrants would not necessarily have been able to meet these criteria. Despite potential problems, however, Ben-Gurion saw these immigrants as an essential factor in the Zionist political struggle for statehood, even if they did not appear as the primary human material from which the State would be built.

Accompanying this calculation, however, was an additional factor that often clashed with Ben-Gurion's acceptance of the survivors as one of the potential population bases for the "State in the making." Constantly aware of his uppermost consideration—the "good of the Jews in Palestine"—Ben-Gurion was occasionally forced to make a decision that appeared to be detrimental to the DPs, such as temporarily sacrificing their immediate good in order to make a political statement. Against this background, it is easier to understand what appears to have been a resolute Zionist debate about where to assemble the survivors—in Italy, which was much more convenient for immigration to Palestine, or in Germany, which was better suited as a fulcrum through which Ben-Gurion could sway world public opinion. Similarly, his attitude explains the instrumental approach adopted by much of the

Zionist leadership, which used the DP camps as a means of inducing Britain to change its immigration policy without regard for the survivors' immediate needs.[27]

While Ben-Gurion was formulating what critics called his cold political calculations, members of the Jewish Brigade were exhibiting a diametrically opposite response toward the survivors. These Jewish soldiers, who had fought as an independent unit in the British Army, rejected the ideological pragmatism espoused by Ben-Gurion and the top echelons of the Jewish Agency—"the instrumentality of realism employed to realize a visionary ideal," in the words of Meir Avizohar.[28] Soldiers like Chaim Ben-Asher, Aharon Hoter-Yishai, Ze'ev Birger, and Yosef Lavi (Levkowitz) responded to the survivors' needs, pushing aside calculations of political party particularism, which, they had been taught, should serve as their uppermost guide. Acting instinctively, these soldier-members made the survivors feel that regardless of their physical and psychological state, somehow or other the Brigade would assist them in reaching Palestine. Indeed, members of the Jewish Brigade played a pivotal role in organizing the illegal immigration of many groups of survivors, including dozens of chalutzim from Kibbutz Buchenwald.[29]

Before negotiating the passage between the reality of liberated Germany and the dream of Palestine that awaited them, the survivors had to cope with a plethora of situations reminiscent of the popular British song "The World Turned Upside Down." In the "kingdom of the absurd" founded by the Allies on the ruins of defeated Germany, image and reality often clashed in a grotesque parody of a mirror world. Kings were reduced to beggary, but every beggar could become a king, provided he could profitably navigate the waters of the black market, which flourished everywhere. In this new kingdom, American GIs discovered that the erstwhile "enemies of humanity"— the Germans—were ostensibly clean, polite, and diligent human beings, while the liberated Jews—the victims of Nazi persecution still living in the liberated camps or recently moved to filthy and overcrowded DP centers, appeared to be dirty and argumentative, if not repulsive. Educational and political emissaries sent by the Yishuv to assist the survivors in the DP camps underwent a similar educational process. As their acquaintance with the survivors deepened, more than one emissary concluded that this was not the ideal material with which to build the Jewish state. Amid all this, the illusory hopes of the liberators met the sobering rationalism of the camp graduates, who, with eyes that had seen the events of a thousand years, dubiously viewed the desperate attempt to restore order to a society that had descended to the depths of chaos.

Into that world, Kibbutz Buchenwald was born.

CHAPTER TWO

From Buchenwald
to Kibbutz Buchenwald

"But no one told me what to do with the Jews."

"And I—where will I go? Where shall I seek my home?"

THROUGHOUT APRIL AND MAY 1945, the liberating Allied forces in Germany slowly became aware of several troubling issues related to the war and its aftermath. The first was the sudden manifestation of nationalist sentiment among liberated prisoners before their repatriation. The second was the lack of any particular directives regarding the treatment of liberated Jews as opposed to other nationalities. The third was the need for a concerted policy with regard to lingering resentment, among both Jews and other liberated prisoners, against the Germans among whom they continued to live. In one form or another, each of these issues was directly connected to the development of American policy regarding Jewish DPs in Germany in general, and the establishment of Kibbutz Buchenwald in particular.

NATIONAL SENTIMENT

The illusory feelings of brotherhood among the camp inmates lasted for barely a week after liberation. On April 19, a memorial service was held for the victims of Buchenwald. Throughout the ceremony, the national flags, prepared during the first week following liberation to represent the entire spectrum of Buchenwald inmates, fluttered in the *appelplatz* (roll-call area, where the prisoners were counted by the Nazi guards), above a memorial that bore the inscription "51,000"—the number of inmates who had perished from the time of the camp's establishment in 1937. No Jewish flag was in evidence. On that day the Jews of Buchenwald took their place as Poles, Czechs, Frenchmen, Belgians, Germans, Dutch, Greeks, and Italians. No speeches were made in Yiddish—rather, Russian, Czech, German, French, and Polish were the order of the day. For the first time since their capture by the Nazis, the various groups in the camp all proclaimed their national identities with fanfare and long-forgotten pride. Anthems were sung, flags pieced together and exaltedly flown, national memories revived, and clandestine dreams expressed. At that time, little if any distinction was made between Jew and Gentile of a particular nationality. Momentarily, then, it seemed that the Jews had gained acceptance as normal citizens by their non-Jewish ex-compatriots, all being survivors of the Nazi terror.

This illusion was shattered less than a day later, when the Belgian, Dutch, and French contingents, Jews and non-Jews alike, set out westward. That moment accentuated the essential difference between these Jews and their German- or Polish-born coreligionists. A distinct note of envy and dejection is discernible in Avraham's description of the first departures from Buchenwald:

> The Frenchmen and the Belgians are going *home*. Yes indeed, they are going *home*, to their relatives, families, and neighbors. They go to those whom they love and who return their love. They are returning to their former lives. They are returning home. And I—where will I go? Where shall I seek my home? Where shall I find my family and relatives? I have neither.[1]

Avraham's longing for a "home" epitomized the dilemma confronting the majority of Polish Jews left in the camp: Where should they seek to make their homes? Was it feasible for them to consider returning to Eastern Europe, in view of the anti-Semitism that they had encountered there and the probability that the situation in Poland would be distinctly unfavorable to the surviving Jews? Why should they consider returning "home," when there was no home anymore: no parents, siblings, spouses to await them; no friends to welcome them back from the depths of hell to a normal existence? Yet how could they remain in Germany, the country responsible for their tortured existence during the past few years? If they decided to leave Germany and not return to Poland, who would grant them asylum? Where could they go?

The general Jewish feeling of homelessness was compounded by the growing contrast with the other DPs' budding nationalism and return home. By the fourth week of April, the repatriation of released Buchenwald inmates was proceeding apace. The first shock of liberation had passed, and the thousands of walking skeletons in the camp, who at war's end had barely retained the physical vestiges of humanity, were showing the first signs of recovery. Physical recovery was accompanied by psychological implications, however. Relatively physically healthy young Jews began to raise their heads and voice the question for which no one as yet had an answer: "What next?"

One answer, which took into account the risk of encountering Eastern European anti-Semitism, was to return home nevertheless to try to pick up the threads of their former lives. Some Jews, released from Buchenwald and other camps throughout Germany, began making their way back to Poland, Hungary, and Romania in the hope of encountering surviving friends and relatives, recovering lost possessions or property, and beginning their lives anew. Others, incapable of grappling with the dilemma, waited passively for instructions from the liberating forces as to where to go and what to do. Yet a third group of Jews, among whom were the founders of Kibbutz Buchenwald, expressed their national identity in the form of Zionist sentiment, which, as we have already seen in the previous chapter, began to take concrete expression throughout liberated Germany by the summer of 1945. A similar phenomenon had already evinced itself in Eastern Poland, where Zionist groups had begun to take shape in the autumn of 1944, almost immediately after liberation.

LINGERING RESENTMENT AGAINST GERMANS

Shortly after their liberation, Jews in Germany were forced to grapple with an issue that put their moral steadfastness to the test: How would they treat the defeated German population that, in their minds, either had collaborated with the Nazis or had stood idly by as the Jews met their gruesome fate? One survivor, now a noted Holocaust scholar, remembers accompanying a group that left a camp in order to wreak vengeance upon the local population in the form of rape, looting, and the like. When the group of young men opened the door of the first house in their path, they found a young German woman with a nursing infant in her arms. This sight of the vulnerable mother and child so unnerved the young survivor that he ran into the woods and was sick to his stomach. His partners in vengeance, however, were apparently not as squeamish as he. Going from house to house, they continued to bring their wrath down on the local population, leaving havoc in their wake.[2]

The same desire for active revenge was evident in Buchenwald, where more than a few Jews chose to act upon their retaliatory impulses by taking out their frustrations on the local population. Initially, visits to nearby villages were meant to secure food, but these revenge-seekers also looted, harassed Germans in general, and raped young German women. Shortly thereafter, a black market began to operate in Buchenwald, with the active involvement of nearly all the young people in the camp. Here, the small group that was soon to found Kibbutz Buchenwald came into play. Poznansky, Gruenbaum, Tydor, and another religious Jew, Moshe Zauderer, found these activities repugnant, and specifically feared their destructive effect on camp youth.[3] Some two weeks after liberation, Avraham Gottlieb described his impressions of the effect of the newly found "freedom" on the Jews of Buchenwald. Officially they were free, he stated, as no barbed wire surrounded them, but practically speaking they had no true liberty. Although officially forbidden by the commandant to leave the camp, many Jews nevertheless made excursions into the neighboring villages. "Some sightsee; others go to 'organize' something to barter: eggs, salami, onions, salt, etc. Others seek a woman. . . . But this is not freedom. We want to live a settled life, to feel its measured pulse. Here there is nothing but forest, no people, only the memory of the camp."4

Gottlieb's poignant analysis of the situation was concretely expressed by Tydor, Gruenbaum, and Zauderer, who approached Chaplain Schacter in a desperate attempt to find a stopgap solution to the rapidly escalating moral bankruptcy. Their analysis of the situation left only one hope for a solution: In the camp there are young people with Zionist backgrounds, they stated. These young men must be removed from Buchenwald as quickly as possible before they are contaminated by the increasing licentiousness in the camp. The best thing would be to find land nearby and establish a training farm where they could train prior to their *aliyah* (immigration; literally, ascent) to Palestine. Did Rabbi Schacter have any idea how to implement this plan?

The decision to approach Schacter was not an arbitrary one. Ever since Buchenwald's liberation, Schacter's function as a religious guide to Jewish soldiers in the American Eighth Army was slowly being supplanted by an intense concern for the problems of the released concentration camp inmates. Consequently, many of the Jewish activists in Buchenwald saw him as a natural audience for their problems, desires, needs, and hopes. Schacter took every query to heart, which earned him a reputation as a savior among hundreds of homeless, indigent survivors. In this case, his own repugnance for the behavior of many young Jewish DPs caused him to give the unusual request extra thought. Like every other officer in the American army, he was aware that the key to the solution lay in the hands of the G-5 division commander, who oversaw the civil administration of the occupied territories.

One evening in early May, Schacter met with the commanding officer for the Weimer region (his name later escaped Schacter's memory), and in the course of their conversation, he broached the issue of the Jews at Buchenwald. Schacter found himself making a moving appeal to the senior officer to ensure the future of at least the young people in the camp by removing them to a more wholesome environment. Unfamiliar with the particular ins and outs of the Jewish DP problem, the colonel replied that he didn't see why the Jews of Buchenwald were causing so much trouble and could not be repatriated to Germany and Eastern Europe. Shocked at what he considered a combination of ignorance and callousness, Schacter, who as he later recalled immediately lost the "last vestiges of his military naïveté," tried to enlighten the officer as to why repatriation in the East was not a viable option for the Jews from those countries. He concluded his plea: "How can they return to Poland, a land saturated with Jewish blood?"5

Schacter's appeal touched a responsive chord in the colonel, who immediately began searching for a practical solution to the problem so abruptly thrown in his lap. This productive action contrasted sharply with the prevailing attitude among members of the American military government toward the liberated Jews. Seen in the light of the general unwillingness of the American military command to admit to the need for special treatment of the Jewish DPs at this early stage, the colonel's active efforts (though Schacter's rhetorical ability undoubtedly swayed him) to seek a solution to the problem of the young people at Buchenwald comprised a most unusual gesture. Within several days, the combination of good intentions and unique administrative ability offered a practical resolution of the problem. Having investigated the conditions on farms in the Weimar region, the colonel in charge became convinced that the most suitable venue was a large estate in Eggendorf bei Blenkenheim, which had been in Nazi hands during the war. All that remained was to inform the Zionist group in Buchenwald of his decision and to hand the estate over to their care.[6]

As the wheels of fortune began to spin for the Zionist-oriented young survivors in Buchenwald, the Jews in question were completely unaware of the new turn of events. The trio that had approached Schacter remained in the dark, having heard nothing about either his conversation with the American colonel or the efforts under way to find them a suitable farmstead. Increasingly concerned about their future, the small band of young men under their care began making rash plans to leave the camp illegally in search of a route to Palestine.

What enabled this particular group of survivors to consider such an undertaking? How did they differ from the majority of survivors who required slow but steady recuperation following years of deprivation and suffering? The key to understanding the handful of survivors—mostly teenagers or youths in their early twenties with Zionist backgrounds—who had already made contact with each other in Buchenwald before the war's end, lies in their nature and wartime pursuits. Even during the most difficult times, the adults in the group—Tydor, Poznansky, Zauderer, and Gruenbaum—remained active, taking the youths in the camps under their wing, helping them to find food, shelter, and protection. After the war, these efforts found their natural extension in the attempt to remove young people from what the adults perceived as the pernicious influence of the camp atmosphere. The group's younger members were also unique, as the large majority were former members of youth movements who had continued their political involvement during the war. Many managed to remain together, even during the death marches. Others possessed acute historical awareness, like Avraham Gottlieb, who felt impelled to keep a personal diary in the camp. Clearly, these were dynamic individuals, who were therefore less in need than some others of an extended recuperative period before returning to full activity.

On May 5, Elik Gruenbaum resolved to leave the camp in order to wander from city to city and from country to country all the way to Palestine, along with anyone who cared to accompany him. Three days later he and Shmuel Gottlieb set forth. Initially they planned to head for Erfurt and to continue their journey from there, but "the travels of Benjamin the Third undertaken by Elik and Shmuel" (as they were dubbed by Avraham in his diary, referring to the famous medieval Jewish traveler Benjamin of Tudella,) lasted a mere twenty-four hours.[7] Their plan, cultivated by their Zionist backgrounds and nurtured by a combination of depression and despair, was unfeasible. The return of the two to the camp, separately, put an end to the plans of illegal departure made by others in the interim.

In the midst of this adventure, the leaders of the youth group received an invitation to meet with the American colonel in Weimar. In a spirit of hopeful trepidation, Tydor, Gruenbaum, and Zauderer set out for what was to be a fateful meeting. They quickly discovered that any fears were misplaced. In the course of the conversation, the colonel proposed that the group move to the Eggendorf farm at the end of May. This startling announcement left them thunderstruck; they had been certain that their request was languishing somewhere in the bureaucratic machinery of the American army. Moreover, the colonel's warm and humane manner contrasted sharply with what they perceived as the indifference of the official Jewish agencies. Avraham's diary reflects the feeling of abandonment felt by many of the Buchenwald survivors who had expected an outpouring of international Jewish sentiment when the story of their captivity and survival became known. Instead, he wrote, no Jewish organization in the Diaspora had contacted them or made an attempt to look after them. Only two American chaplains—Rabbis Herschel Schacter and Robert Marcus—had taken an interest in the Jews. Similarly, the young rabbis had also made contact with the Jews in the Bergen-Belsen, Leipzig, and Altenburg camps. "But all this is at their own initiative, and when we inquire 'What will happen to us?'—they have no reply."[8]

Schacter and Marcus were only two of the dozens of chaplains who were then playing a major, even crucial, role in the initial rehabilitation of the camp survivors. Putting personal and military considerations aside, time and time again these rabbis used their military and personal standing—at times risking their careers—in order to assist their newly liberated coreligionists.[9] Schacter's story was typical. His immediate superior officer was an Irish Catholic priest, an anti-Semite described by Schacter as a "drunken S.O.B." The young Jewish chaplain's energetic measures on behalf of the survivors antagonized his superior. Recalling an exchange with his superior, Schacter tried to describe the gap dividing the two men:

PRIEST: Chaplain, I fail to understand you. I thought your job was to serve American soldiers. What the devil are you doing in that camp?
SCHACTER: Father, there are many Catholics in the camp who would surely appreciate a visit from an American Catholic chaplain.
PRIEST: Certainly, there must be priests there. They don't need me.[10]

This conversation had its aftermath. During the second week of June, Schacter's commanding officers concluded that he needed a rest after carrying a double load for many weeks. Their unspoken aim was to halt his activity among the survivors and to restore him to his original function—looking after the spiritual needs of American soldiers. This was not the only attempt to remove a problematic Jewish chaplain from the scene in order to prevent further anomalies. Throughout 1945 and 1946, chaplains who evinced special attachments to Jewish DPs were more often than not temporarily removed from their posts in order to halt unwanted "fraternization" with the problematic survivors. It took an unusually understanding commanding officer with the ability and desire to turn a blind eye to situations in which chaplains procured U.S. army goods for DP use, or even forged documents to aid illegal immigration, to allow such enterprises to continue smoothly. For example, in what they euphemistically termed "a good night's work," Schacter, together with Tydor, made liberal use of U.S. Army rubber stamps and passes during his superiors' absence. Most were used in order to forge emigration forms to enable overage young survivors from Buchenwald join a Red Cross transport of liberated children to Switzerland. In another case, he provided passes for three liberated women—two young women in their twenties and their mother, in her early fifties—stating that all were in their late teens, in order to enable them to join the same children's transport. Fearing that the mother's haggard looks would endanger the entire endeavor, he made her swear to remain in the toilet of the train throughout the entire journey in order to avoid detection by the strict and anti-Semitic Red Cross nurse in charge of the voyage. Similarly, he was later instrumental in "borrowing" U.S. military supplies to help the founding members of Kibbutz Buchenwald begin setting up their agricultural training farm.[11]

Schacter's attachment to the founders of Kibbutz Buchenwald stemmed from more than the original chemistry that had attracted him to the young survivors. In comparison with the general run of survivors with whom he had contact, he was amazed that these underweight, overburdened young men were able to consider the greater good even after all they had been through. Forty years after the fact, he recalled how the vast majority of survivors with whom he came in contact were solely concerned with their physical recovery and the search for their relatives. "And here was a group of older men, almost 'musselmen' [starving concentration camp inmates], whose primary concern was saving the younger people in the liberated camp. To this day, I wonder where they found the strength to think and plan for the collective good, so soon after liberation," he remembered.[12]

The announcement of the imminent move to Eggendorf surprised the young people as much as it had the group's organizers. On May 25, Elik informed his "guys," and Moshe Zauderer told the religious youths, that within the space of a few days they would be moving to a farm some thirty kilometers from Buchenwald. Naturally, this announcement was enthusiastically received. Tydor, having nearly succumbed to typhus, lay in the camp hospital during those weeks, hovering between life and death. Here, too, Chaplain Schacter played a significant role in his recovery. Aware that large doses of vitamin C would hasten the older survivor's recovery, he "borrowed" oranges—a practically unobtainable luxury—from the army PX in order to supply Tydor with the necessary vitamins. Until his dying day, Tydor remained convinced that the unique combination of physical and spiritual—the prayers of his survivor friends and Schacter's "liberation" of U.S. Army oranges—were the secret to his rapid and unique recovery.

THE ESTABLISHMENT OF KIBBUTZ BUCHENWALD

While Tydor lay recuperating in the Buchenwald hospital, the remaining sixteen young men of the various Zionist groups connected with him, Greenbaum, and Poznansky began making plans to move out of the camp and into their new abode. Taking possession of the farm was a complex matter, one that involved far more than the physical transfer of youthful survivors and essential equipment from one location to another. It raised questions of principle that went far beyond logistics and technical difficulties. Some were connected with the issue of lingering Jewish resentment toward Germany. The chalutzim abhorred the thought of remaining in Germany even temporarily, and wrestled with the implications of farming what they referred to as "*diese verfluchte deutsche erde*" (German for "this accursed German soil"). Unanimously, they reached a decision not to remain in Germany even a day longer than necessity dictated. Nonetheless, they bowed to pragmatic exigencies. Reiterating that their goal was not to cultivate German soil, but that at present they were homeless, Avraham Gottlieb described the psychological and practical methods by which the young pioneers attempted to cope with the dilemma at hand:

> We aspire to help build a healthy Jewish society in its own land, and we ourselves hope to live there. And since we cannot go "there" at present— "there" being Eretz Israel [the land of Israel]—we must content ourselves with finding a place, with founding a collective on a confiscated German estate, and

with waiting for the day when we can realize our dream. Meanwhile we will
engage in productive work. Can our endeavor succeed?[13]

Avraham was not the only one to voice doubts. The American military
administration stationed in Weimar—both its commanding officers and
Jewish chaplains—as well as the Jewish inmates at Buchenwald, expressed
skepticism as to whether this gar'in (nucleus of a pioneering group) could
successfully implement its goals. First, they questioned the very notion of
setting up a hachsharah. Although hachsharot had been established in
postwar Poland, no such precedents existed in occupied Germany. Moreover, the hachsharot in Poland were urban collectives, not farming communities, whose only goal was to reach Palestine as quickly as possible. Thus
they differed in structure and activity from the hachsharah envisioned by
the former Buchenwald inmates. Second, it was difficult to imagine that
this group could so rapidly surmount the effects of years of suffering and
enslavement.

It is important to remember that the events described were set in motion
but a few days following the German surrender. During the first month after
liberation, the majority of the Jews in Germany either remained in the liberated camps, or wandered through various towns in a desperate search for
family and friends. Historian Abraham Peck claims that at that time, the
survivors were perceived by their liberators "as the passive objects of history,
awaiting with resignation and despair the acting out of a drama in which they
could play little if any role."[14] Although this description was perhaps not
correct in the long run, it accurately depicts the immediate postliberation
period. Even at this stage, however, there were notable exceptions. Among
those who appeared to the liberators as "a dense dark forest populated by
skeletons"[15] were individuals who refused even momentarily to submit to the
status of "passive object" and insisted, almost immediately, upon inscribing a
new page in the history of the she'erit hapletah in Germany. These were the
chalutzim of Kibbutz Buchenwald.

On Sunday, June 3, a group of sixteen chalutzim moved to the Eggendorf
farm. Their first step was to inventory the existing supplies, and to prepare to
operate a farm in territory under foreign conquest. A brief tour apprised
them that they had "inherited" some cows, horses, oxen, wagons, fields, a
garden, fruit trees, a two-story house, a broken tractor, and an inoperable car.
The transportation problem was solved by "borrowing" a tractor from the
camp, but other problems—such as the shortage of food and workers—were
not as readily conquered. The food shortage emanated both from the nature
of the farm itself and from the conditions prevailing in postwar Germany.
The farm at Eggendorf was far from self-supporting; even in its heyday, it
had never fully provided for its residents' needs. This problem was solved by

the various organizations involved in feeding the survivors. Provisions were supplied at first by the American army, and later by UNRRA.

The problem of training a suitable workforce posed more of a challenge, as it involved both ideological and practical repercussions—those pertaining to the Zionist national ideal as well as those stemming from the general resentment toward Germans evident among survivors during the early period following liberation. Following the Zionist ideological affirmation of "Jewish labor," the kibbutz members prepared themselves to run the training farm single-handedly. Because most of the young men had not managed to spend any length of time at one of the prewar or wartime hachsharot, however, the abstract concept of Jewish labor was rarely backed by practical agricultural training. In view of the unpostponable necessity of milking the cows, pruning the trees, and preparing for the late summer harvest, the survivors were forced to overcome their repugnance for their German neighbors and to employ local workers to operate the farm.

Nevertheless, the young founders refused to compromise on one matter of principle, that of collectivism, which was well known to anyone familiar with the tenets of socialist Zionism. In the spirit of socialism, the young men decided to operate the kibbutz as a commune, with a central dining hall and a duty roster. Thus, every member would be responsible for a rotating set of duties, and the onus of running the hachsharah would be equally shared by all. The decision to administer the training farm along cooperative lines was, in truth, a continuation of the clandestine wartime communes formed by each of the groups in Buchenwald to assure mutual assistance and ensure the survival of all members, both weak and strong. Consequently, Kibbutz Buchenwald's administrative pattern drew upon prewar parallel ideological and practical roots that had set the configuration for both hachshara kibbutzim in Europe and permanent kibbutzim in Palestine, and wartime practices that had enabled the various groups to fight and survive the daily odds in the Nazi camps.[16]

The group expanded daily. Young survivors from Buchenwald and other nearby camps came to observe the pioneering way of life. Only a minority had Zionist leanings; the majority were attracted by the option of choosing an alternative to their idle existence in the liberated camps. Naturally, each person hoped that by joining the Buchenwald group, he would expedite his departure from Germany. Whatever the motivation, workloads were assigned according to physical ability, not Zionist affiliation.

This was the kibbutz's founding period, its initial groping toward a truly cooperative way of life. At this juncture, at Tydor and Schacter's urging, the kibbutz adopted an official name—Kibbutz Buchenwald—reflecting the camp origin of its founding members. This decision was reached at the kibbutz's founding party in early June. In his speech on this occasion, Schacter noted a theme that he hoped would become the kibbutz's hallmark—the sense of a shared Jewish fate. The entry that Avraham Gottlieb made in his diary following the party is the first documented expression of what was to be Kibbutz Buchenwald's leitmotif—cooperation and unity, transcending prewar political and religious particularism. Marveling at the fact that Schacter, as a rabbi, had no intention of coercing the entire group to be religious, he noted the chaplain's request that they not allow ideology to divide them, as it had before the war, but instead become one band with a place for each individual with a declared wish to live as a Jew among Jews. "Each person is free to imagine the way of life that best suits him and the ideological viewpoint he sees as most correct," wrote Gottlieb, "and at the same time we should organize our life together in a democratic fashion, with the right wing displaying tolerance for the left, and vice versa, with secular Jews showing tolerance for religious Jews, and the converse."[17]

COMMUNALISM

At first glance, Kibbutz Buchenwald appears to be a communal framework, formed in response to the sudden plight of displaced Jews in liberated Germany to enable them to improve their lot. Indeed, it appears that almost all the kibbutzim that sprang up in postwar Germany, both inside and outside the Displaced Persons' camps, were created for that purpose. It was in these camps, established by the Allies to house the tens of thousands of liberated prisoners who could not—or would not—be repatriated to their homelands, that tens of thousands of liberated Jews were concentrated. During the first postwar years, many of them found solace in joining the communal frameworks that ultimately took form within the larger framework of the camp.

Unlike the case of most of these survivors, for whom communal frameworks were only a means to an end, for many of Kibbutz Buchenwald's members the communal framework also had an ideological significance. More than half the members of Kibbutz Buchenwald's initial gar'in had belonged to Zionist youth movements before or during the war. Some were graduates of prewar or wartime hachsharot, which they had joined voluntarily. For these youths, the founding of a kibbutz in the postwar period marked the continuation of the path chosen years earlier. Consequently, they viewed life on Kibbutz Buchenwald as the pinnacle of their dreams, in which the utopian element naturally played a major role.

Interestingly, no comparable communal phenomenon is evident among other groups of DPs following the Second World War. At the war's end, some seven million displaced persons were found in Germany; in late summer 1945, there remained some one and a half million, who had lacked either the desire or the means to return to their homelands. The DP camps housed thousands of Poles, Yugoslavs, Ukrainians, Hungarians, Romanians, Russians, Greeks, and Albanians, as well as Spaniards who refused to return to Franco's Spain. In reports on those DPs submitted by UNRRA and other welfare workers, no communal phenomenon is noted, whereas the descriptions of the She'erit hapletah are replete with references to the various kibbutzim.[18] One possible explanation for Jewish collectivism is that the Jews had to cope with conditions far worse than those of other DPs. Whatever the reason, the impetus to organize kibbutzim to satisfy the individual's daily needs was far stronger among Jews than among other groups. Moreover, conceptually, Jews in the DP camps were familiar with the Zionist tradition of founding kibbutzim. As for other DPs, those drawn to communal frameworks on a socialist basis could return to their now almost exclusively socialist homelands, and join collectives like the *kolkhozy* (agricultural communal settlements) that operated throughout the Soviet Union. The fact that these DPs refused to be repatriated perhaps indicates their problematic attitude toward socialism in general, and collectivism in particular.

FINDING A NEW KIBBUTZ SITE

Before concluding his visit to the farm, Schacter informed the pioneers that according to the Potsdam Agreement, Thueringia—the area where the kibbutz was located—was to be turned over to the Russians in a few weeks' time. In practical terms, if the group were to remain on the Eggendorf farm, the Soviet takeover—and with it, the Russian freeze on emigration—would put a halt to their plans to reach Palestine. Even the Soviet repatriation agreement with the Polish government stipulated a summer 1945 deadline for leaving the USSR in order to return to the Polish homeland. It was therefore vital that the kibbutz move west prior to the Soviet takeover, in order to remain in the American zone. Naturally, this announcement radically altered daily routines on the farm. Plans for further development were shelved in favor of discussions about how to find an alternative site in the American zone. Concurrently, the members discussed life under Communist rule, in debates reminiscent of those within the Polish group on the day after the camp's liberation. Nonetheless, no practical steps were taken to find a new site for the kibbutz. In addition, despite the news of the impending Soviet takeover, new members—young men and women survivors of various camps who had heard of the Zionist experiment from Allied soldiers, as well as members of the Jewish Brigade and other survivors—continued to arrive daily. They all realized, however, that the kibbutz was in limbo until the question of transfer was clarified.

Efforts to locate a suitable farm site went into high gear only after a surprise visit from the Russian advance party. One morning in mid-June, a German-speaking Russian general arrived at Eggendorf from the direction of

Buchenwald. Although he was surprised to see young Jews operating an agricultural venture, he had no inkling that they would perceive the Russian presence as anything other than welcome. In anticipation of their excitement, he turned to the chalutzim with a broad smile and inquired, "Comrades, aren't you glad that we are arriving soon?" Luckily for those standing nearby, the general did not expect a reply.[19]

Tydor, Gruenbaum, and Zauderer were men of action. That very same evening, they made plans to head for Frankfurt, Tydor's former home, to seek a solution; but this was easier said than done. At that time, finding a means of transportation was a problem in and of itself. Operable motor vehicles were a rarity in postwar Germany. An American officer hit the nail on the head when he said, "Cars are virtually nonexistent. Even the American army has difficulty obtaining vehicles, and when someone finally 'organizes' wheels, he usually finds he has no gasoline."[20] The chalutzim, fully cognizant of this problem, appealed to Rabbi Schacter to accompany them to the regional commander in Frankfurt in order to explain the urgent need to move the kibbutz. Unable at that time to get away, Schacter placed both his army jeep and his driver, Haim Shulman, at their disposal. The evening prior to their departure, Zauderer, Tydor, and another chalutz, Victor Hirshkowitz, prepared a list of possible alternatives to Eggendorf. The potential sites included a former training farm belonging to the Bachad (the acronym for Brit Chalutzim Datiyim— League of Religious Pioneers) movement at Geringshof. No one knew whether the farm was accessible; therefore, they decided to proceed directly to the American military government in Frankfurt in order to tender a formal request. The three set out, accompanied by "our friend Haim," as they called Schacter's driver, choosing a route that took them through the Fulda district north of Frankfurt, where the Geringshof farm was located.

As they neared the area of the former training farm, Tydor impulsively suggested that they detour to Geringshof to check out the farm. With a sense of daring expectation, the trio entered the offices of the mayor of Hattenhof, the closest village to Geringshof. The sudden appearance of these uninvited guests embarrassed the "host," who refused to accompany them back to the farm. Having failed in their attempt to see the estate, the three then set out for the offices of the commander of the American military government in Fulda, Lieutenant Finkelstein, a Jew. At their request, he checked the records concerning Geringshof, and following a brief telephone conversation, confirmed that indeed it was now owned by a German family that had fled the Russians. Warming to the occasion, Lieutenant Finkelstein immediately dictated a letter to the village mayor, designating the farm as henceforth the exclusive property of the Jewish community of Hattenhof. He concluded his missive with a clause to the effect that the bearers of this letter were this Jewish community's official representatives.

Armed with this very official-looking letter, the "representatives of the Hattenhof Jewish community" returned to the village to claim their estate. Left with no alternative, the village mayor reluctantly accompanied them to the farm to oversee the meeting with the German tenants. From this moment on, matters progressed rapidly, far exceeding their wildest dreams. Tydor recalled their exceptional reception at Geringshof:

> Its new owner, a Volksdeutsche (German term for ethnic German) and his family, hesitated to grant us access, but surrendered upon seeing the warrant. We entered and took a quick look at the main building and its contents. Nearby stood a storage shack for stockpiling wood for the winter months.
> Instinctively . . . I went over to the shack, opened the door, and saw torn scraps of parchment from a *Sefer Torah* [Torah Scroll] scattered in the woodpile. We removed the wood and gathered the parchment scraps in order to turn them over to trustworthy hands. I can still visualize the expression on the *Volksdeutsche*'s face, as if he were inquiring: "What are you looking for here?" I could not bring myself to look him in the eye. When the shack was completely empty, we found written in chalk on the rear wall—"*Wir werden wiederkehren*"— [German for] "We shall yet return." This was the last will and testament left by the remaining members of the training farm before their expulsion. We continued our survey of the estate, and decided that we must "redeem it" by putting down our temporary roots here until our aliyah to Eretz Israel.[21]

Prior to returning to Eggendorf, the three representatives inventoried the farm's supplies. They also decided to allow the owner to remain temporarily, making him responsible for looking after the farm and its contents. Toward evening, after the official arrangements for transfer of ownership were completed, the group turned eastward to bring the eagerly awaited news to Eggendorf.

The behavior of each of the parties involved in the establishment of Kibbutz Buchenwald and its transfer to a "temporarily permanent" home on German soil must be examined within the historical context of liberated Germany. Variations of this triangle—the American army, Germans, and Jews—appeared in liberated Germany in various contexts. Was the interaction between the sides described here—with the Americans represented by Rabbi Schacter and Lieutenant Finkelstein, the Germans by the village mayor and the Volksdeutsche, and finally, the Jews by the chalutzim from Eggendorf—typical of postwar Germany?

THE AMERICAN ARMY

Rabbi Schacter's generosity in extending to the loan of his official jeep in order to enable the Eggendorf representatives to benefit from the services of the U.S. Army, conformed to the actions of dozens of Jewish chaplains who devoted themselves to assisting the survivors. The same held true for Jewish rank-and-file soldiers, some with Zionist backgrounds, who circumvented and even contravened army procedures for the benefit of their newly liberated brethren. One such soldier was Akiva Skidell, a European-born activist in the Zionist Habonim (The Builders) movement. Skidell knew of the Eggendorf farm, and visited there several times prior to its transfer. On each occasion, he left a package containing food, cigarettes, and newspapers. He even brought the group its first Bible. Concerning the Bible, Skidell wrote to his wife, "It was received, let me tell you, with real enthusiasm. They had asked for a *Tanach* [Bible] the night before but the chaplains told them they had no hope of getting one for them: Where would they find it? Oh, these modern rabbis! Undertaking a perilous journey across the seas without a Bible in their pockets. Well, perhaps they know it all by heart."[22]

Skidell's contact with the kibbutz did not cease with its transfer to Geringshof. Indeed, during the entire time he was stationed in Europe, the young American soldier continued to visit the group and to assist it to the best of his ability. He maintained contact even after the group reached Palestine.

The reception given by Lieutenant Finkelstein to his guests was by no means the typical attitude of U.S. Army commanders toward liberated Jews in Germany. Leonard Dinnerstein documented the callousness of many American army personnel in Germany in his study of the American attitude toward Holocaust survivors.[23] In addition, the majority of the commanding officers were both physically and psychologically isolated from the Jews under their aegis, and were unaware of their distress. Moreover, their ignorance about how to treat the Jews, as reflected in the comment made by the sympathetic officer who found the Eggendorf farm for the Buchenwald group, stemmed at times not only from lack of knowledge but from a lack of interest as well. According to Rabbis Herschel Schacter and Mayer Abramowitz, the American army establishment had its share of anti-Semites.[24] One of the more infamous was the Third Army's George S. Patton, who wrote in his diary that others "believe that the Displaced Person is a human being, which he is not, and this applies particularly to the Jews who are lower than animals."[25] While British pressure on American policy did not as yet play an influential role, negative feelings toward Jewish DPs were in evidence.

In light of this psychological gap and these anti-Semitic tendencies, the measures taken by the commander of the Fulda district were remarkable. As a Jew, Lieutenant Finkelstein felt a special obligation to aid his fellow Jews, even if this meant bending army regulations. His insight into the emotional needs of the survivors enabled him to perceive that for these young Jews, true rehabilitation could only begin outside the camp environment, in a setting where they could actively determine their own future. Consequently, his behavior toward the chalutzim, both at this time and on future occasions when they requested his assistance, went above and beyond the call of duty.

Nevertheless, the steps taken to enable the organized departure of the young people from the camp, such as confiscating the estates at Eggendorf and Geringshof, did belong to a pattern typical of the immediate postliberation period. From May to November 1945, estates, farms, apartments, and various buildings were confiscated from Germans in favor of the homeless Jews. This occurred not only at Eggendorf and Geringshof, but at Gersfeld, Zeilsheim, Frankfurt, and elsewhere.

THE GERMANS

On the German side of the triangle, here again, the issue of postwar interaction between Jews and Germans comes into play—but with a twist, owing to the fact that the contact in question was taking place under the watchful eyes of the American army. The behavior of the village mayor, and of the Volksdeutsche from Geringshof, was consistent with the usual pattern of interaction with American army personnel in cases where liberated Jews were concerned. The cool reception initially given the Eggendorf group contrasted sharply with the polite behavior evident upon their second meeting with the village mayor, which took place under the auspices of the military governor's warrant. This change in attitude is attributable to two factors—a clearheaded evaluation of the situation, and the German tradition of obedience to authority. Similar patterns of interaction are evident in later cases of Jews from the DP camps who came into contact with Germans, particularly during the first postwar months. The complex relationship between the members of Kibbutz Buchenwald and the local Germans slowly metamorphosed from antagonism into working relationships during late 1946 and 1947, mirroring the changing composition of the She'erit hapletah in Germany and the ensuing difference in the Jewish attitude toward the local population. Naturally, the entire question of Jewish–German relations in occupied Germany was infinitely more complex, and merits separate, in-depth study.

THE SURVIVORS

The third side of the triangle, the Eggendorf group, represents the main actors in this drama and renews the issue of postwar national aspirations. Their motivation, behavior, and hopes have already been described in detail with parallels drawn to other ethnic groups. In addition, it is important to note the existence of a psychological factor, definable as a sense of mission, of completion, or the closing of a circle. A significant number of the members at Eggendorf—particularly the founders, for whom Zionism was not an abstract concept but a concrete ideal—had identified with pioneering movements before the war, or had undergone agricultural training during its course, in preparation for immigration to Palestine. From their perspective, the founding of a kibbutz training farm represented the renewal of both personal and institutional Zionist activity that had been so cruelly and suddenly terminated by the Nazis.

The sense of closing a circle was related to the second site chosen for the kibbutz. Geringshof was a training center whose activity had likewise been dramatically arrested at the height of the war. The parting injunction scribbled on the wall of the shack at Geringshof—"We shall yet return"—only strengthened the determination of the young people from Buchenwald to pursue their chosen path. By creating a new kibbutz society at Geringshof, the young survivors saw themselves as closing a double circle that had been cruelly broken during the war. The first was their own, suddenly broken with their incarceration in ghettos and camps; the second was that of Geringshof, one of the last hachsharot allowed to function in Germany, whose members' activities were cruelly terminated with their deportation in 1943. The further history of the hachsharah at Geringshof bears witness to this feeling. Up to their final day on German soil, the members of Kibbutz Buchenwald continued to see themselves as the standard-bearers of Zionism, both for themselves and in memory of those who had failed to escape destruction by the enemy.

Did the Zionist movement in Palestine consider these survivors worthy of bearing this standard? The answer to this complex question would become apparent in two stages: first, with the visit of the Zionist movement's representatives to Geringshof during the summer of 1945, and later, after the founders of Kibbutz Buchenwald reached Palestine in the autumn of that year.

CHAPTER THREE

The Initial Period at Geringshof, Summer 1945

"We were as dreamers."—Psalm 126:1

THE MOVE FROM EGGENDORF to Geringshof opened a new chapter in the lives of the members of Kibbutz Buchenwald. The event was laconically noted in the official kibbutz diary by Haim Meir Gottlieb in a brief entry that reveals little of the true adventure behind the move:

Sunday, June 24. We, [that is] fifty-three members of both sexes, arrived at Geringshof, near Fulda, after hours upon hours of travel over hill and dale in one bus and two trucks. Thus we accomplished Kibbutz Buchenwald's move to its new site. (Some members remained behind and will arrive over the next few days by horse and wagon.) . . . We immediately set to work. In the fields, barn, stable, and yard Jewish hands are at work, the hands of our members. At night, two members stand guard. In the evenings, after work, discussions are held; songs echo in Yiddish and in Hebrew; life goes on.[1]

In truth, the entire undertaking, summarized in the one sentence "Thus we accomplished Kibbutz Buchenwald's move to its new site," was characterized by a playful sense of adventure. The move began on Saturday afternoon, July 23, when UNRRA placed vehicles at the disposal of the chalutzim. Fourteen people, mostly religious chalutzim, who had remained at Eggendorf, planned to join the group the following day. At dawn, the group took a last tour of the farm that had served as their home for such a short while. Then someone came up with an idea: Buses are good for transporting people, he said, but not a farm. Instead of leaving all the livestock for the incoming Russians, why not at least take the horses with them? "Thus, we hitched four horses to two wagons and took a splendid journey through Germany—through Erfurt, Gotha, Eisenach," one of the adventurers recalled. "I remember the castles we passed; I even purchased picture postcards on the way. The roads were filled with wandering DPs, Germany was bombed out, people wandered—Germans, Russians—and we, we traveled by wagon for four days."[2]

Upon their arrival, the travelers immediately noticed the poor conditions—particularly the lack of beds and food—that their fellow members had endured for the past few days at Geringshof. This contrasted sharply with their experiences during their journey. While on the road, they had reported each evening to the local village mayor, who had then provided for all their needs, from a place to sleep to a shoeshine. Here, basic necessities were lacking.

That same day, two of the venturesome horsemen remounted their steeds in order to secure supplies for their friends. One was Avraham Gottlieb: "We must have suffered from wanderlust," he recalled. "We suddenly remembered that before the move we had brought two sacks of flour to the mill, and decided to go and fetch them." Things were not so simple for the team of chalutzim who dared to venture back to the Soviet-occupied area. Avraham continued: "From the time we reached the mill and until we managed to rent a car, the Russians appeared. They showed no interest in us, and we proceeded westward until we were stopped by American soldiers. We returned to the nearby village in order to cross the border there. A chase developed—with the Americans only a few meters behind us. But they did not send us back, and we managed to bring a carload of flour back to Geringshof."[3]

This almost surrealistic account illustrates the feeling of detachment that characterized many members of Kibbutz Buchenwald throughout their stay at the hachsharah (training farm). To placidly make a decision to take the horses and wagon from Eggendorf to Geringshof on a journey of several days was one thing; to turn around practically upon arrival in order to go back and pick up two sacks of flour, braving both American and Soviet troops without any identification papers, was another. It was inconceivable to imagine the majority of the survivors in Germany undertaking, only two months after liberation, an adventure that would put them into such precarious dependency upon the Germans—mayor and villagers alike—en route. In this, the members of Kibbutz Buchenwald differed from the bulk of the survivors, living either in the liberated concentration camps or in the early DP camps, for whom contact with German reality was a daily affair. These survivors were much more wary of the difficulties of Jewish–German interaction, more conscious of the fact that they were still a despised minority in the midst of a German majority. Being in constant contact with Germans, they were also more aware of their own smoldering resentment toward this majority who, only weeks before, had been at best oblivious of their plight or, at worst, their captors.

Yet in another respect, the story of the two young riders was emblematic: As a group, the survivors were affected by wanderlust. Travel, generally in search of relatives or better living conditions, played a significant role among the survivors. Descriptions of journeys, short and long, fill the pages of Avraham's diary, the kibbutz diary, letters from the period, and even in the memoirs of UNRRA workers. For some, travel was a means of expressing newfound freedom. "After years of imprisonment, we wanted to travel as much and as far as we felt like going," recalled a young Bergen-Belsen survivor who spent a short period at Geringshof.[4] Her childhood friend, who spent the war in exile in Siberia, added his own explanation, which stems from the fact that the majority of the survivors had no real activity to challenge them. "Under the circumstances, the survivors always sought *something*, as they were well aware that seeking *someone* was pointless," he recalled, "and they sought this something by journeying throughout Europe. These were the true wanderings of the survivors, motivated by a strongly internal, personal need."[5]

Chaim Meir Gottlieb's assertion, "Life goes on," was quickly adopted as the ad hoc kibbutz motto; but orderly life must have some type of measured tempo, all the more so if it is to continue in a collectivist framework. Consequently, for Kibbutz Buchenwald to succeed in its pioneering Zionist purpose, steps had to be taken to ensure the smooth functioning of the kibbutz. As a first step in organizing the band at Geringshof, it was suggested that a *va'ad* (committee) be chosen to coordinate the various daily activities according to the pattern adopted by a majority of the members. On the lines of the worn joke concerning two Jews on a desert island who have three synagogues ("yours, mine, and the one we don't attend"), however, there were even differences of opinion over the question of whether it was necessary to choose a va'ad at all; perhaps an amorphous structure with no binding rules or regulations was preferable. Others felt that both demographic and political circumstances—the increased number of members and the impending struggle to enter Palestine—dictated its creation. Another proposal insisted that the committee be chaired by a "kibbutz leader," whose main function would be to negotiate among the various groups represented at Geringshof. The debate found expression in the official kibbutz diary, in the first entry to hint at the heterogeneous composition of its founders. The original groups forming the kibbutz had espoused a broad spectrum of political and religious proclivities before joining together—from Tydor and Zauderer's band of orthodox youths, who had been far removed from socialist Zionist ideology, to Poznansky's labor movement pioneers and Greenbaum's radical left-wing young men, some of whom were ideologically antireligious:

> It is a fact that the kibbutz is comprised of a medley of individuals affiliated with various political movements. It is also true that while all are Zionists—some are observant Jews while others hold secular views—there is a "right" and a "left," etc. Understandably then, the majority of kibbutz members oppose placing individuals on the steering committee who as yet have not won the trust of *all* the members.[6]

In the end, it was resolved to establish a six-member council to represent the broad spectrum of views on the kibbutz, and to elect Yechezkel Tydor "Kibbutz Paterfamilias," in Chaim Meir Gottlieb's words. Tydor was also the sole person to win the support of all the diverse factions.7 Initially, Tydor refused to accept this position, as it now appeared that his stay on the kibbutz would be a temporary one. Shortly after liberation, he had learned that his two young children had been rescued during the war and had been taken to the United States. At some point in the not too distant future, he would have to go to the United States in order to bring them to Palestine. Was the group willing to be led by someone who would not be able to join in their venture in Palestine? he asked. The unequivocal answer was: "See us to our allotted haven" (Deuteronomy 12:9), and then go to your children. Tydor succumbed to this emotional outburst and agreed to serve as kibbutz leader. However, he stipulated two conditions that he considered essential for coexistence between the various groups composing the kibbutz, particularly in issues concerning religion: strict observance of the Sabbath in the kibbutz's public domain, and an official policy of tolerance between the various factions. Only under these circumstances would it be possible to maintain a modus vivendi on daily matters, in the full knowledge that no group would attempt to chastise another for its chosen lifestyle; only then would the Sabbath—a sensitive issue for observant members who could finally observe the day in the orthodox manner after years of spiritual deprivation in labor and concentration camps—be a day of rest and not one of constant ideological strife. Even when he was tested by some of the kibbutz's more antireligious members in matters pertaining to Sabbath observance, Tydor maintained his policy of tolerance, leading, in turn, to a grudging general acceptance of his conditions in the knowledge that they were stipulated for the public good.[8]

At first glance, the forty-two-year-old survivor's altruistic step—his willingness to delay his reunion with his children in order to see the kibbutz to Palestine—seems incomprehensible. Was it conceivable that Tydor placed the collective good above and beyond his paternal desire to be reunited with his children after a seven-year separation? Practically speaking, Tydor was aware that technical reasons—postwar restrictions on travel from Europe to the United States—inhibited his reunion with his children no less than did his sense of obligation to the kibbutz. Moreover, he reasoned that as it was his ultimate intention to bring the children to Palestine, it was preferable for him to go there first in order to prepare their future home. These, among other considerations, motivated Tydor to accept the position of kibbutz leader, but they also determined the limited duration of his tenure in this post.

Tydor's longing for his children found a vicarious outlet in a relationship that developed with a young female survivor, Yehudit Harash, Itka to her friends. The thirteen-year-old Itka was the sole surviving member of her family, and had arrived at Geringshof with a group of women from Bergen-Belsen. Her resemblance to his daughter of the same age brought Tydor and Itka together, and a close relationship developed between the two. Tydor unofficially adopted her as his daughter, while she saw him as an authority and paternal figure combined. As Itka recalled, "I remember how difficult it was for me to call him 'Yechezkel' at first, as that was also my father's first name. I used to address him respectfully as 'Herr Tydor' until I became accustomed to the idea that using his first name was acceptable."[9]

The multifaceted nature of Tydor's post as kibbutz leader quickly became apparent. Called upon to arbitrate internal disputes, to represent the kibbutz before local authorities, the U.S. Army, and emissaries from the Yishuv who reached Germany during the summer of 1945, Tydor found himself serving as arbitrator, legislator, diplomat, and translator all rolled into one. The burden of his office prevented him from overseeing the day-to-day functioning of the kibbutz. This was effectively vested in the hands of various committees, such as the supplies committee headed by Elik Gruenbaum, the culture committee in which Avraham Gottlieb played an active role, the admissions committee, the disciplinary committee, and others. Fears that instituting a formal administration would detract from the open nature of the kibbutz proved to be unfounded. Kibbutz members continued to conduct their collective way of life with a maximum of flexibility, all the while maintaining the unique character of the kibbutz.

It was during this formative period that the members of Kibbutz Buchenwald actually defined to themselves for the first time what this unique character entailed: the maintenance of a communal way of life based upon the aspiration to build an egalitarian society with no cultural or religious barriers. By internalizing this goal, it was possible for the kibbutz to accept so heterogeneous a membership and yet maintain its equilibrium as an independent but unified entity; by being aware that such a venture would be impossible without certain ground rules, the members were able to agree to Tydor's stipulations regarding the hachsharah's outward character. As the kibbutz's membership grew constantly over the summer months, welcoming members from all strata of the survivor spectrum, the values of cooperation, communality, unity, and tolerance grew and strengthened. Thus it was unimportant that many of the kibbutz members had little understanding of the principles of collectivism or even of Zionism, and of minor significance that a goodly number of them regarded the kibbutz instrumentally as a rapid method of leaving Europe and reaching Palestine. All that was important was to have a strong nucleus of activists who would set the tone for the majority, and who intended to continue in a united pioneering supraideological lifestyle—preferably together—upon reaching Eretz Israel. These activists could sweep the newcomers into a psychological and practical atmosphere far removed from that of the liberated concentration camps, thus allowing for their physical and spiritual rehabilitation after years of oppression.

The Members and Their Lifestyle

Who were these newcomers to Kibbutz Buchenwald? How did they come to hear of the kibbutz, and what induced them to join? The answers to these questions may be found in the nature of life among the DPs during the summer of 1945. Following liberation, many survivors roamed throughout Europe searching for relatives and friends, for their ties to the past. In the course of their wanderings from camp to camp, these survivors came in contact with members of the Jewish Brigade and with Jewish soldiers in the U.S. Army, who brought the kibbutz to their attention. Some people came to the kibbutz simply out of curiosity, with no prior ideological commitment to Zionism or to kibbutz life. One of these was twenty-four-year-old Rita Wasserman, who had been released from a labor camp in Leipzig and heard about the kibbutz while wandering around postwar Germany with several released women friends, all in search of Jews. She recounted: "Upon our liberation, we met up with Jews who informed us that not far from where we were was the Buchenwald camp, where the kibbutz that we joined had originated. At that point, I had no idea even of what a kibbutz was—I only saw it as a way of getting to Palestine."[10]

Wasserman was typical of one type of survivor to join a postwar Zionist group in occupied Germany and indeed, in many areas of liberated Eastern Europe: those whose burning desire to leave Europe—usually with the intention of reaching Palestine—was a major factor in their decision to join up with a Zionist collective or, in this case, a hachsharah kibbutz. A great number of those requesting to join the kibbutz had no Zionist affiliations before the war, nor had they any real understanding of the efforts necessary to build and maintain a cooperative venture along socialist Zionist lines. All they knew was that they needed "out"—out of the liberated concentration camps, out of the newly formed DP centers, and out of occupied Germany, which reminded them daily of their wartime travails. Joining any type of Zionist-oriented enterprise was the best and fastest way of ensuring an "out" when that would become possible. Throughout the first postwar years, dozens of self-styled Zionist collectives operated in the DP camps without incorporating the principle of hachsharah, thus providing their members with the hope of illegal immigration to Palestine. In spite of the fact that the hachsharah at Geringshof was a more demanding framework than were these ad hoc collectives, for many it was in fact just another venture, albeit a more challenging one, that could help them reach their ultimate goal.

A second group of newcomers, including Esther Landgarten and Chava

Yuskowitz, joined relatives already at the kibbutz. Esther came from Bergen-Belsen to be with her brother, and later took charge of the kibbutz's kosher kitchen. "While we were traveling in search of my brother, I was told he was at Buchenwald. There, I was informed that he was at Eggendorf. That's how I came to join the hachsharah."[11] Chava Yuskowitz was also reunited with her brother at the kibbutz. She felt no need to grapple with the question of whether the kibbutz was an autonomous ideal, or simply a means of reaching Palestine. "I made no connection between the two," she recalled. "The kibbutz was one thing, and immigration to Palestine another."[12] Some found kibbutz life a sufficient goal in and of itself. According to Lola Sultanik, "The ideal of kibbutz life appealed to me: equality and cultivation of the soil."[13]

This succinct description—equality and farming—accurately sums up one aspect of life at Kibbutz Buchenwald, but the kibbutz had other features apart from its being a collective farm. Collectivism took a unique form among people left with no personal possessions after the war.

From its very inception, the kibbutz adhered to the principle of collectivism. This was especially true with regard to basic supplies. Initially, food, clothing, footwear, and other personal amenities were distributed by the district commander, Lieutenant Finkelstein, and his aide, Second Lieutenant Rosenbaum. At a later stage, UNRRA stepped in as the main provider. All provisions reaching the kibbutz were divided equally among the members, regardless of whether the recipient was the kibbutz leader or its youngest member. Tydor recalled that as kibbutz leader, he had his own room, which quickly turned into a storage room for the entire kibbutz. As it contained only a bed, a table, and one chair, when others wished to consult with him they had to bring chairs from their own rooms. "I had almost no personal effects," he remembered. "What I had was what everyone had. I even had no watch and was constantly asking others for the time. One day a member of the Jewish Brigade asked where my watch was. When I replied that I had none, he removed his and gave it to me. I hesitated to accept, but the soldier pressed me until I agreed." On another occasion, a group from the kibbutz went to Fulda to be outfitted with suits. They also received personal items—a comb, a hairbrush, a toothbrush, and vital accessories, like toothpaste. "This was my first taste of a German 'war product'," continued Tydor, "the chloroform-flavored toothpaste used by the Germans throughout the war. Well, I must say that I didn't really feel especially sorry for them," he concluded with a half-smile, alluding once again to the prevalent attitude of survivors in Germany with regard to the local population.[14]

Making do with little was not a universally shared philosophy. Many members availed themselves of every opportunity to stockpile goods in preparation for the move to Palestine. Despite explicit opposition to black market trade, not all were able to resist temptation, but even those who refrained from profiteering benefited from the generosity of members of the Jewish Brigade and the U.S. Armed Forces.

Representatives of the occupying powers who visited the farm were bombarded with requests for such things as food, personal items, books, and even ritual objects, and generally, the soldiers tried their best to meet these requests. Apparently the majority of the kibbutz members maintained a sense of proportion, adapting their requests to circumstances. For example, since no *kippot* (skullcaps) were available, the religious members wore ordinary caps. The kibbutz jointly owned several pairs of *tefillin* (phylacteries), *tzizit* (ritual fringes), and prayer books. However, kosher meat was unobtainable. Therefore, on the Sabbath, the observant Jews ate such dairy products as they managed to procure. Tydor recalled how the religious group's first aim in the realm of kosher food was to arrange for dairy Sabbath meals. It was especially difficult to obtain challah. "We brought some loaves of bread from Fulda, and from the point of view of those who today strictly observe *chalav Israel* or *pat akum* [the prohibition against consuming milk or bread prepared by non-Jews] our efforts to find a bakery that didn't use lard to grease the baking pans may seem somewhat ludicrous." Later on, when he had occasion to travel, the leader of Kibbutz Buchenwald discovered that this was the case in most camps. Only in large cities, where remnants of Jewish communities remained, was it possible to observe the fine points of Jewish law. "Kosher food barely existed. It was enough for most not to eat *trafe* (non-kosher food)," he concluded. During the first few weeks, the kibbutz received tinned goods from the army and/or UNRRA. This posed yet another problem in maintaining any type of a kosher kitchen in the hachsharah. "Certainly, many tins were of questionable origin, but we couldn't keep watch over everyone," recalled Tydor, recounting the difficulties for observant Jews on the kibbutz. "There were lots of tins of sardines, which we kept for the main course of our Shabbat [Sabbath] meal. Someone joked about this in Yiddish: "In a place where there are no men, strive to be a man" [Ethics of the Fathers 2:6]; and in a place where a Jew has no carp, then herring must also strive to be a 'Sabbath fish.' "15

A comparison of property at Kibbutz Buchenwald with the situation of most survivors in Germany at that time reveals significant differences. During the early days following liberation, few survivors in Germany had any personal possessions, other than those provided by the liberating armies, mostly clothes and foodstuffs. As time passed, the occupying authorities began to provide the DPs with a minimum of clothing and personal toiletries. With the establishment and growth of black market trade, however, survivors began to fall into two categories—the haves and the have-nots. Those in the first category either knew how to "organize"—reminiscent of the days in camp when one's survival depended upon this ability—or had contacts in the black market framework. Those in the second category were either too weak to participate in trading, or decided not to partake in the exercise for reasons of their own, usually ideological. Many of the latter were therefore drawn to the cooperative frameworks then being established in the DP camps, although belonging to such a group did not preclude their being active in a black market network—this time for the common, and not the personal, good.

This shared responsibility, found among members of all collective frameworks in postwar Germany (and Eastern Europe), had its parallel on Kibbutz Buchenwald, albeit on a larger scale than that of possessions and foodstuffs alone. Generally speaking, life at Geringshof did not conform to the usual pattern of a kibbutz training farm. There was no scheduled compulsory wake-up call, and apart from those engaged in household and other daily tasks, the members were not obligated to work. Furthermore, despite the kibbutz's aim of preparing its members for agricultural life in Palestine, few evinced any interest in the agricultural ideal, and fewer still were prepared to devote time to studying its practical implementation. Part of this reluctance stemmed from the perception of Germany as an accursed land whose soil should not be cultivated beyond the bare minimum required for subsistence. In isolated cases, some members claimed that society owed them a debt, that due to their traumatic wartime experiences they should not be expected to work at all. They, in turn, tried to convince others to accept this view, a step that Tydor found greatly upsetting, and antithetical to his attempt to create a harmonious atmosphere on the kibbutz. Much discussion was devoted to this issue both among the members and in the kibbutz journal.

A similar attitude was prevalent during the early postwar period among many survivors who found it difficult to conceive of returning to a normal existence while they were living in DP camps throughout Germany. In a DP film made in 1947, *Lang is der Weg* (*Long is the journey*), the protagonist tries to organize the young survivors in his camp into workshops, in order to train them for their future, preferably in Palestine. However, with the first technical setback, the enterprise comes to a dismal failure, owing to the fact that most of the DPs are unable (or unwilling) to enter into a productive life when there is no immediate hope of leaving Germany. Written, acted and produced by survivors in Germany, the film ends on an upbeat pastoral/Zionist note: The hero leaves the DP camp for some sort of hachsharah in Germany. In the final scene, he is seen trudging off into the sunset before joining his wife, mother, and newborn child under a spreading tree, talking about how they will soon join the rest of the Jewish people in Palestine.

Reality, however, usually took a different turn than the unbounded enthusiasm and hope characterizing the film's end. True, workshops were often established in the DP camps by enterprising survivors who realized the futility of inactively sitting and waiting. The same people also comprehended the unique problems of DP youngsters who had lost years of education during the war and therefore lacked any type of productive training for life. Other such enterprises were initiated by groups who came to assist the survivors in Germany—the international Jewish vocational training organization ORT (Organization of Rehabilitation and Training), and social welfare organizations such as the JDC (Joint Distribution Committee). Nevertheless, there were still numerous groups of survivors who could see little beyond tomorrow; their hopes centered around today, with its many needs and few promises. It was only after months of existence in the DP camps that such groups agreed to join study circles, and even longer before they were able to maintain the internal discipline necessary to keep a vocational workshop going.

Kibbutz members recall debate and discussion as a prominent feature of life at Kibbutz Buchenwald. Itka Harash, the kibbutz's youngest member, recounted: "We hardly slept. We spent hours discussing every topic under the sun, and for me—a thirteen-and-a-half-year-old girl alone in the world, having lost seven brothers and sisters, these idealists embodied the height of perfection."[16]

Talks at the kibbutz took two forms—spontaneous and organized. Most popular and well-attended were the kibbutz's Friday night Oneg Shabbat parties. Word of these parties spread, drawing Jews from the nearby area, soldiers and civilians alike. The highlight of the evening was always the skit performed by Elimelech Wiener, the kibbutz comedian. At times, these gatherings lasted so long that they could almost be considered a *melaveh malkah*—a party ushering out the Sabbath on Saturday evening. Another formal activity was educational: Six Hebrew lessons, six English lessons, three Yiddish lessons, and two lectures on Jewish history were scheduled on a weekly basis. Additional lectures were delivered at the request of the kibbutz's cultural committee. This variegated educational activity provides yet another contrast to the general population of survivors in Germany, who, by and large, were unable to devote energy to cultivating the intellectual sphere so soon after liberation.[17]

Were the members themselves pleased with life at the kibbutz? How did they perceive its role in their plans for the future? Some, like Lola Sultanik and Itka Harash, viewed their stay at the kibbutz as an interim period, a time-out prior to making decisions regarding their future. Others, like Avraham Gottlieb, felt the need to prepare themselves for the future by resuming the studies interrupted by the war. Still others saw the kibbutz as a fleeting phenomenon, one incapable of long-term survival in its present form. Avraham Gottlieb recorded his impressions regarding this issue in late July 1945, expressing his lack of regret on founding the kibbutz but also voicing his apprehension that the kibbutz was an experiment that had failed: "For we . . . all differ in nature and intelligence; each of us lacks some quality and has difficulty finding himself, in truly knowing his 'I.' Not one of us truly knows where he is bound, or where his heart pulls him, to whom his longing takes him, or why his bubbling laughter is followed by intense sadness. Yet I know that there is no place better than this kibbutz, for sadness dogs the steps of all those who have evaded death's embrace. I do not believe that it can be evaded." Was there an alternative, he asked, one that would be viable for the majority of survivors in Germany? "Perhaps the answer lies in individual existence, in a family and not in a kibbutz setting? Or does happiness lie in the collective existence? And, are we, who differ so from one another, all suited to the collective life? I have no answers, only questions."[18]

EARLY DIFFICULTIES OF COOPERATIVE KIBBUTZ EXISTENCE

Avraham's critical musings were not the only expression of concern and even discontent among the group of young Zionist pioneers, many of whom had little understanding of the meaning of Zionism and pioneering life; of kibbutz members who had only a partial comprehension of the nature of collective existence, with little or no grasp of the ideology behind the experiment. Consequently, despite the idealized descriptions of a pastoral existence enlivened by singing and dancing, cracks soon appeared in the foundation of Kibbutz Buchenwald's earthly paradise.

One set of difficulties stemmed from the heterogeneous composition of the kibbutz membership, comprised of people who had only recently undergone inconceivably traumatic experiences. It was therefore not surprising that the kibbutz had its share of internal dissension. Memoirs and recollections of the chalutzim reveal three main areas of conflict: religion, national origin, and ideology. Of the three, religion presented the least problem, and was the first to be resolved. One example was the debate over what day would be the official day of rest on the kibbutz, a question initially raised at Eggendorf. Naturally, the observant Jews wanted Saturday, while Elik and his circle opted for Sunday, in accord with civil practice. Finally, a compromise was reached whereby Saturday was declared the official day of rest, but those who wished to take Sunday off as well were free to do so. The same principle was applied to *kashrut* (Jewish dietary laws). While most of the members ate whatever was available, a kosher kitchen supplied food for the observant Jews. By all accounts, the figure responsible for this spirit of tolerance was the kibbutz leader, a religious Jew who made no attempt to impose his way of life on the collective and created an atmosphere best characterized as "Live and let live." As Arthur Poznansky recalled, "On the first Saturday at Geringshof, Elik wanted to go horseback riding. He consulted Tydor. 'Today is the Sabbath,' he replied. 'I cannot give you permission, but neither will I tell you what to do.' " Tydor's tolerant attitude had a pervasive influence.[19] Even Elik Gruenbaum admitted as much. As the person in charge of household management, he made certain that there was ample kosher food for those who wanted it. "We also wanted to keep the idea of Sabbath, to take a direction as yet unheard of in Palestine," he recalled. "We wanted to keep their Sabbath, that of the religious; at the same time we didn't want them to tell us what to do." Did such an enterprise have any promise? "I believed there was a chance, even a good chance of success, because after what we went through . . . we knew . . . that a Jew is a Jew, whether he has *payes* [Yiddish for sidelocks], a beard, and a *shtreimel* [fur-edged hat worn by Hasidic Jews] or is clean shaven, he is a Jew."[20]

Apparently, within the initial group at Geringshof, tensions related to the realm of religious observance were quickly and satisfactorily resolved. A trickier area of conflict revolved about the different national origins of the leadership—German Jews—as opposed to the membership—largely Polish Jews. Over time, segments of the membership developed feelings of being discriminated against on the basis of their Polish origins. The following entry from the kibbutz diary, dating from mid-July, sharply delineates this sense of discrimination.

There are two camps in our kibbutz—"us" and "them." This phenomenon must be noted and clarified. "Us" means the majority, and "them" means Zauderer, Poznansky, and perhaps Tydor as well. I am not suggesting that these are hostile camps; I am simply noting their existence as something undesirable in and of itself. The underlying cause for this division is thus: We are all ordinary members, and though we may differ in degree of development or intellectual ability, this is not noticeable due to the open and friendly relations that prevail among us. But Zauderer and Poznansky come from an entirely different environment. They are true *Yekkim* [Yiddish term for German Jews], who find it hard to get along with us, sometimes even with regard to trifling matters. They act as if they are the masters and we are the workers in some work camp or other. Perhaps they mean well, but we resent their patronizing behavior. It often turns out in the course of disagreement that "they" are right, but we are not inclined to give in, in order not to convey the impression that we are taking orders. . . . We all realize that Zauderer and Poznansky merit recognition, but we cannot tolerate "masters" in our kibbutz. . . . Anyone who tries—wittingly or unwittingly—to create classes in our kibbutz meets with stiff opposition from the members, who are perhaps too enamored of battle. This situation promotes rebellious feelings and gossip all around the camp, and fights as well. None of these brings any benefit.[21]

This bitterness was not universally felt; it reflects rather a minority view. The members' responses to questions regarding this issue reveal that while some displayed extreme sensitivity to the "national rupture," others failed to notice it until the issue was raised at a kibbutz meeting. Itka Harash agreed that some friction existed between the German-born and the Polish-born members. "The Germans conversed in German, or even Hebrew, while the members from Poland spoke Yiddish," she recalled. "Some of the German-born adopted a condescending tone toward the others. But Tydor managed to smooth things over. As a *Yekke* of Polish origin, he spoke both fluent German and a *geshmakte* [flavorsome] Yiddish, and everyone respected his desire to make peace among the *chaverim* [members]."[22]

Indeed, logic dictated that the official kibbutz representatives be German born. Given the circumstances, "it could not be otherwise," remarked Tydor. Although there were leaders among the Polish-born factions, such as Elik Gruenbaum and his circle, in order to represent the kibbutz effectively to the outside world, it was necessary to use someone fluent in the local language—German—and familiar with the local procedures as well. "Therefore, it was only natural that the kibbutz's representatives for external affairs be of German origin," he concluded.[23] Another leader of the German group, Arthur Poznansky, recalled being called upon to conduct official visitors around the kibbutz. He also traveled to Fulda and Frankfurt on kibbutz business, appearing before the authorities as its official representative.[24]

The us-and-them controversy is emblematic of the third realm of conflict—the ideological split. An obvious source of friction was the heterogeneous nature of the members' Zionist leanings. At Kibbutz Buchenwald, veteran chalutzim, members of existing trends within the Zionist movement; newly initiated chalutzim, who barely knew what a party was; and non-chalutzim were represented as well. At Kibbutz Buchenwald, the schism between the veteran pioneers and the "new Zionists"—rather than party differences—sparked the most volatile internal debate. On occasion, these differences of opinion irritated outsiders more than they bothered the members themselves. During a visit in mid-July, Rabbi Robert Marcus, the U.S. Army chaplain who together with Rabbi Schacter assisted the Buchenwald survivors, complained that word had reached him of lack of discipline among the members. This comment aroused an angry response from those who but moments before had been deeply involved in an ideological debate regarding the nature of the ideal society to be founded in Palestine. "Can we determine now that we will always dance to the same tune?" retorted Avraham. "Is any harm done if religious members study *Mishnah* [Oral Law] together, while in a different corner of the dining room another group learns English, or if yet a third group of young men and women prefers a walk in the woods to study? The important thing is that the members share a single goal—to work in Palestine for the Jewish people."[25]

As long as they remained confined to the abstract realm, these differences could be bridged, but the moment real-life questions were at stake, battle lines were drawn, emphasizing the gaps between the various groups: veteran Zionist movement members versus newcomers, secular versus orthodox, those originating in Germany and those from Poland. In other locales throughout occupied Germany a similar process was making itself felt, particularly in the close confines of the DP camps, where groups based upon origin, religious affiliation, and ideology were a common occurence. The pinnacle of postwar DP partisanship were the fistfights between various groups in the camps—Zionist and non-Zionist, or orthodox and secular— over various practical issues. Even an issue such as matzah baking on Passover could cause unprecedented strife between orthodox and ultraorthodox in these camps, as documented by letters of the Religious Department of the Joint Distribution Committee responsible for supplying ritual articles to the DPs in Germany.[26]

In the case of Kibbutz Buchenwald, one such divisive issue was the question of entry certificates to Palestine. From the beginning, there were those who advocated issuing certificates only to the "deserving," that is, only to those with deep-seated Zionist convictions. Naturally, this approach angered many of the members, who felt that the entire kibbutz should remain together as a group. When the latter opinion prevailed, the issue was seemingly settled. Not so. Nevertheless, as long as aliyah remained an unfulfilled dream, it seemed absurd to continue this debate.

The members began to despair of ever reaching Palestine. In early July, Avraham noted that the group's patience was at an end. "We argue endlessly," he wrote. "The information that has reached us proves that our residing in Germany is a dead end. We shall remain here forever, while all those who reach Paris and make contact with the Palestine office in Paris will end up in Palestine."[27] Actively encouraged by Rabbi Schacter, the members began to seriously consider leaving Germany for France as a group, without waiting for the services of intermediaries. Rabbi Marcus, Schacter's the more senior of the two Jewish chaplains, requested that the members delay their departure by two weeks. In the interim, Marcus himself promised to try to expedite the matter of the certificates. If, within this two-week period, he failed to achieve results, the members would be free to proceed unrestricted.

Following this conversation, the kibbutz members penned a letter to the Palestine office in Paris. The letter, signed by Avraham Gottlieb, politely but firmly stated their unswerving resolve to leave Germany. It also clearly implied that if their request was denied, the kibbutz members would not hesitate to employ unconventional means to reach their goal. "Do you really believe that agricultural training is our true aim?" they wrote. "Are we in need of physical or spiritual training to be worthy of living in Palestine? . . . We have already undergone a six-year trial period that forged us in iron, immunized our bodies against illness and earthly troubles, and prepared us to be fearless emotionally. We will march bravely toward our set goal, paying stumbling blocks no heed," they concluded forcefully.[28]

Historical circumstances favored the chalutzim. The very same week that Rabbi Marcus delivered their letter to the Paris office, Eliyahu Dobkin, assistant head of the Jewish Agency's immigration department, was there. Succumbing to pressure from Marcus, Dobkin agreed to grant the kibbutz seventy certificates remaining from the prewar reserves of five thousand.[29] Rabbi Marcus brought these glad tidings to the kibbutz upon his return, on July 15, but he also forwarded an accompanying request; that the group remain at Geringshof until the certificates would be delivered, some six weeks hence.

This by no means comprised Rabbi Marcus's only significant contribution to Kibbutz Buchenwald. Throughout his travels in the summer of 1945, Robert Marcus conducted an intensive publicity campaign on the kibbutz's behalf. Unceasingly disseminating information about the hachsharah to his audience in Germany, he also took steps to ensure that news of the kibbutz's existence reached the Jewish press in Palestine by publishing an article about the farm in the Palestine Labor movement's daily, *Davar*.[30] In addition to spreading publicity about the kibbutz, Rabbi Marcus brought his listeners to the farm itself. Through his mediation, British and American military officers, as well as Jewish and non-Jewish welfare workers, reached the farm. One such visitor, Dr. Joseph Schwartz, European head of the Joint Distribution Committee, was so impressed that he immediately promised to cover the kibbutz's monthly operational deficit of approximately five thousand marks.

Members of the Jewish Brigade were also counted among the frequent visitors to the kibbutz. Two—Chaim Ben-Asher, "a Brigade member from [Kibbutz] Giv'at Brenner," and Arieh Simon, "an officer of the Jewish fighting division from Ben-Shemen"—made brief entries in the kibbutz diary when they came to lecture the members on the need to enlist concentration camp survivors in the struggle for a Jewish state.

By coincidence, that same day Eliyahu Dobkin himself arrived at the kibbutz and was given a reception in keeping with his standing as the person who would shortly award the members the much-awaited certificates. In the course of their meeting, however, Dobkin shocked the kibbutz members by suggested that they could better serve Zionist aims by rejecting the certificates and remaining in the Diaspora in symbolic protest against British immigration policy. Their immediate reaction was one of outrage, but Dobkin would not back down. Although he had certificates at his disposal, the group would receive them only if no "worthier" group were found. Dobkin's laconic entry in the kibbutz chronicle—"May we soon meet again in Eretz Israel"—contrasted ironically with his squelching of the group's hopes.

This meeting with Dobkin marked a turning point for the members of Kibbutz Buchenwald. Even the most naïve realized that they had been drawn unwittingly into a political game. For them, the training farm at Geringshof had symbolized both a new way of life and a means of reaching Palestine. Suddenly, they were struck by the thought that for the Yishuv leadership, they were simply another bargaining chip in the struggle to establish a Jewish state. If their immigration would in any way further the Jewish Agency's political interests, they would be sent to Palestine immediately, given the availability of the certificates. If not, the members at Geringshof feared, they would be left to rot in the Diaspora until the coming of the Messiah or the founding of a Jewish state, whichever came first.

This somewhat simplistic view regarding the attitude of the Yishuv's leadership to the survivors does not do justice to the complexity of the situation. At that time, the Zionist leadership had no clearly defined or consistent policy toward the survivors. Substantial differences in attitude divided the leadership in Palestine from those in direct daily contact with the survivors, such as members of the Jewish Brigade. However, both groups recognized that in the fluid postwar European context it was impossible to try to persuade the Jewish DPs—both the Zionist oriented and the undecided—that their future lay only in Palestine. In Ben-Gurion's opinion, this was the sole means of achieving a "Zionist solution" to the Palestine issue.[31] Consequently, after his visit to Germany in the autumn of 1945, Ben-Gurion decided that disseminating Zionist propaganda among the survivors would be given top priority. Even before that date, the Yishuv leadership had intuitively concluded that the European Jews' strong desire to leave Europe could be channeled from a mass emigration to any destination into a longing for Zion, even among those with no professed Zionist leanings. The only question was how to go about doing so.

THE FIRST CONFERENCE OF JEWISH SURVIVORS IN GERMANY

Meanwhile, preparations for the General Conference of Jewish Survivors in Munich were under way. The conference opened on July 25, at St. Ottilien, a former Benedictine monastery not far from Munich. During the war, it had served the Nazis as a hospital, and at war's end, the Americans transformed it into an assembly center for Jews from the surrounding areas. The forum convened at eight P.M., and discussions continued uninterrupted for eleven consecutive hours, until the following morning. Among the ninety-four delegates were five from Kibbutz Buchenwald—Yechezkel Tydor, Elik Gruenbaum, Simcha Dimant, Paltiel Rosenfrucht, and Leib Gruenfeld. In turn, each delegate presented the problems of the camp, population, or particular group he was deputed to represent. As kibbutz leader, Tydor addressed the plenum. "Each group spoke of its problems and maladies," he recalled. "Then it was my turn to represent a group that had taken the initiative to leave the camp, to live in a healthy environment in preparation for aliyah. In light of our success I suggested that others take advantage of the fluid situation to 'appropriate' confiscated estates while it was still feasible."[32]

Despite the successful precedent of Kibbutz Buchenwald, Tydor's words fell on deaf ears. Representatives of the London-based orthodox Va'ad Hatzalah (Rescue Committee) opposed this idea most vociferously, contending that if large numbers of Jews were removed from the camps, it would create the misleading impression among the Allied governments that they no longer needed to address the DP question. This would engender difficulties for survivors and welfare agencies alike. Nor were the Zionist organizations anxious to implement Tydor's suggestion. Prior to 1946, with the arrival of Polish pioneers in Germany, no similar initiatives had been taken. The underlying causes were complex. The stewards of the Zionist movement feared that by founding additional kibbutz training farms, the survivors would take root in Germany, whereas their sense of dislocation was viewed as a useful tool for shaping world opinion in favor of a Jewish state. Thus, on the one hand, the pioneering movements in Germany missed a unique opportunity to set up dozens of training farms outside the DP camps; but on the other hand, the Zionist leadership already visualized a role for the survivors in its future policy. While this role clashed with the survivors' immediate interests, it was clear to the Zionist leadership that in order to achieve the greater good of a Jewish state, the immediate needs of the survivors had to be sacrificed.[33]

This first conference of survivors aroused mixed feelings among the Kibbutz Buchenwald delegates. It was, of course, a moving symbolic public demonstration of independence by those who had so recently been released from their shackles. The pinnacle of this declaration was the decision to hold the closing session at the infamous Munich Burgerbrau beer cellar. On the other hand, the majority of speakers emphasized that the survivors were as yet unable to determine their own fate. The sense that their superficial independence masked an ever growing dependence on foreign agencies was acutely felt by the Kibbutz Buchenwald delegates, who had not yet recovered from the impression left by Dobkin's visit to the farm. Then surprisingly, once again fortune smiled upon the members of the kibbutz. Within the space of a few days after the delegates' return, the kibbutz members were informed that they had been granted eighty immigration certificates, a number that even exceeded the kibbutz membership. Consequently, it was decided to induct new members both to fill the quota, and to ensure the continuity of the hachsharah following the first group's departure for Palestine. Up to that point, almost anyone who expressed a desire to join the kibbutz had been accepted. In light of the new situation, this policy underwent a change, expressed succinctly in Avraham Gottlieb's diary: "We have eighty immigration certificates, but our kibbutz does not have eighty members," he wrote. "Therefore, we can induct new members to accompany us to Palestine. But now we will not admit members casually; we seek only those worthy of aliyah."[34]

This phrase—"worthy of aliyah"—was destined to epitomize the most serious rift among the founders of at Kibbutz Buchenwald. A potential source for new members was the Hechalutz pioneering Zionist center at Bergen-Belsen; thus, Arthur Poznansky and Simcha Dimant were dispatched to make overtures to the group. Their reception at Bergen-Belsen destroyed any remaining vestiges of political naïveté at Kibbutz Buchenwald. The Hechalutz group request that the Kibbutz Buchenwald members consider the general good and flagrantly return the certificates in protest. Eighty certificates were certainly insufficient to redeem the surviving remnant of European Jewry. Moreover, the kibbutz members should be the last to go; first priority should be awarded to those who might sink into a life or crime or degeneracy.[35] This request generated an uproar in the kibbutz. Following intense debate, the kibbutz resolved to reject the proposal to return the certificates. Avraham Gottlieb summed up the decision by saying that they may have been naïve, but they were not stupid:

> We had beautiful slogans, like bringing the idea of unity to Palestine, and justifiable rationales for using the certificates, like the argument that they came from the old prewar quota, and that none of the Yishuv leaders who visited the kibbutz had even hinted at the possibility of returning them in protest. But we were well aware that even if we returned the certificates, they would not be framed and hung, but used by "VIPs" in our stead. Idealism is a beautiful thing, but we were not so innocent as to believe that all the Hechalutz members themselves were ready to take this step.[36]

It quickly became evident that Avraham's suspicions were not unfounded. Two days after Dimant and Poznansky returned from their mission, members of Poznansky's former hachsharot began arriving at Geringshof. The arrival of these young people caused a "minor revolution," to quote the author of the entry in the kibbutz diary for that day. "Upon their arrival we suddenly saw a different sort of person, unlike us," he wrote. "Young people, whose past in pioneering movements is apparent, modestly dressed, lively, at home from the moment of their arrival, subject to group discipline, placing the movement above all, constantly laughing and singing."[37]

The minor revolution was followed by an aftershock. On the evening of their arrival, one of the chalutzim, Herbert Growald, contended that the certificates should be given to movement members more worthy of aliyah than they. Moreover, he claimed to have heard that the members intended to strip the farm upon their departure, and issued a warning that if they did so, the long arm of justice would pursue them in Palestine. Shock swiftly gave way to anger directed not only at the newcomers from Bergen-Belsen, but mainly at Poznansky, who now appeared to some as a traitor. This impression is reflected both in the kibbutz diary and in Avraham Gottlieb's personal notes. "We expected to welcome them as equals, with no barriers," he wrote. "But throughout the day, a sort of coolness emanated from them, for which we had no explanation. All day long they were involved in discussions among themselves, and Arthur with them. We had no inkling of the topic of discussion, nor did we care. Now we understand."[38]

The entry in the kibbutz diary was even more explicit, breaking the last taboo of keeping at least an apparent semblance of complete unity within the group:

> In his sick view of the world, of mankind, and of us, Arthur has evolved strange ideas about us, sounding off preposterous notions to his friends. In so doing, Arthur has doubly sinned against us. He has defamed us to outsiders. It seems that he saw our ship sinking, and with no pangs of conscience transferred to a passing ship. Furthermore, from there he helped sink ours. And all this while serving as a responsible member of the *va'ad* [committee]. And his other sin. He has misrepresented us, thereby creating a negative impression of us among the new members.[39]

There was a sequel to this story. Several days later, Poznansky announced that he intended to waive his right to leave for Palestine with the first group in order to stay on with the new members. From this point on, he was openly aligned with the Bergen-Belsen faction—all veteran members of Hechalutz, all German born. Thus two avenues of friction—the ideological and the national—coalesced.

Was this feeling general, or was this sharp reaction confined to the small group of activists that had emerged early in the summer? "Those poor certificates!" recalled Tydor ironically, chronicling the never-ending saga of the immigration passes. "It appears that we were never intended to use them. First there was the scene with Dobkin, and Rabbi Marcus's pleading with the Paris office until they granted the entry permits. Then there was the demand that we return them in protest, and finally, the request that we grant them to movement members." How did the group react to the attack on their only venue for leaving Germany? "Some of us paid no heed, some laughed, others got angry," he concluded.[40]

What position did the newcomers to Geringshof take regarding the issue that threatened to split the kibbutz not only internally but with regard to the new members, that of the relationship between the newcomers and the kibbutz founders? Ernst Simcha (nicknamed Pize in allusion to a popular prewar German comedian) attempted to explain the position of the Bergen-Belsen faction after having met the chalutzim from Geringshof: "Herbert's warnings were not unfounded," he stated categorically. "We had been in contact with the group almost from its inception and knew that some of the people there were capable of taking things from the general pool for their personal use."[41]

Additional insight into the attitude of the Bergen-Belsen faction was given by Hilda Gruenwald, one of the leading Hechalutz coordinators in the camp. According to Gruenwald, the prevailing view among the Hechalutz federation at Bergen-Belsen regarding those "worthy of aliyah" differed from the one presented by Herbert Growald. "We believed that it was precisely the sick, the stragglers, and the weak who should go first, since we, the movement's members, would certainly reach Palestine," she stated. "In fact, we, that is Arthur's band, were promised eight or ten places in the first group, but we declined to go, sending others in our stead so we could ensure the continuity of the hachsharah at Geringshof."[42]

The relationship between the members of Kibbutz Buchenwald and the Hechalutz center at Bergen-Belsen was a complex one, even before the issue of immigration certificates loomed upon the horizon. The central pioneering center had been established at Bergen-Belsen by a group of activist Zionist survivors—both men and women—immediately after the liberation. Maintaining close contact with Kibbutz Buchenwald even before its move to Geringshof, the Hechalutz center made no attempt to interfere in the nature or running of the kibbutz until it was necessary to recruit new members. At that point, Hechalutz entered the picture, sending several dozen chalutzim to the farm, including the young newcomers alluded to in the kibbutz diary. This particular mixture of founders and newcomers was fraught with tension; even during a brief period of coexistence, a state of cold war prevailed between the two groups. The battle lines were clearly drawn: Hechalutz members versus the "mixed multitude"; members from German-based hachsharot versus members from Polish-based ones, or those with no prior training farm experience at all; Geringshof's new residents, who had just begun the process of acclimation, versus its longtime residents, who had one foot on the boat, so to speak; and, most important, those intending to enter Palestine illegally as opposed to those holding legal liberation certificates. The dichotomy that developed between the "Buchenwald veterans"—as the kibbutz founders were called by the Bergen-Belsen group—and the new chalutzim marked an era of conflict that lasted until the first group's departure for Palestine. At that point, the Bergen-Belsen faction essentially took charge of the training farm at Geringshof, completing the practical and ideological Hechalutz takeover of the hachsharah.

The New Groups at Geringshof

The increased politicization engendered by the newly appended group alarmed the kibbutz secretariat, which attempted to take countermeasures before leaving for Palestine. The first was to try to attract members from other trends in the Zionist movement. To this end, Tydor traveled to Frankfurt to make contact with other Zionist-oriented survivors, while another member made overtures to a group of young women from the ultraorthodox Po'alei Agudat Israel movement who wished to go to Palestine. The young survivors, aged eighteen to thirty, were hesitant to join the hachsharah, and finally delegated two of their number to investigate and report on life at the kibbutz.

The ultraorthodox vanguard arrived at Geringshof during the second week of August, and was immediately referred to Tydor, as kibbutz head. Expounding upon the principles of the unique hachsharah to these two young women from the Beth Jacob center, the orthodox girls' school network that had been reestablished at Bergen-Belsen, Tydor extended an invitation for them to stay over the weekend in order to assess their compatibility with kibbutz life. The offer was particularly tempting to the two young women, who wanted to experience firsthand what life on Geringshof was like before committing the entire group to a Zionist nonpartisan pioneering life. "The Sabbath we spent there was a positive experience, and at its conclusion there was no doubt in our minds that we would return to Bergen-Belsen for the rest of the young women," recalled Rivka England, the younger of the two emissaries. "However, the technical arrangements took time, and we reached Geringshof only on the evening before the first group's departure for Palestine. As a result we spent only that one, but unforgettable, evening together," she concluded.[43]

This idyllic but simplistic portrait was only a partial impression of the duo's experiences regarding the merger with Geringshof. Rachel Shantzer, the other Beth Jacob emissary who spent the weekend at Geringshof, recalls that matters were infinitely more complex. Some girls opposed the idea of a mixed secular-religious hachsharah, and after much discussion, they addressed a question on this matter to Rabbi Moshe Munk, an UNRRA representative who was then living in a town near Bergen-Belsen. "Was it permissible to join a kibbutz with secular Jews in order to obtain immigration certificates?" we asked. "He gave us an affirmative answer, based upon the rationale that all possible means should be employed to leave Germany. Nonetheless, some of our members still hesitated. It was our meeting with Tydor that tipped the balance. I remember my overwhelming astonishment that the kibbutz leader was an ultraorthodox Jew from Frankfurt."[44]

Despite the desire for immediate travel to the hachsharah, a number of practical obstacles delayed the implementation of the decision to go. The young women did not want to make the transfer unaccompanied, so they co-opted several ultraorthodox young men from Bergen-Belsen on the pretext that the group would need at least a few men for religious purposes. With the demographic balance within the group resolved, a second question arose: Should the ultraorthodox survivors join the existing hachsharah at Geringshof, or should they move to a neighboring affiliated farm, which they could run according to their own specifications? The small band was divided on this matter and eventually deemed it advisable to move to Geringshof proper. Nevertheless, it was understood that some of the women would later move to a separate nearby hachsharah that would be started at the Gersfeld farm.[45]

Within a few months, the hachsharah at Gersfeld, an orchard-bounded farm several kilometers from Geringshof, became an independent center and continued to function as a collection point for chalutzim until 1948. Its inception is shrouded in obscurity. Tydor recalled taking the young women to Lieutenant Finkelstein, who appropriated for them the small farm near Geringshof that was slated to become a separate hachsharah. Others claim that the farm was taken over in September 1945 in order to catch the overflow from Geringshof when the "mother hachsharah" became overcrowded.

Pize, the Hechalutz activist from Bergen-Belsen who subsequently became one of the leaders of the second group training at Geringshof, recalled Geringshof and Gersfeld as being one hachsharah, separated only by geographical distance. "There was constant movement between the two," he stated. "I cannot recall how or when the hachsharah at Gersfeld came into being, but the rationale for the move was clear: Geringshof was full, and if we wished to retain our members and accept new chalutzim as well, we had to be able to offer tolerable conditions."[46]

The issue of living conditions on the hachsharah, and the possibility of solving problems of overcrowding, was yet another facet contrasting Kibbutz Buchenwald with the DP camps then being established throughout the American sector of occupied Germany. These camps, characterized by serious overcrowding, lack of any privacy, and the ensuing tensions, were a far cry from the pastoral setting of the Zionist training farm. Consequently, a major attraction of the young kibbutz was the physical living conditions, which were immensely gracious in comparison with the early postwar conditions in the survivors' living centers.

IMMIGRATION TO PALESTINE

While these new members were being absorbed, the veteran group was preparing for aliyah. On a few days' notice, the outgoing group had to pack its belongings and turn the farm over to the incoming group. On Sunday evening, August 26, the hachsharah's administration was transferred to a temporary committee drawn from among the new members, including Isaac Juker, Pize, Aharon Gafni, and Rivka Englard, each representing one of the subgroups that had recently joined the kibbutz. Following the ceremony, during which an inventory of the farm's property was signed by both the incoming and the outgoing committees, the farewell party began. After the speeches were over, the members danced into the night around a campfire in the kibbutz garden. The climax of the farewell party took place at midnight, when the entire group stood in a circle watching a swastika burn in a symbolic act of spiritual revenge.

The kibbutz diary devoted but a few lines to the first group's departure, noting only that it traveled to Fulda in five U.S. Army trucks. American GI Akiva Skidell included a more colorful description in a letter to his wife in which he explained how it came about that the pioneers traveled in army trucks, not UNRRA buses. "Officially they are supposed to be going through UNRRA, but UNRRA is becoming the standard joke around the place, like the Joint [Distribution Committee], for that matter," he wrote. "When UNRRA sends clothes, it is rags, worse than what they have taken out of the concentration camps." In the case of Kibbutz Buchenwald, UNRRA was supposed to provide transportation but did not. Consequently, it was decided that the chalutzim, led by Tydor and including almost all the founding members, would travel by army train from Fulda to Marseilles. "To Fulda they went by army trucks, arranged for by the Jewish major [Rosenbaum] from town that I wrote you about. The major was there yesterday, came to say good-bye and see what they need, and they told him their plight. So he said, five GI truck will be waiting for them right on the farm at 6 A.M. Otherwise they would have to travel half the night or more by cart to meet the train at Fulda," Skidell concluded.[47]

From Fulda, the group set out for the port of Marseilles, traveling through Germany and France for a week. The the trip was punctuated with stirring moments, some inherent in the trip itself, and others in the timing, the pre–High Holy Day season. A high point was the recitation of the *Selichot* (penitential prayers). Tydor recalled poignantly how the group began to recite Selichot on Saturday night, on the way to Marseilles: "A member with cantorial ability recited the refrain, *'Be-mozei menuchah'* ['When the day of rest ends']. Most joined in the prayer, and everyone felt a great spiritual uplift."[48]

Not all those present had precisely the same recollection. Avraham Gottlieb gave the "spiritual uplift" a different twist in the description appearing in his diary:

The door of the car is open. Below stands a mixed group of members laughingly reciting the prayer calling the congregation to Selichot. This is our group of practical jokers, who have once again decided to mock us, waking everyone on the pretext that tonight is the first night of Selichot. What clowns! . . . All the passengers are awake. Some got angry and shouted at the *meshigeners* [crazy ones]. Others laughed, while a few got off their hard beds and joined the group. Now they are gathering on the grassy bank of the tracks, and the violinist, who has awakened, is playing his violin, and the group is singing along. No prayer or plea is on their lips: rather it's simply a noisy way to spend a sleepless night. Songs resound in Hebrew, Yiddish, Russian, and Polish. Now someone is giving a nonsensical speech, and everyone is choking with laughter.[49]

A totally different aspect of the trip was the opportunity for revenge. At one stop, the group chanced upon American soldiers guarding a sealed train. Brief inquiry revealed that "not people, but SS men"—in the words of the anonymous entry in the kibbutz diary—were being held there. "We greeted them as they deserved. Rocks hailed down on the cars holding the SS men. If not for the whistle indicating our departure, not a stone would have remained at the station."[50]

Yet another facet of the trip centered around the number of chalutzim traveling to Palestine and the legal means by which they would be admitted. Throughout the journey, Tydor, Zauderer, and Gruenbaum wrestled with the problem of the certificates. Although eighty permits had been promised, the group, which had swelled by new members, now numbered approximately one hundred. How would this "surplus" reach Palestine? As the train pulled into Marseilles, no solution had yet been found.

In Marseilles, the group was greeted by another little surprise regarding this matter—only seventy-eight certificates had been provided. According to the kibbutz diary, two members were struck from the list of immigrants. One of them could enter Palestine legally through Youth Aliyah, the immigration framework for unaccompanied children and teenagers. The day after their arrival, the group boarded the SS *Mataroa*, an aging British ship. On September 4, the ship weighed anchor and embarked for Palestine.

The immigrants sailing on the *Mataroa* were more than a thousand Jews who had come from Switzerland, Belgium, France, and Germany. Among them were David Frankfurter, who had attempted to assassinate the Swiss Nazi leader Gustlaf, and Rabbit Robert Marcus, in his capacity as World Jewish Congress representative. Paltiel Ben-Chaim recorded his impressions of the travelers in the kibbutz diary, categorizing them both demographically and anthropologically:

The human material is varied. It spans the elderly, women with children who did not suffer under Hitler, alongside concentration camp survivors who miraculously survived; women with painted lips and nails alongside muscular chalutzim with calloused hands. The concept of unity that we uphold has attracted much sympathetic interest among the Jews aboard our ship, especially among the former concentration camp inmates, as opposed to the Swiss Jews who had no experience of the camps, who have not yet been penetrated by the moral lesson of six million dead. They continue to adhere to their outdated party principles.[51]

Another account of the trip was delivered to the Mapai (Israeli Labor Party) secretariat by emissary David Shealtiel, who traveled with the immigrants. His reaction to the passengers' behavior bordered on disgust. The young men repeatedly attempted to gain entry to the women's cabins, while the young girls "went only with the sailors, sponging off them."[52] Both Shealtiel and Rabbi Marcus spent most of their time policing the ship in an attempt to instill order. In the midst of the general atmosphere of licentiousness, the Kibbutz Buchenwald group was a notable exception. Shealtiel praised the group and predicted a rosy future: "These individuals are bound by emotional ties and shared experiences," he wrote enthusiastically. "They have decided to try their hand at living together on a kibbutz, when they are settled. . . . Wonderful material, and disciplined, I think Dobkin took the right step in granting them certificates. We believe their example will encourage the hachsharah movement in Germany."[53]

At Rabbi Marcus's request, the group put out a newspaper at sea, *Hed Hagalim* (Echo of the waves). The paper included two articles prepared by Shlomo Gruenfeld and Avraham Gottlieb, as well as coverage of shipboard events and a humorous sketch by the kibbutz comedian, Elimelech Wiener. The newspaper was printed in spite of the stormy weather conditions in order to assure its distribution before Rosh Hashanah (the Jewish New Year).

"We finally sighted land rising from the mist" on the morning of the second day of Rosh Hashanah, wrote Ben-Chaim in the kibbutz diary. "Tears of happiness welled up in many of the passengers' eyes. The mist lifted as we approached the shore. British boats approached with greetings. Cheers of joy from the immigrants erupted in response. Singing 'Hatikvah' ["Hope," now the Israeli national anthem], we reached Haifa port at 2:30 P.M."[54]

How did other Kibbutz Buchenwald members react to their first glimpse of Mount Carmel, upon sighting their long-awaited goal? Here are impressions of the thoughts and hopes of four members: According to Lola Sultanik, "When I saw the mountain I thought: At last I have realized my parents' dream! I have achieved what my family could not." Shmuel Yuskowitz remembered: "I felt that I had realized an innermost childhood dream. I expected to experience marvelous feelings upon first treading on the soil of Eretz Israel." In the words of Avraham Gottlieb: "It was a climax. We saw the Carmel as the physical embodiment of a dream." Itka Harash, the group's youngest member, described her feelings at that moment more fully:

> At first we could only see the mountain range from afar. I was surrounded by men and women, young and old, whose eyes brimmed with tears, and I, I couldn't cry. I couldn't really take in what I was seeing. That we were nearing Eretz Israel, that I knew. That we were approaching Haifa, of that I was also aware. But this mountain—I wasn't sure what it was. When I inquired, the people standing nearby laughed, and answered: "That's Mount Carmel." And I stood whispering to myself: "That's the Carmel, the Carmel from which we drank the wine."[55]

The ship docked at Haifa in the afternoon, on the second day of Rosh Hashanah, 1945. In the course of a day, its passengers left their status as the remnants of the European Diaspora behind to become full-fledged members of the Jewish Yishuv in Palestine. This step inadvertently brought with it the seeds of change. Although the group was exhilarated at reaching its goal, divisive forces began to act upon its members. Due to the sanctity of the day, the authorities allowed the religious passengers to remain on the dock until the conclusion of Rosh Hashanah. Instead of remaining together as a group, most of the Kibbutz Buchenwald members left for the Atlit transit camp, leaving the handful of religious members behind at the pier, seated on orange crates. At that moment, the religious members were not particularly troubled by the larger group's departure. Nonetheless, the secular majority's willingness to part company so readily with the religious minority indicates the fragility of the ostensibly inviolable principle of unity. At this juncture, the members had no inkling of the selection process they were about to undergo at the hands of the party representatives at Atlit, or of the increased dropout rate of religious members following the kibbutz's move to kibbutz Afikim. Nor could they have foreseen the political homogeneity of the future groups from Geringshof that subsequently would join them in Palestine. Finally, they had no knowledge as yet of the virtual impossibility of coexistence within the sociopolitical context of the Yishuv. At that moment they cared for one thing only—the fact that they had finally reached their homeland.

Tydor recalled what had happened to the group's "illegal" immigrants: "We were lucky," he stated. As the British were anxious to be rid of the group and knew that it was impossible to board ship at Marseilles without a certificate, they didn't bother counting the group when its members disembarked at Haifa. The orthodox chalutzim remained on the Haifa docks until sundown. Tydor remembered:

> We waited for the holiday to end. We sang, amused ourselves, recited the evening prayer. We were surprised that the stars came out at seven in the

evening, and not at eight or nine P.M. as in Europe. We traveled to Atlit to join the other members. That night a single emotion dominated our thoughts: that we had reached the end of our wandering, wandering that had lasted for years and encompassed many lands, peoples, and the sounds of foreign languages. Now we found ourselves at the end of a road that also marked the beginning of a new way of life.[56]

Thus, a mere hundred days after sixteen young men had left Buchenwald for Eggendorf, the first group of pioneers from Kibbutz Buchenwald arrived in its homeland.

THE EARLY HISTORY OF KIBBUTZ BUCHENWALD IN HISTORICAL PERSPECTIVE

Kibbutz Buchenwald, organized during the formative months of June through September 1945, was, in its history and development, both like and unlike the general formation and activity of the other DPs in occupied Germany. The characteristics that distinguished Kibbutz Buchenwald from other projects undertaken by survivors during this period are discernible in an examination of two fundamental concepts as they related to the survivors—*ichud* (unity) and *kibbutz*.

The Unity Movement

The pioneers' idealistic, perhaps even naïve, belief that representatives of different Zionist political trends could live peacefully under one roof, keeping company with pure souls as yet untouched by the odium of politicization, was not only a byproduct of the war; it had a prior history. A close look at the history of the ichud movement shows that the members' faith did not emerge in either an ideological or a practical vacuum. Within the Zionist movement in the 1930s and 1940s, two separate unity movements emerged, one in Europe and the other in Palestine. Initial signs of ichud emerged in Poland, in the 1930s, within the framework of the Hechalutz movement, an umbrella organization in which all the labor and left-wing Zionist pioneer movements participated. Joined by the left-wing Hashomer Hatza'ir (Young Guard) and Gordonia Zionist movements on an autonomous basis, the unity movement in Poland as it was created under Hechalutz marked the inception of a general bloc of pioneering movements that was politically and practically identified with one of the two major kibbutz movements of the time, Hakibbutz Hameuchad (Unified Kibbutz).[57] Although unification was based upon purely practical political considerations, this did not affect its implementation. Both Gruenbaum and

Poznansky were active members of Hechalutz at this time, so they were certainly familiar with this unity trend.

During the war, the tendency to form umbrella unity organizations intensified in Europe, but for practical reasons and not for the political reasons that had caused the initial inception of a unity trend. It was not political necessity that dictated unity during wartime, but rather a deeply felt internal Jewish need. The desire to relieve Jewish distress and hardship often led to temporary alliances between such diametrically opposed political movements as the left-wing Hashomer Hatza'ir and the ultraorthodox pioneers of Po'alei Agudat Israel. Such alliances occurred in both Western and Eastern Europe. In France, for example, the French Jewish youth movements united in December 1941, and in Poland, in the same year, the united Irgun Brit Zion (IBZ) (Zionist Organization) movement was created in the Kovno ghetto. Internal forces dissolved the alliance in France shortly after liberation, even prior to the arrival of emissaries from Palestine who were the potential bearers of divisiveness. In Poland, however, the alliance was more enduring in nature. The members of IBZ continued to adhere to the concept of unity, and promoted it among the survivors in Germany. Moreover, IBZ played a crucial role in the founding of two branches of the unity movement—the Nocham (No'ar Chalutzi Meuchad—United Pioneering Youth movement) kibbutz movement, which began to function in August 1945, and the United Zionist Organization (UZO), founded in September of that year.

It is the first of these organizations, Nocham, to which Kibbutz Buchenwald eventually belonged, which is of particular interest to us when attempting to understand the role of the kibbutz within the organizational framework of the she'erit hapletah in Germany. Founded largely at the instigation of Mapai members serving in the Jewish Brigade, the organization initially encompassed the majority of the pioneering movements in Germany. However, in late 1945, Nocham began to disintegrate due to growing factionalism among its members. When the unified front ultimately dissolved in early 1946, Nocham became almost totally identified with Mapai, thus losing its suprapolitical nature and becoming yet another almost particularistic kibbutz movement.

Later particularism notwithstanding, it appears that during the first months after liberation, a majority of the survivors espoused a trend toward unity, grounded in the belief that their shared experiences far outweighed any differences between the various groups. The formation of a division of survivors from Eastern Europe in 1944, after the liberation of Poland's eastern sector, was an additional expression of this feeling of a common fate.[58]

A parallel trend of unity movements existed in Palestine, but the underlying rationale for this trend differed from that of its European counterpart. In 1943, members of the Mapai secretariat in Palestine proposed the formation of the Unified Hechalutz with the cooperation of all pioneering movements.

Unlike the European version, this was motivated solely by political grounds. Mapai sought to dominate the various pioneering movements by controlling the Jewish Agency's emissaries. To this end, Mapai, which was on the verge of a split, hoped to engineer the transfer of the Unified Hechalutz to the Jewish Agency. In this way, it endeavored to control the future of the immigrants from Near Eastern countries and from post-Holocaust Europe alike. This proposal aroused sharp opposition within Hakibbutz Hameuchad circles, which immediately suspected a political trick.[59] For manifold reasons, the Unified Hechalutz program was never implemented in Europe, but the very proposal sheds light on the distinction between the unity trends in Palestine and in Europe. While the unity trend in Palestine most resembled the prewar European variety, which was directly influenced by party divisions in the Yishuv, unity among the survivors emerged from their shared trauma. Cold political calculations in Europe were not a part of their initial view of reality.

Nevertheless, the survivors' desire for unity should not be viewed solely as the result of unbounded emotional idealism. Apart from the almost visceral longing for unity, as a group, supporters of the unity trend among the survivors soon realized what the espousers of the unity trend in the Yishuv had realized long ago: that unity could also provide them with a strong power base. Unlike in the case of the Yishuv, though, where political pragmatism was usually the overriding consideration, the dictates of political necessity among the DPs were often accompanied by an almost messianic sense of mission, by a desire to serve as the model for continued Jewish existence in the post-Holocaust world. This desire, however, was not unique to the groups espousing unity. Throughout occupied Germany this sense of mission strengthened and grew among a number of groups of survivors, leading to the establishment and reestablishment of various ideological trends—Zionist, religious, non-Zionist socialist, and the like.

The Unity Concept in a Kibbutz Setting

These prior attempts to achieve unity do not seem to have influenced the pioneers at Geringshof. In the spring of 1945, when the kibbutz was founded, its members were unaware of either the Unified Hechalutz in Palestine or of IBZ in Europe. Thus, although their desire for unity was not unique, it appears that they arrived at this concept independently. What was unique, however, was the way Kibbutz Buchenwald implemented this concept within a kibbutz framework. Although the Geringshof group accepted the classical definition of a kibbutz—constructive socialism within an agricultural setting—it created a hybrid, characterized by a weak agricultural training program with strong collective content.[60] This approach suited the members who had come to appreciate the importance of unity during the war, but whose emotional and physical limitations disposed them against cultivating German soil. Despite the problems with the physical aspect of pioneering in Germany, Kibbutz Buchenwald did operate as a training farm, the first among the DPs in Germany. From June to October 1945, it remained the only kibbutz hachsharah functioning in Germany, while Kibbutz Chafetz Chaim, founded near the DP camp at Zeilsheim by members of Po'alei Agudat Israel in October 1945, was the second. Indeed, some of the latter kibbutz's membership came from groups that had left the hachsharot at Geringshof and Gersfeld.[61] The emphasis on agricultural training distinguished these two enterprises from other kibbutzim that sprang up in DP camps in the early postliberation period. While these other kibbutzim espoused a socialist pioneering outlook, only the socialist aspect was implemented. In recording his impressions of postwar Germany, Dr. Chaim Hoffman (Yahil), head of the Palestinian delegation to the DPs (the Welfare Units), commented that these kibbutzim, imbued with a pioneering spirit, gave it practical expression in the form of shared living quarters, a separate kitchen, separate cultural activities, and a greater number of workers than among the rest of the camp population.[62]

By virtue of their location in the DP camps, these kibbutzim, like their urban counterparts in Poland, were unable to provide agricultural training. Nonetheless, they served an important function by providing a spiritual and economic refuge for those repelled by the moral corruption in the camps and troubled by the constant food shortages. In addition, there were ad hoc kibbutzim formed solely for the purpose of emigration. The leaders of these "aliyah kibbutzim" were vested with sweeping powers, but unlike Kibbutz Buchenwald, these associations were only temporary in nature.[63] Although initially they were affiliated with the Nocham line of unity, as time passed, many of these ad hoc kibbutzim aligned themselves with political parties, especially when party representatives appeared on the scene. This was only natural under the circumstances. As their stated goal was to reach Palestine, the kibbutzim sought powerful patronage in the interest of rapidly achieving this goal.

Thus, the phenomenon of Kibbutz Buchenwald as a training farm in the spirit of unity is understandable against the background of the immediate postliberation period. It maintained this ideal even in light of separationist trends that later developed among large sectors of the DPs. During the summer months, the chalutzim at Geringshof lived in a secluded sanctuary, conducive to fostering the ideal of unity. Their isolation resulted from a combination of geographical, technical, and ideological factors. First, although Geringshof was centrally located in the heart of Hesse, near Fulda, the farm itself was off the main road, physically removed from the atmosphere of politicization that engulfed the DP camps. A second factor contributing to the kibbutz's isolation was the lack of a telephone. Contacts with the outside world had to be on a personal level, and information reached the kibbutz via the comings and goings of various individuals. Even the visitors who reach the farm—welfare workers, U.S. Army chaplains, Jewish soldiers serving in the Allied forces, members of the Jewish Brigade—were struck by the cooperative atmosphere and refrained from introducing divisive feelings. The party representatives whose presence in the Welfare Units heralded the advent of factional discord first reached Germany in December 1945. Throughout the summer, only one official Yishuv representative visited the farm—Eliyahu Dobkin, head of the Jewish Agency's aliyah desk. The unofficial nature of these visits and the absence of any attempt to introduce the schismatic political heritage of the Yishuv fostered the atmosphere of tranquillity at Geringshof. While visits provided an opportunity to exchange information with outsiders, it appears that they served more as an opportunity to publicize the kibbutz than as a means of bringing in the outside world.

This combination of factors—geographical distance from DP centers, the apolitical nature of visits from the outside world, and the absence of an unmediated connection with the external society—reinforced the barrier between the kibbutz and its surrounding environment. This barrier was not impermeable; rather, it allowed a selective flow of information to the kibbutz. However, the creation of a protective environment was crucial at this juncture of the rehabilitation process, as its members were desperately in need of a respite. All around them, other survivors were involved in a storm of political activity and organization. In the pastoral atmosphere at Geringshof, it was possible for the kibbutz members to diffuse their internal pressures and deal with personal traumas without interference from external agencies.

Nonetheless, this isolation had its negative aspect. It encouraged the naïve belief on the members' part that the principle of unity as practiced at Geringshof could be transplanted unaltered to Palestine. While Kibbutz Buchenwald's isolation barred divisive ideological forces from the kibbutz, it also deprived it of essential knowledge regarding the political reality in Palestine. Indeed, the majority of kibbutz members adhered to their ideal until their jarring encounter with the Yishuv and its political scene.

In addition to being the first pioneering venture among the survivors in Germany, Kibbutz Buchenwald was also distinguished by its unwillingness to accept "ordinary" (that is, politically unaffiliated) Jews. While its founding group had a strong Zionist orientation and intended to remain within a kibbutz framework in Palestine, this was not the case for many of those who subsequently joined the kibbutz over the summer. They regarded Kibbutz Buchenwald as a refuge from loneliness, as an adventure, and most of all, as a means of expediting their immigration to Palestine. The desire to emigrate was not always grounded in Zionist leanings; in truth, while Palestine was not the sole option for survivors seeking to leave Europe, it was usually geographically the nearest option and, in spite of the illegality involved, often the most organized. Like those who had joined Hechalutz in the 1930s in order to acquire certificates, those who joined Kibbutz Buchenwald could be considered expedient Zionists, many of whom had no ideology or desire other than to leave Europe as soon as possible. Nonetheless, the kibbutz rarely rejected any applicants, hoping that the Zionist idea would eventually grow on its members, who would choose to remain in a kibbutz framework after reaching Eretz Israel. This hope was based on the belief that by not choosing other options available to the DPs—usually immigration to Central or South America—the survivors had indirectly professed their Zionist leanings, even if they were unable to verbalize their commitment overtly.

Kibbutz Buchenwald's guiding principles of unity, collectivism, and unselective absorption as formulated in the summer of 1945 were soon put to the test, both in Palestine and in the Diaspora. Three factors eventually would change the character of the kibbutz: its members' politicization, the withdrawal of separatist groups at the urging of their parent parties, and the Yishuv's suspicion of unity movements as a threatening foreign transplant. The initial encounter with Yishuv society constituted a test of Kibbutz Buchenwald's ideological principles and prepared the members for the reality of their new homeland. The "reception" at Atlit by party representatives anxious to "make provision for their own households," in the words of historian Anita Shapira,[64] negated Kibbutz Buchenwald's aspiration to be guided by a sense of unity, shared fate, tolerance, and friendship. Although the firm stand taken at this juncture testifies that at this stage, the ideal of unity was still an essential component of the ideological baggage imported from the Diaspora, it was no longer firmly implanted in their hearts. Just as travelers eventually tend to put down their baggage in order to continue unhindered, thus, in the months following their aliyah, the members of Kibbutz Buchenwald gradually shed the unity principle. In late summer 1945, however, the idealists among the members still believed that it was possible to bring the message of unity to Palestine, and even the greatest skeptics believed that separation lay in the distant future. This was the summer of 1945, the first summer after liberation, when everything seemed possible, that difficult and magical summer when the survivors were reborn.

1. "Papa Juker" and another member of Kibbutz Buchenwald removing the Torah scroll from its hiding place in the attic (*Netzer Sereni Archive*)

2. Founders of the kibbutz in the 1980s. Left to right: Lola Ahuvia, Avraham Ahuvia, Rabbi Herschel Schacter, Penina Schacter, Shirley Tydor, Yechezkel Tydor, Hilda Simche (*Netzer Sereni Archive*)

3. The Geringshof main building (*Moreshet Archives, Givat Haviva*)

4. Members of Kibbutz Buchenwald outside the main building at Geringshof (*Netzer Sereni Archive*)

5. Special Shavuot (Pentecost festival) prayer at the liberated Buchenwald Concentration Camp (May 1945) led by Chaplain Schacter (*Netzer Sereni Archive*)

6. Singing and dancing at Geringshof (*Netzer Sereni Archive*)

7. The communal washroom at Geringshof (*Netzer Sereni Archive*)

8. The clubroom at Geringshof. The words on the far wall read in Hebrew "Adam, Avodah, Teva" (Man, Work, Nature) (*Netzer Sereni Archive*)

9. Members of Kibbutz Buchenwald in the Geringshof dining room (*Netzer Sereni Archive*)

10. Members of Kibbutz Buchenwald (*Netzer Sereni Archive*)

11. The founders of Kibbutz Buchenwald less than three months after liberation (*Netzer Sereni Archive*)

PART TWO:

THE REALITY

CHAPTER FOUR

The Kibbutz in Palestine, 1945–1947

"Everything looks different from over here."

ATLIT. Sand, mud, rows of shacks surrounded by barbed wire. Atlit, the British detention camp for illegal immigrants established on the northern coast of Palestine in 1938, which in wartime served as a quarantine center for persons from enemy states. Atlit, which in the spring of 1945 merited this description: "The common rooms are empty shacks furnished with wooden pallets . . . like shelves with straw blankets. . . . Everything is drowning in mud, the first Hebrew word [botz] each new immigrant learns here."[1] Atlit, a camp lacking streets, roads, blankets, and a central office; the initial collection and distribution point for immigrants from liberated Europe. Atlit, Kibbutz Buchenwald's first stop in its new homeland.

Kibbutz Buchenwald's members were transported directly to Atlit upon their arrival at the port of Haifa in early September 1945. As it was the second day of Rosh Hashanah, the kibbutz's religious contingent was permitted to remain at the port until the holiday's conclusion. In 1945, it was still standard procedure to send all immigrants, both legal and illegal, to Atlit, where they remained briefly until they were placed by the kibbutz movements, or until they made contact with relatives or friends. In Kibbutz Buchenwald's case, the projected stay was two weeks to a month, enough time to allow initial adjustment and find a temporary home.

With the exception of mealtimes, camp life had no fixed routines. The daytime was mainly devoted to filling out forms and to meetings with representatives of the Yishuv bureaucracy—kibbutz movements, health plans, the Histadrut (the workers' federation; literally, Organization), and workers' movements. The remainder of the day was spent in discussion and debate, in socializing with friends and relatives who came to welcome the newcomers. As is usually the case where idleness is the rule, much time was spent in anticipation of the meals dispensed by the camp's central kitchen.

Each *chaver* (kibbutz member) reacted differently to the stay at Atlit. Some found their first exposure to collective existence in Palestine a positive experience. As one young woman recalled, "We were a close-knit happy group. We danced and sang. As we were among the first immigrants to reach Palestine, many local residents came to the fence seeking information about their relatives."[2] A man recalled, "Our group cohesiveness and contacts with Yishuv activists helped us overcome the feeling of 'You may view the land from a distance, but you shall not enter it' [Deuteronomy 32:52]."[3] Another succinctly stated, "I saw the Atlit camp as a way station only. I was well treated during my stay there, and looked forward to moving to our new and permanent residence as soon as possible."[4] Others reacted negatively to what they perceived as a loss of freedom, even if only temporary. "Atlit was difficult for me," reported one member. "It meant being confined in a camp again."[5] For some, the camp's physical appearance itself elicited a negative response: "Once again we were greeted by barbed wire. How could we be expected to feel?"[6]

For the new immigrants, Atlit represented their initial encounter with life in Palestine, their first exposure to its searing Middle Eastern heat and the ever-present sand that found its way into every corner. It was also their first experience with the instrumental politics characteristic of the Yishuv, destined to affect their lives even before they left Atlit. At Geringshof, the chaverim had been isolated from the Yishuv's politicalization due to both the kibbutz's ideological affiliation and its offbeat geographical location. This was not the case at Atlit, where the Jewish Agency had been granted jurisdiction over the camp by the government of the British Mandate. Consequently, the internal division of tasks took place according to party lines and with the external backing of the various parent parties active in the Yishuv. During the years prior to the establishment of the State of Israel, the local political scene in Palestine was characterized by intense internal rivalry. Each political faction expected to amass enough clout to determine the future of the state. These internecine conflicts had both local and European ramifications, as party representatives competed fiercely for adherents among the survivors both before their immigration and after their arrival.

The Yishuv's leadership had long been aware of the political significance of the survivors in their long-range calculations. Their initial contact with the refugees who reached Palestine via Teheran in 1942 had been singularly disenchanting. On that occasion, Eliyahu Dobkin had expressed cautious pessimism regarding the "human material" that was likely to survive the war. Subsequently, before the war's end, both the Jewish Agency and various political parties had devoted several sessions to a discussion of the survivors' potential role in the Zionist program. By late 1944, the Zionist establishment clearly realized that the DPs constituted a major human resource. However, at this stage, plans for the Yishuv party emissaries to contact this group were as yet only tentative. Only after the liberation were full-scale plans formed to reach the survivors and to attempt to draw them into the political framework of the Yishuv. These plans were two-pronged: on the one hand, to send educational and political emissaries to the DPs still in Germany; on the other, to recruit adherents from among the survivors upon their arrival in Eretz Israel.[7]

Palestinian members of the Jewish Brigade—the "live bridge" to the Diaspora, as they were known—were the first representatives of the Yishuv to make contact with the survivors. Of the Yishuv officials, only Eliyahu Dobkin reached Europe during the immediate postliberation period. In October 1945, David Ben-Gurion toured the German DP camps—a "tour of a theater of operations," in the words of historian Meir Avizohar.[8] Ben-Gurion's firsthand observations convinced him that the she'erit hapletah had a major role to play in the future of the Zionist enterprise. Thus, he directed the survivors toward Bavaria, in the American zone, where they would be crowded into DP camps, calculating that he could best serve his political aims by having them pressure world public opinion from inside those camps. In Avizohar's estimation, this plan was the "instrumental use of misery for the sake of redemption," and thus acceptable in Ben-Gurion's eyes.[9]

The Yishuv's leadership was not alone in casting its eyes on the potential human reserve that the She'erit hapletah represented. Faced with a severe shortage of labor, the kibbutz movements in Palestine also hoped to benefit from this available workforce after its arrival in the Zionist homeland. As word that unity movements had been founded in Eastern and Central Europe reached the movements' leaders, they feared that the survivors would "lapse politically" and be lost to the parent parties in Palestine.[10] To offset this potential problem, various movements—along with political parties—decided to send emissaries to the DPs, ostensibly to supplement the work of the welfare agencies, which were already providing services to the survivors. In practice, the emissaries were also to engage in intensive political propaganda among the survivors, with an eye to stabilizing or even increasing their movement's or party's membership.[11]

After long bureaucratic delays, the kibbutz movement's emissaries finally reached Germany from the Yishuv in December 1945. Headed by Chaim Hoffman (Yahil), the Yishuv's Welfare Units were staffed by social, health, and education workers.[12] Party representatives, often traveling in the guise of cattle dealers, fish breeders, experts in aluminum production, and even as stowaways, reached Europe somewhat later.[13] While members of the Jewish Brigade who had provided immediate assistance to the survivors during the summer of 1945 had rarely shown political particularism, this "second generation of emissaries"[14] aggressively represented its parent organizations.[15] Furthermore, while the Brigade had adopted a primarily emotional attitude toward the survivors, the new emissaries developed a more functional attitude. This difference was mirrored in the very language used by the emissaries. Jewish Brigade members referred to the DPs empathetically as "brothers" and "flesh of our flesh." Over the course of 1946, the later emissaries adopted abstract, almost derogatory terms of reference, such as "elements," "refugees," and "wraiths."[16] This was not simply a semantic shift; rather, it reflects the instrumental approach adopted by some emissaries to cope with a group whose demographic composition radically and rapidly altered before their very eyes. Furthermore, the impressions conveyed to the Yishuv from Europe had wider implications, as they shaped the Yishuv's image of the she'erit hapletah.[17] Nevertheless, regardless of their disconcertingly ambivalent feelings, the emissaries spared no effort to create a Zionist framework within the DP camps, and to transmit Jewish and Zionist values to their inmates.

Efforts by the Yishuv and its representatives on the survivors' behalf did not stop there. Another major endeavor was the promotion and organization of illegal immigration to Palestine. These were the years of a state in the making, the pre-State era when organized illegal immigration was practically the sole means of reaching Palestine. Although, as Aviva Halamish has noted, written sources sometimes convey the impression that this was "an immigration wave without immigrants," the survivors did actively try to reach Palestine.[18] While many failed to reach their goal, the vibrant human mosaic of deportees continued in Cyprus its struggle for a Jewish state.

The second method of strengthening the existing political or kibbutz movements was to recruit adherents from among the new immigrants soon after their arrival. From the war's end until the founding of the State of Israel, some 70,000 immigrants, mainly Holocaust survivors, sailed for the shores of Palestine.[19] Of these, some 2,500 illegal immigrants successfully evaded the British manhunt and entered Palestine; the *Exodus*'s 4,500 passengers were returned to Germany; and 52,000 illegal immigrants were deported to the Cyprus detention camps. The remaining 11,000 individuals were apprehended by the British upon entry and detained at Atlit until they could be granted entry permits out of the monthly quota.[20]

The arrival of each new group of immigrants was the signal for the various political factions to send representatives to Atlit to recruit members. This represented their first, and perhaps only, chance to influence any unaffiliated immigrants before they entered the mainstream of Israeli society.[21] One by one, Kibbutz Buchenwald's members entered the distribution hut to meet with party and kibbutz movement representatives. Inquiries were made regarding each member's political orientation, attitude toward Jewish religious tradition, and future plans. Direct and oblique attempts were made to convince them to abandon their decision to remain united but separate from the existing movements and instead to join established kibbutzim. When this came to Tydor's attention, he decided to be present at all interviews in his capacity as kibbutz leader in order to prevent the premature breakup of unity before its realization in Palestine.[22] Tydor recalled making particular efforts to be present at the interviews of the young people who had to decide where to continue their education, as schools in Palestine were also politicized. The young survivors were given three choices: an ultraorthodox school in Kfar Saba, the labor-oriented Ahavah institution north of Haifa, and the modern Religious Youth Village (Kfar Hano'ar Hadati), connected with the Mizrachi political party. "Initially, the questions asked were along the lines of: 'Did your father have a beard? What did your family do on Friday night?' I immediately objected to this line of questioning. At interviews where I was present, a more concrete tack was pursued."[23]

The young people were ultimately distributed among three schools. Four attended the Ahavah school in Kiryat Bialik, one went to the Mikveh Israel Agricultural School, and the kibbutz's youngest member, Itka Harash, chose to study at the Religious Youth Village. Although members of Kibbutz Buchenwald maintained contact with the young survivors who continued to consider the kibbutz their home, in practice they were divided up among various political movements and were placed under their influence for several years.

Then it was the adults' turn. Kibbutz Buchenwald's arrival created a stir in the Yishuv, drawing visits from friends, relatives, and Yishuv officials. Among those welcoming the newcomers were Chaim Rokach for the Histadrut, Eliyahu Dobkin for the Jewish Agency's Aliyah Desk, Rabbi Robert Marcus for the World Jewish Congress, and Rachel Katznelson for the working women's movement. Kibbutz Buchenwald's members consistently informed all and sundry Yishuv officials that they wished to create a new social model, a unity kibbutz. Not all their visitors gave this announcement a sympathetic hearing. Eliyahu Dobkin, for one, made several attempts to enlighten the members, explaining the idiosyncratic nature of their goal in the Yishuv's political scene, and strongly advising them to adapt to the local political climate, but his arguments went unheeded.[24] Nor did party representatives unanimously endorse the unity trend. Whereas Mapai envoys perceived Kibbutz Buchenwald as personifying their dream of a Unified Hechalutz, Hashomer Hatza'ir and Hakibbutz Hadati (religious kibbutz movement) representatives were skeptical, even downright pessimistic, regarding the group's chances for success. They cautioned against further Mapai attempts to co-opt additional elements in the guise of sponsoring unity.

In the Hakibbutz Hadati organ *Yedi'ot Hamazkirut* (News of the secretariat), Hapo'el Hamizrachi (religious Zionist pioneering movement) leaders described the propaganda campaign waged by them to lure Kibbutz Buchenwald's religious members to their fold. Despite these pleas, Kibbutz Buchenwald's religious contingent opted to remain with their kibbutz for hachsharah: "The religious immigrants are aware that they have chosen a difficult path of doubtful outcome, but they feel obligated to take the plunge despite the failure of prior similar attempts . . . whereas we are convinced that the kibbutz will disintegrate rapidly. More's the pity. So much effort will have been for nought."[25]

Hapo'el Hamizrachi's leaders attributed the religious immigrants' obstinate refusal to leave the Kibbutz Buchenwald framework not solely to the desire to continue past relationships. Rather, they believed that the immigrants had been duped by promises of settlement assistance and support made by Histadrut, which were at best half-truths, and at worst, outright lies. Hapo'el Hamizrachi reserved its harshest judgment for itself, however. The news item concluded with self-flagellation for the movement's failure to reach the immigrants before their "contamination" by the unity trend: "Clearly, if we had succeeded in reaching the religious members earlier, and in explaining Yishuv reality to them, we could have prevented the creation of this 'original' conception."[26]

The new immigrants had to find a home. Their public declaration of unity notwithstanding, during the initial period at Atlit, each individual member wrestled with the dilemma of whether to stay or leave, whether to pursue an individual or collective existence. This decision addressed a question broader than that of remaining within the unity trend: whether to remain on a kibbutz altogether. Some members were convinced by friends or relatives to make a new life for themselves in town. Others, who had joined the kibbutz in Germany with the sole intention of expediting their immigration, now acted upon their earlier decision to leave the kibbutz upon reaching Palestine. In any event, only half of Kibbutz Buchenwald's original contingent expressed the desire to continue their hachsharah.

Now the remaining chalutzim faced a different problem: finding a framework in which they could continue their training. As early as their first week at Atlit, three alternative sites were proposed: a kibbutz near Haifa, a hachsharah site near Merchavyah in the Jezreel Valley, and Kibbutz Afikim in the Jordan Valley. The first site was rejected when Kibbutz Buchenwald's members learned that there was no agricultural training program there, that only outside employment was available. The second proposal, the hachsharah site, was already in use; therefore it was logistically impossible to house another hachsharah there. This left Kibbutz Afikim as their sole option. On September 17, Chaim Rokach arranged for an Afikim member to meet with the Buchenwalders and to answer their inquiries. The questions asked disclose the group's state of mind, its fears and expectations. Most of the questions raised were related to the climate: If they suffered from the heat at Atlit, how would they be able to cope with the Jordan Valley? After six years of hard labor in European camps, would they be able to work in the Jordan Valley's extreme heat? Rokach assuaged their fears by citing examples from Kibbutz Tirat Tzvi, where survivors worked in conditions similar to those at Afikim. Another issue raised was the needs of the group's religious members. Rokach replied that although there were no religious kibbutzim in the Jordan Valley, there was a Hamizrachi hachsharah at Afikim itself, as well as a synagogue and a kosher kitchen where the members could share meals. The final question raised at the meeting concerned the unity trend. Would Afikim's members be prepared to accept a group with this political orientation for hachsharah?[27]

Indeed, of all the existing kibbutzim, Afikim was uniquely suited to absorb an atypical group. A member of Netzach (No'ar Tzofi Chalutzi—Young Pioneering Scouts), Kibbutz Afikim functioned autonomously within the Kibbutz Hameuchad framework. As early as 1930, Netzach had won the right to maintain independent ties to its Diaspora branches.[28] This long-term arrangement affected two main areas usually under the sole jurisdiction Kibbutz Hameuchad: control of chalutz movement branches in the Diaspora, and distribution of new immigrants to the various settlements. Thus, within Hakibbutz Hameuchad, Kibbutz Afikim, as part of Netzach, constituted an internal opposition movement; accordingly, for Kibbutz Buchenwald, it symbolized pluralism.[29]

On September 20, Rokach, Tydor, Zauderer, and three other chalutzim traveled to Afikim to attend a general membership meeting. At this meeting, a motion was presented to accept the Kibbutz Buchenwald group for "hachsharah, work, and kibbutz living," in the words of the kibbutz newsletter.[30] Despite objections raised regarding the difficulty of absorbing an autonomous group that involved maintaining two kitchens and separate dining areas, the motion was passed. The article notes that at the meeting's conclusion the Afikim members gathered to "listen . . . to the new immigrants, who held them spellbound with accounts of their suffering in the ghettos, at forced labor, and in the concentration camps. Much was said about the encounter with the land and the creative spirit that characterizes the kibbutz movement; indeed, the entire labor movement."[31]

At first glance, this description of survivor–Yishuv veteran interaction seems to diverge from the classic pattern; usually, the Yishuv distanced itself from accounts from hell. Nonetheless, the wording of the report reveals another aspect of this pattern of dissociation—not an unwillingness to listen, but the inability to comprehend. The juxtaposition of the term "suffering" with the kibbutz and labor movements' "creative spirit" conforms to the stereotypical, almost propagandalike spirit of the times. It also foreshadows the tenor of future relations between Afikim members and Kibbutz Buchenwald's survivors. In the future, the program at every public ceremony, festivity, or holiday at Afikim would include a presentation by a survivor, recounting impressions of that holiday in the camps, or other events from the past. This was not primarily intended to promote catharsis, nor to provide a sympathetic hearing; rather, stress was put upon the contrast between past and present reality, and upon the acquisition of new values and patterns of life—on labor movement values in particular.

The chalutzim greeted the news of the impending transfer to Afikim enthusiastically. They were eager to leave Atlit, to begin their new lives. Hungry for even a glimpse of their new homeland, some people spent hours standing near the fence, gazing at the surrounding scenery. Now they would be able to walk in the green fields, to work together under fruit-laden trees, to cultivate the land. Naturally, these feelings of eagerness were mingled with apprehension. First and foremost, the chalutzim doubted their ability to adjust to the climate, to carry out physical labor under conditions of intense heat and poor health. Second, they feared the possible effect of the move on the group's political ideology. At Atlit, they had already been exposed to attempts virtually to coerce them to adopt a strict party line. Now they feared they would be forced to endorse fully the Kibbutz Hameuchad line. Consequently, shortly before their departure for Afikim, the members of the "Active" (active members) formulated seven cardinal guiding principles: (1) unity; (2) avoidance of propagandizing for a particular way of life; (3) mutual toleration by those originally from different backgrounds; (4) freedom of religious observance; (5) maintenance of a kosher kitchen; (6) Shabbat (Saturday) as the official day of rest; and if necessary, (7) disciplinary measures to be taken against those who broke the rules.[32]

The period at Atlit was not the final stage of Kibbutz Buchenwald's insulated physical and ideological existence. Rather, it represented the initial stage of adjustment to a new environment, to the supposed paradise that would unexpectedly be revealed as a hellish climate, and to a political scene intolerant of European-born unity. Not simply in another stage of dependence upon outside agencies, having left the UNNRA framework for the Jewish Agency's support, Kibbutz Buchenwald was to reach its pinnacle as a kibbutz movement dependent.

The two-week interim period at Atlit served several purposes, all of which involved change and adaptation. It provided time for physical adjustment to a new climate, to its heat and humidity; for individual decision-making about whether to remain with the group; and for the collective to reorganize following the departure of the "urbanites." Moreover, the group's political-ideological image shifted as well. To the Yishuv representatives in Europe or on the boat to Palestine, they had represented an ideological avant-garde, an example of the healthiest sort of rebirth that the survivors could undergo; to the political representatives at Atlit, they now appeared to be little more than a political anomaly, even a nuisance in view of the accepted codes of the Yishuv's political division. A sociological adjustment was called for as well, as the group's status changed. From being Jewish survivors among a sea of liberated strangers, they now became strangers among their Jewish compatriots. Primarily, though, the Atlit period served as one of psychological adjustment, affording an opportunity to formulate their goals and expectations from hachsharah in the Yishuv.

Like the Exodus from Egypt, Kibbutz Buchenwald's transfer to Afikim was hastily executed. On September 21, only a day after the kibbutz general meeting, and the eve of Sukkot (Feast of Tabernacles), Kibbutz Buchenwald's fifty-four members left Atlit for Afikim to continue their training. With the song "Kibbutz Buchenwald Chai Vekayam" (Kibbutz Buchenwald yet lives) on their lips, the chalutzim made their way to the Jordan Valley. For many, their initial visual encounter with their new homeland came as a shock. "Where is the biblical land flowing with milk and honey?" inquired one upon seeing bare fields at the roadside. "There is nothing but dry earth and a scorching sun beating down on our heads." "And the Arabs," commented another, "why are they so poor, so dirty?" Then Kibbutz Afikim came into view. "A manmade paradise blessed by God," wrote Avraham in the kibbutz diary, making an oblique reference to the heat as well: "Green, green, green, shade, shade, shade! This is a land flowing with milk and honey!"[33]

Following initial logistical arrangements, the hachsharah turned to its next organizational task: choosing a new steering committee. Before the holiday, Tydor had announced his intention to reunite with his children. Having brought the kibbutz to "its allotted haven," he now wished to leave Afikim for Jerusalem as soon as possible to make contact with the officials who could arrange the necessary paperwork. Therefore, the group decided to meet immediately after the holiday. Two committees, composed of three members each, were chosen—a general committee and a culture committee. With this act, Kibbutz Buchenwald's original organizational chapter came to an official close.[34]

LIFE AT AFIKIM

Kibbutz Buchenwald's members spent nearly two years at Kibbutz Afikim. When they arrived, Afikim's membership numbered some 670 individuals. The kibbutz extended over close to a square mile of land, used to raise grain, grow bananas and other fruit, cultivate olives and grapes, and serve as pasturage.[35] From the outset, the hachsharah functioned as an autonomous group within an independent collective. The arrangements made for the Buchenwalders' housing, social life, and meals emphasized this fact. To begin with, the group requested separate living accommodations. The Afikim secretariat acceded to this request, placing several small shacks in a small wood at their disposal. This area became known in kibbutz parlance as the "Buchenwalders' enclave."[36] Moreover, they organized their own cultural club in a former kitchen shack, a move that took many veteran Afikim members by surprise. Further evidence of their separate but equal status is provided by the continuation of their Oneg Shabbat parties, which Afikim members attended as invited guests, while the Buchenwalders served as hosts. Even the dining room arrangements highlighted the group's unique status as a separate institution within the organized kibbutz. At first, the hachsharah mixed with the Afikim membership, but this practice suddenly ceased. In a brief letter in the Afikim newsletter titled "Why Do We Sit at Separate Tables?" Avraham explained the sudden change. After describing the shift to separate tables, he stated that because everyone had noted the change, he wished to explain that this step was not a separatist act: "If joint meals have all the advantages outlined above, they also serve an important function within the society itself. Just like a family, all members of a society should eat together. But some of our members, the religious ones, ate at separate tables, the ones where kosher food is served. Understandably, we could not allow our religious and nonreligious members to dine separately throughout the entire hachsharah period."[37] Consequently, the members of Kibbutz Buchenwald agreed that in order to keep their smaller "family" together at all costs, they would all eat at separate tables to enable to observant members to remain part of the whole.

Full integration was achieved only in the realm of the pioneering endeavor. Within a brief period, the new immigrants had been absorbed in all branches of kibbutz work. Avraham's description of the kibbutz at Geringshof—"In the fields, barn, stable, and yard Jewish hands are at work"—was realized at Afikim in the orchards, in construction, in the kitchen, and the carpentry shop. Older immigrants were placed at the kibbutz's Kelet Afikim plant.

Nor were the new immigrants' cultural and spiritual needs neglected. In addition to talks held at the culture club, formal education was also provided. As new immigrants, Kibbutz Buchenwald's members were entitled to one day of classes per week in lieu of work. This arrangement, universal among all Hameuchad and Haartzi kibbutzim that absorbed new immigrants, was designed to increase the newcomers' knowledge of Jewish and Hebrew subjects, and more to "equip the immigrant with the requisite knowledge and values necessary to enable him to become a conscious participant in our creative struggle,"[38] as one counselor of immigrants stated at a seminar held at Giv'at Hashloshah. The four topics of instruction chosen for immigrants— Zionism, the Land of Israel, the Labor Federation, and the kibbutz—were grounded in this conception.[39] This orientation was not implemented at

Afikim, where both veteran members and the Buchenwalders had other ideas. They sought to stress Jewish- and humanistically-oriented topics instead. Thus, at Afikim, the day of study was devoted to classes in Hebrew language and literature, Bible, and history. For the Buchenwalders, these classes served an important function. Not only did the lessons foster their acclimatization by providing a formal cultural context and knowledge, they also met the survivors' thirst for education, both formal and informal. Young survivors in particular characteristically sought to complete the educational process interrupted during the lost years in the ghettos and camps.

While all their teachers expressed admiration for the survivors' thirst for knowledge, only in one case did this interest extend beyond the formal teacher-student relationship. The Hebrew teacher, Aliya (Gurevitsch) Evyasaf-Levi, a talented young woman who joined the kibbutz through marriage, befriended the Buchenwalders. At the time, because the younger members of the group were the only ones close to her in age, she felt drawn to the "merry crew," as she called them, spending many hours with them both inside and outside the classroom.[40]

This unique relationship brings us to the question of intergroup interaction at Afikim in general. How did Afikim veterans react to the presence of an alien group in their midst, with its distinctive background, culture, and ideology? Governed by Zionist, pioneering, and secular values and imbued with a visionary sense of mission, Afikim society in general fit the pattern of a broad sector of Yishuv society: irreligious, ideologically committed to Zionism, politically associated in the broader sense with the labor movement. In many respects, the Afikim–Kibbutz Buchenwald encounter was absolutely unique; nonetheless, it was not Afikim's first experience with Holocaust survivors. In 1943, Afikim had absorbed a substantial number of "Teheran children," a group of Polish children who reached Palestine via the Soviet Union, Persia, and India. Due to their previous familiarity with the poor health, wartime-based fears, and food hoarding that characterized the children, Afikim's members considered themselves experienced in dealing with Holocaust-induced traumas, but with the Buchenwalders' arrival, they quickly discovered that a yawning gulf separated what the survivors of Auschwitz, Ravensbruck, Bergen-Belsen, and Buchenwald had experienced from what the Teheran children had suffered. While the latter group had suffered hardships, they had not been exposed to the terrors of the camps; while the children had left Europe in early to mid-1942, the survivors had witnessed the "Final Solution" and its aftermath. Each group reacted differently to its experiences and thus underwent a different process of absorption in their new homeland.

Kibbutz Afikim's veteran members utilized the only two tools at their disposal to bridge this gap: They reached out to build personal relationships, and they involved the survivors in the pioneering venture. Many kibbutz families adopted individual Buchenwalders in an attempt to confer a feeling of home, of belonging. Some acted out of a sense of personal commitment; other were motivated by pity. These relationships did not always last, however. Even when both parties made serious attempts to cement these personal ties, obstacles to intimacy remained. Of these, the psychological barrier between survivor and kibbutz veteran was the most difficult to overcome. This distance was reflected by the reception given to the Buchenwalders' account of their experiences "over there." "Speech was our therapy," recalled Elik Gruenbaum, "but they couldn't understand us."[41] Lola Sultanik added, "The chaverim listened to the stories, although I am not certain that they really wanted to hear them. When I began to suspect that my tales were being received skeptically, I stopped telling them."[42] How did the Afikim veterans react? As Aliya Gurevitsch recalled, "Some [survivors] talked incessantly, while others kept their mouths shut. Many chaverim were unable to hear the stories of atrocities, and conveyed this feeling to the survivors."[43] Rita Wasserman recalled uncomfortable moments, even with those who expressed a desire to hear. "Initially they displayed a lot of interest, but the first question was always the most embarrassing. They unfailingly inquired, 'Why did you go like sheep to the slaughter?' "[44]

Nonetheless, Kibbutz Afikim's veteran members were aware that they could not simply erase the newcomers' past. A modus vivendi evolved whereby the survivors' experiences were given official recognition. As mentioned earlier, the program at every ceremonial, holiday, or festive occasion now incorporated a pertinent recitation by a Buchenwalder. It is not clear, however, whether this compromise reflected sincere recognition of the events' historic importance, or whether it was an institutionalized means of dealing with a phenomenon that kibbutz society had neither the emotional nor practical tools to address. This step represented recognition of the survivors' emotional need to speak out, but it was also an attempt to isolate the atrocities of the past in a ritualized stratum, thereby neutralizing their personal and painful elements.

COLLECTIVE MEMORY

This attempt to incorporate pieces of the past into the mosaic of the present brings us to the question of how Kibbutz Buchenwald proceeded to build its collective memory, the first stage of three in its collective absorption.[45] The underlying premise that guided this process recognized that past and present were inextricably linked: Only by formulating a collective memory could the survivors shake off the traumas of the past in order to concentrate on building a new life in the present.

What is a collective memory? By what elements is it nurtured, and how can it be built and enhanced? In his book *Zakhor,* historian Yosef Chaim Yerushalmi distinguishes between Jewish history and Jewish memory, that is between recorded history and events as absorbed by the collective national memory.[46] Kibbutz Buchenwald's members were aware of this distinction, and devoted attention to both realms. First, the group utilized the kibbutz diary for its historiographical record. Although primarily a chronicle of the present, the diary did include memories from the past. At the same time, the Buchenwalders fostered the dimension of collective memory by recounting experiences from their past at group functions.

A number of aspects of their past found their way into Kibbutz Buchenwald's collective memory. Since they did not seek to create a "myth of heroism," their collective memory incorporated many elements of what Lawrence Langer has termed "agonizing Holocaust memory"—memories grounded mainly in feelings of helplessness.[47] In an attempt to mitigate the harsh emotional difficulties involved in recalling the past, painful memories were cast within the ideological framework of cooperation and unity.

Practically speaking, this collective memory was built during their initial year at Afikim by the Buchenwalders' taking every available opportunity to remember the past, the contrast it with the present. On occasion, this occurred before a broad audience, including all of Kibbutz Afikim's members. At other times, this activity was of a more intimate nature, restricted to the Buchenwalders' more limited circle. Descriptions of this process, as found in the kibbutz diary and the Afikim newsletter, reflect its cathartic dynamic. The Sukkot issue of the Afikim newsletter contains the first evidence for this process, as perceived by an Afikim veteran:

> At the conclusion of the first day of Sukkot we held a reception for Kibbutz Buchenwald in the dining hall. . . . One of the new immigrants spoke, further heightening the tension. His restrained remarks hammered like heavy blows. The listeners sat with bated breath. They were astonished that he could speak after long years of inhuman suffering that suppressed all feelings, all emotions. . . . It was miraculous that brotherly love could melt the ice; that repressed feelings could be aroused. . . . The strains of "Hatikvah" concluded his remarks. One song— the song of those incarcerated in the camps, of those fluttering between life and death in flaming ghettos—with its final desperate cry for help, commingled with another, a song of hope and encouragement, life and creativity. . . . We were close to tears. But once again the never-ending stream of life triumphed in a storm of song and dance that engulfed the audience.[48]

These remarks sound as if they were directly lifted from a propaganda script entitled *The Pioneering Life Cures All Ills.* The pervasive tone of pathos, the glowing description of the miracle wrought by brotherly love, the sharp contrast between those fluttering between life and death in flaming ghettos and the song of hope and encouragement, life and creativity, all indicate an unwillingness—or inability—to confront the Holocaust's deeper significance. Afikim veterans found it easier to employ hackneyed phrases to mask their inability to comprehend, while the Buchenwalders also preferred to hide behind broad generalizations in order to defer the need to grapple publicly with their past. In this sense, the stereotypical descriptions provided an honorable loophole for both parties. Remembering, even reminding, was acceptable, but picking at the still-festering wound was not.

Chanukkah saw the continuation of this process. In an entry in the kibbutz diary, "Chanukkah . . . Here and There," Avraham described the last Chanukkah at Buchenwald. This piece, which surrealistically transformed the crematoria fires into Chanukkah candles, was read at a members' party, but only to the restricted circle of Buchenwalders, not to the kibbutz membership at large. Chanukkah differed from Sukkot by virtue of its more intimate setting, which enabled the group to confront the past more profoundly. The ever increasing chronological distance from the past facilitated this process. Despite its limited distribution, the essay had a sentimental tone, especially in its description of the holiday at Afikim: "How different it is from the holiday at Buchenwald! Rows of free people, marching in a procession . . . standing erect . . . and in the distance an armed Hebrew watchman makes his rounds, protecting and guarding us. . . . And here, at the top of the tower a comforting fire glows, spreading light and faith, calling to life and progress . . . 'Garb yourselves, gird yourselves with strength for the nation's benefit' " [poem by Chaim Nachman Bialik: "To the Volunteers"].[49] Evidently, even the Buchenwalders had difficulty bridging the gap between past and present; consequently, they idealized the Zionist experience.

The festivals of Tu Bishevat (the fifteenth day of the Hebrew month of Shevat, marking the beginning of spring) and Passover 1946 marked two additional turning points in this process. Both the focal point of the memory process and its role at public functions underwent a change. At the Tu Bishevat party, representatives of the new immigrants met with schoolchildren from Haifa to mark the forty-fourth anniversary of the Jewish National Fund's founding. They spoke about "Concentration Camp Life and Allegiance to Palestine in Those Days."[50] Here the weight of memory shifted from the past to the present, from their Holocaust experiences to their Zionist leanings during their internment in the camps. Passover saw the furthering of this process with the reduction of the role of the past at public functions. Unlike on previous occasions, at the Passover party, which was also a welcoming reception for the second group of chalutzim from Geringshof, the past took a minor role. At center stage were current concerns. The Anglo-American commission and other geographical, demographic, and political problems were the topics of the day. Similarly, a Palestine-centered orientation—not a focus on the camps—characterized the Afikim membership at large during this period.[51] Three factors promoted this altered orientation. Unquestionably, during those months political events overwhelmingly captured the interest of the entire Yishuv. The Palestine-centric trend that appeared in microcosm at Afikim simply reflected developments in the greater Yishuv macrocosm. There was a sense that the Yishuv's political future stood at a critical juncture, that all secondary goals were to be deferred in favor of the ultimate goal—the founding of an independent political entity. Second, following a period of suppression, the Yishuv's egocentric tendencies, an intrinsic component of its nature since the 1920s, began to reassert themselves. This approach, which treated the Yishuv as the avant-garde of the Jewish world, did not emerge from the Yishuv's sense of mission; rather, it served as a psychological crutch to mask its dependence on that Jewish world in terms of human resources, financial backing, and even emotional support. Last, a third factor underlay the renewal of the Yishuv's egocentric inclination: It had wearied of coping with the survivors' traumas. Kibbutz Buchenwald's chalutzim themselves recognized this phenomenon; thus they resolved to engage in building their collective memory within an intimate setting, not in the presence of the entire kibbutz membership. From that point on, only survivors engaged in intensive examination of the past. At shared public occasions, remembrances of the past receded into the background.

The anniversary of Buchenwald's liberation, the twenty-eighth day of the month of Nisan, fell a week after Passover. At Afikim, the former camp inmates marked the occasion by calling a convocation. The official program included memorial prayers, a poetic presentation of experiences from the past, greetings from Jewish Agency Executive and National Fund representatives, as well as the transfer of a gift of three hundred trees donated to Kibbutz Buchenwald by students at the Shalvah High School in Tel Aviv. Although they had been invited, Labor party representatives failed to attend. The news coverage of the convocation concluded with an account of the trip taken the next day by the participants to the Sea of Galilee and the Susita (Hippos) fortress.[52]

The convocation held on Nisan 28 marked a major milestone in the building of Kibbutz Buchenwald's collective memory. In and of itself, the convocation represented an innovation, unique in terms of its compass, and in the response it elicited from the surrounding society. While days of mourning were declared by the she'erit hapletah in Germany to mark the death of their sisters and brothers in the various Nazi concentration camps, the Kibbutz Buchenwald convocation was the first memorial service held by former camp inmates in Palestine.[53] Second, it was a Yishuv-wide convocation of all Buchenwald survivors, not just a restricted gathering with Afikim members. For their part, Afikim members greeted the service with understanding and admiration, but they maintained their distance. This distance was reflected in the coverage given the convocation in the kibbutz newsletter—unsentimental straightforward reporting, thus illustrating how much their attitude toward public accounts of the Holocaust had changed since the Buchenwalders' arrival on Sukkot. Their initial thirst to hear had been replaced by the need to keep their distance.

Once again, what happened at Kibbutz Buchenwald reflects, in microcosm, the broader picture in the Yishuv as a whole. The absence of Labor party representatives illustrates the political establishment's prevailing attitude toward attempts at public expression by survivors: at best, indifference; at worst, alienation. Their reluctance to recognize the she'erit hapletah as a group with a distinct identity motivated this attitude. The Yishuv's political establishment saw the she'erit hapletah as a vital resource; at the same time, it denied its right to exist as a separate entity. The Yishuv establishment closed ranks against this foreign implant on two planes. On the social-collective plane, it opposed the creation of kibbutzim composed solely of survivors; on the political level, it failed to integrate the she'erit hapletah leadership into the Yishuv's institutions, and later those of the State. In addition, avoidance of Holocaust memorial services stemmed from Ben-Gurion's policy of "statehood," which placed the Yishuv and later, the State, above all other internal or external loyalties. The "rejection of the Diaspora" played a central role in this conception, which viewed the State of Israel as the lodestone for Jewish loyalty. Seen in this light, how could Yishuv leaders attend a gathering or mark an event that legitimated the very Diaspora condition that had made the Holocaust possible?[54] It was only in the 1950s that this hard-line attitude softened—with respect both to the Holocaust in general, and to the survivors' attempts at self-definition in particular—as a result of the effects of the decade's political, social, and psychological processes on Israeli society.

This desire to absorb the survivors within the fabric of society without giving them collective expression also made itself felt on the individual level. Yishuv society was in the throes of an intense political struggle that left little patience for the survivors' self-absorption. Although the Yishuv leadership recognized the survivors' special needs in theory, in practice they were guided by formulas developed in response to earlier waves of immigrants.[55] One overriding axiom called for the radical transformation of the immigrant's identity. Developed during the Second Aliyah (wave of immigration to Palestine, 1904–1914), this principle demanded that new immigrants discard their Diaspora birthright, regardless of the cataclysmic circumstances that may have motivated their immigration. Upon reaching the shores of Palestine, the new arrivals were expected to exchange, cheerfully and unhesitatingly—or even eradicate—their Diaspora identity in favor of a new Palestinian persona. In cases where this was not self-evident, the process was to be encouraged by means ranging from gentle persuasion to intense social pressure. In retrospect, this attitude may seem paternalistic and condescending, perhaps even bordering on cultural obtuseness, but it must be remembered that this policy was not callously or maliciously fashioned. In the antipluralistic atmosphere of the Yishuv, its members sincerely believed that this was the most efficient means of helping newcomers both to overcome the traumas of the past and to integrate them quickly and successfully in the Zionist endeavor.[56]

The objects of this policy responded to this blindly Palestine-centric vision, which demanded that they rebuild their lives in its image, with enforced discretion. Discerning survivors quickly learned that it was advisable to maintain a low profile not only regarding the expectations of Yishuv society, but with respect to their wartime and postwar experiences as well. Given the clash between the Yishuv's image of the survivors and the reality of their lives, this reticence is understandable. Two conflicting components nurtured the Yishuv's image of the survivors: The Yishuv idealized the heroism of the ghetto fighters and partisans, the first survivors with whom it had contact; at the same time, it grotesquely assumed that the remainder had survived at the expense of others. This dichotomy naturally led to a distorted perception of the she'erit hapletah, one that embodied diametrically opposed moral standards. In this view, the survivors exemplified both the Zionist myth of heroism and Diaspora parisitism. The exemplars of this conception were powerless to change this distorted image. Accounts of Nazi atrocities were countered by tales of "wartime adversity" in Palestine. Yishuv society found "martyrdom" and "sanctification of life" anachronistic as compared to "real" heroism as they understood it—that of the ghetto fighters and partisans. Exploits patterned on Tel Chai or Masada, not the day-to-day struggle to survive, captured the imagination of the Yishuv. Instead of being incorporated into the Yishuv's national consciousness, the Holocaust assumed personal, intimate, and at times embarrassing dimensions for its survivors.[57] It took nearly twelve years for the Holocaust to achieve official recognition as a component of the State of Israel's collective memory, with the passage of the 1959 Holocaust and Heroism Remembrance Day Law.[58] Meanwhile, the survivors learned to remain silent.

The 1946 Rosh Hashanah party marked the end of Kibbutz Buchenwald's first year in Palestine. It also closed a circle in the group's collective memory-building. Held within the restricted circle of survivors, the gathering was the type of occasion that legitimated bringing up memories from their recent tragic past. This license to remember notwithstanding, wartime experiences played but a minor role at this party. The program was largely devoted to a survey of the formation of Kibbutz Buchenwald's pioneering nucleus, and to reminiscing about their aliyah. Only a small corner of the club dedicated to "those not privileged to be here today" recalled the appalling terrors of the past.

Three factors—psychological, pragmatic, and social—contributed to what appears to be a unique choice: the decision to concentrate upon the Zionist content of collective memory, even in a setting with no external constraints, one in which the Buchenwalders had no need to consider the needs or desires of onlookers who were not survivors. The psychological factor was a function of the group's image as perceived by the surrounding society. The chalutzim realized that as long as the Yishuv regarded them as alien, they would be unable to put their social message into effect. Therefore, the kibbutz leaders deliberately refrained from mentioning events that emphasized the gap between survivors and Yishuv veterans. Moreover, practically speaking, although the kibbutz leaders did not belittle the cathartic process, they felt that the survivors' limited reserves of strength should not be directed at the past, but rather should be preserved for the greater struggles to come in the future. Finally, internal social tensions between new groups that had arrived from Geringshof in the course of 1946 created a need for intensive social integration prior to the move to an independent collective farm. It was felt that the short time at their disposal could best be utilized in creating a sense of belonging to a broader community rooted in Yishuv reality—to the Zionist body politic, the movement body politic, and the kibbutz body politic. Therefore, the shared history of the kibbutzim in Palestine was stressed, not Kibbutz Buchenwald's distinctive European past.

Thus the policy adopted deliberately downplayed the past, or related to it only in terms of the present. The obligation to "those not privileged to be here today" was fulfilled by collective remembrance of the Holocaust at every public gathering. From that point on, however, the past served a tendentious function. It was elicited to legitimize further the demand for a Jewish state and to provide convincing proof that the Zionist axiom of negation of the Diaspora was correct.[59]

SOCIAL INTEGRATION

The second phase of collective absorption, which was intrinsically related to the problem of social integration and group identity, can be termed: from collective memory to collective concern—the relationship to past, present, and future kibbutz members. At this level, the kibbutz was primarily concerned with maintaining contact with former members; ensuring the kibbutz's survival by preventing its current members from dropping out; building the collective; and last, with ensuring a future base.

During the initial months at Afikim, a wave of departures swept the kibbutz, affecting founders and younger chalutzim alike. These dropouts from collective life can be classified in five categories. First, some left in order to be reunited with family members. Tydor belonged to this group. Noting that the survivors' first task was usually to seek relatives, he recalled that from the moment he learned that his children had been rescued and were living in the United States, he knew that he would have to go there and bring them to Palestine. Many other members had similar experiences. Since liberation they had believed themselves their families' sole surviving members. Suddenly they discovered relatives in Tel Aviv, Jerusalem, or elsewhere in the Yishuv or the world. The desire to be with family exercised an immense pull—often overriding the incentive to remain within the kibbutz framework.[60]

Many of those who left in order to be reunited with their families maintained contact with the hachsharah for an extended period, and even dreamed of rejoining their friends at some future date. For its part, the hachsharah at Afikim served as a second home for former members who wished to preserve their connection to their second family—the family of chalutzim.

A second group that dropped out was composed of those no longer capable of performing physical labor. One such individual was Elik Gruenbaum, who recalled how he had reached Afikim with the sole intention of joining the kibbutz. "What happened? When the Jews left the desert, they were simply asked: 'Who are the ones to go?' [Exodus 10:8]. So too, at Atlit. All those remaining who wished to join the kibbutz were free to do so. But the [political] parties had depleted our ranks, and mostly younger members remained." Being older, Gruenbaum simply wanted to find a home. He then went to Afikim, but a few days there sufficed. "Why? We were almost the first Holocaust survivors to reach the Yishuv, and they didn't quite know what to make of us. For example, the Afikim member in charge of work assignments asked me what I had done before the war. I told him that I was 'in construction,' so they assigned me to throw bricks to the second story. I was physically incapable of this task. But truthfully, I was extremely embarrassed by my inability to contribute to the kibbutz. Therefore, I decided to leave."[61]

Elik's feelings were shared by other older members of the group who could not function in the Jordan Valley's extreme heat. The majority moved to the coastal plain or hilly areas to be with friends or relatives. By and large, members of this group stayed in touch with the kibbutz as well, but they recognized that their departure was final.

Social problems were a third factor that motivated members to leave Kibbutz Buchenwald. Some left for personal reasons—to find a mate, for example. Some expressed a more "general dissatisfaction with the group's social life" as recorded in the kibbutz diary. During Kibbutz Buchenwald's two years at Afikim, this category comprised the largest group of dropouts. While it was always aware of the problem, the hachsharah was galvanized into intense consideration of its implications only when one of the pillars of kibbutz society, Avraham Ziegler, left the kibbutz. A long entry in the kibbutz diary explored the roots of the problem in an attempt to stem the tide of this painful phenomenon. This entry sheds light on the members' self-image and the hachsharah's group dynamic:

> Generally we learn that a member is leaving at the end, not the beginning. The dropout informs us only after having completed all outside arrangements. Two weeks, or a month, prior to departure, he deliberately tells one member, so word will spread among the others. We have become accustomed to commenting, "He's in a bad mood." But this is temporary. Then the Social Committee suggests that he leave. And now two things occur. We worry that he will not hear what's right and what's wrong. At the same time we tease him with jokes, making fun at his expense. Does this affect him in any way? No, it does neither good nor harm—he has already made up his mind to leave. . . .
>
> What causes this phenomenon? . . . It is our society. The change is sparked by his first disappointment. He did or said something, made a request or suggestion—and the group, in its apathy, failed to understand him, or made jokes at his expense or (indifferently) opposed his suggestions. And this stings. At first he stops participating in talks, fails to attend lectures or classes. If this member is the type that can overcome this situation, he does so by glossing over the incident, by making efforts to be active socially. Yes, our group loves strong, nonmoody personalities, members who laugh, dance, and sing—"good sports." Heaven help those with weaker personalities! (Do they have no place in the kibbutz?) He cannot make fun of himself in this lively company, as the strong person can. And thus he suffers. Following work in the fields, he feels dissatisfied at home. Whatever he hears, I imagine, he believes directed at himself. He becomes a loner. And the result: contacts with urban friends, with whom he believes he will find social fulfillment.[62]

The kibbutz did act upon these impressions. Although no steps were taken to contact those who had already left, measures were taken to strengthen the collective cohesion of the remaining members.

A fourth small group broke with the kibbutz over the issue of professional training. For example, the kibbutz secretariat rejected Mordechai Nussbaum's request to be trained as a dental technician by his brother-in-law on the grounds that the kibbutz had no need for this skill. On that occasion, the kibbutz diary only noted laconically that Nussbaum "was leaving the group."[63] It will never be certain whether his motives were strictly professional, or whether Nussbaum wished to be reunited with his urban relatives. Such cases, like the socially motivated departures, were not limited to Kibbutz Buchenwald. Rather, they reflected the reality of collective existence in the Yishuv. During that period, the individual was expected to suppress his personal ambitions and career for the greater collective good.[64]

The fifth and final group of dropouts, its religious members, was unique to Kibbutz Buchenwald. During its formative period in Germany, the hachsharah's rallying cry had been unity—between veteran chalutzim and newly recruited pioneers; between political factions; between religious and secular members. The broad-based implementation of this unity concept distinguished Kibbutz Buchenwald from prewar hachsharot. It also set a precedent for other Nocham kibbutzim established by the she'erit hapletah in its image.

Meanwhile, the Yishuv, divisive forces were at work. The first to secede were the members of Hashomer Hatza'ir. An intense campaign by party representatives at Atlit, combining preaching with promises, caused the unity movement's first casualties. Nonetheless, even without these individuals, the group that reached Afikim encompassed a broad spectrum of pioneering movements: Hashomer Hatza'ir, Dror, Gordonia, Hapo'el Hamizrachi, and Po'alei Agudat Israel. The early months of hachsharah were marked by special concern for the spiritual and physical comfort of the group's religious members. Many contemporary entries in the kibbutz diary were devoted to this topic.[65]

This idyll was short-lived, however. Gradually, the number of religious members decreased. Some joined their urban relatives; others went to different kibbutzim. As Lola Sultanik recalled, "I served food to those who observed *kashrut*. As the weeks went by I served fewer portions, not because they had begun to eat Afikim food, but because hardly any religious members remained on the kibbutz."[66]

Reinforcements for the religious contingent arrived on the *Tel Chai* in March 1946. But their stay at Afikim was brief. Some two months later, the last religious Jews that had sailed on the *Mataroa* or the *Tel Chai* left Kibbutz Buchenwald for Kibbutz Tirat Tzvi or Kevutzat Yavneh. This move was directly influenced by the Hapo'el Hamizrachi movement, whose attempts to draw Kibbutz Buchenwald's religious members to its own kibbutzim dated from the arrival of the original Geringshof delegation.[67] Now that Kibbutz Buchenwald's religious members had expressed their willingness to leave Afikim, Hapo'el Hamizrachi received them with open arms. "It only after deep emotional soul-searching that we have decided to leave Kibbutz Buchenwald," wrote the religious members' representative. In a parting letter saturated with pain, this member laid bare their emotional reservations: whether or not to remain in the company of those with whom they had experienced liberation; whether or not to remain part of the dream to build a new society, a dream that had given them hope after years of suffering. For months, the religious members tried to find a place within the collective, but fate—and the political parties—dictated otherwise. Increased partisan pressure, and the breakup of Nocham in Europe, greatly reduced the kibbutz's chances for establishing an independent Nocham settlement in the Yishuv. Soon the kibbutz would be forced to join one of the existing settlement movements, none of which could accommodate a joint secular-religious kibbutz. Therefore, separation was inevitable. The entry ended on a note of despair, in a description of unity's "Via Dolorosa": "Again, a murderer appears, saying: 'I am not yet satisfied by [your] sacrifices, my altar is not yet sated with your blood.' The time is not ripe. The Yishuv is still not worthy to receive the doctrine of unity."[68]

Hakibbutz Hadati leaders received the news that Kibbutz Buchenwald's religious members had decided to secede from the hachsharah with self-congratulation and elation. Enthusiastic news items appeared in the Kibbutz Hadati's *Yedi'ot Hamazkirut* and in the party mouthpiece, *Alonim*. Under the title "Go in Peace!" *Yedi'ot Hamazkirut* described "the end of the Kibbutz Buchenwald affair." After citing the decision by Hapo'el Hamizrachi and Po'alei Agudat Israel members to leave Afikim, the author inveighed against what he saw as the real reason that Kibbutz Buchenwald's experiment of religious-secular cooperation had the backing of certain elements in the Yishuv: "With this step the sorry episode of Kibbutz Buchenwald comes to an end. At the same time, it serves as living proof of the Labor Federation's attempt to dominate pioneering activity in the Diaspora."[69]

An even sharper reaction appeared in *Alonim*, the religious kibbutz movement's mouthpiece. This item appeared in the "Miscellanea" column: "The council notes with satisfaction the eradication of the joint 'experiment' combining religious and nonreligious Jews at Kibbutz Buchenwald. This fact, and preceding ones, prove that a religious chalutz who chooses kibbutz life has his proper place only with the Kibbutz Hadati framework."[70] The final parting of the ways came in late spring 1946, some twelve months after liberation and less than a year after the kibbutz's founding. The secession of the kibbutz's religious members meant that an essential aspect of full unity was abandoned. After the spring of 1946, no religious Jews arrived in the contingents from Geringshof. Apparently, observant Jews in Europe understood much earlier than their Yishuv counterparts that true coexistence between themselves and secular survivors was an impossible dream in the political and social climate of Eretz Israel.

CONTACT WITH YOUTH AND GROUP COHESION

What remained to engage Kibbutz Buchenwald's members following the collapse of their dream of unity was concern for their present membership and the need to guarantee a future population base. Kibbutz Buchenwald's first delegation included not only those at Afikim, but also youth studying at various institutions in the Yishuv. Throughout this period, Afikim was their home on the Sabbath and holidays. For their part, the chalutzim at Afikim tried to maintain regular contact with these younger members, to be attentive to their problems. Ongoing entries in the kibbutz diary indicate that the youngsters studying at Ahavah and Mikveh Israel adjusted well, but this was not the case for the group's youngest member, Itka Harash, who had been placed in the Kfar Hano'ar Hadati (Religious Youth Village). Although her knowledge of Judaism was minimal, she had requested to study at a religious institution. In her words: "I remember telling Moshe Ya'ari, the Youth Aliyah representative at Atlit, that although I was from a religious home, I was not observant at present. I wanted to know what I didn't believe in, but I also wanted a place where I would not be coerced."[71]

Avraham visited Itka in early November 1945, in order to bring her to Afikim for a vacation. He returned to the kibbutz without her, with the impression of an unhappy child who had not found her place in that educational setting. As he wrote in the kibbutz diary, "I could see that she was unhappy. I understood—she is no longer a child and cannot be with children. She has no special friend; she has neither the desire nor the ability to make one."[72]

When Avraham tried to take her to Afikim for a visit, the counselor contended that vacations were allowed only after a three-month stay at the institution. Avraham replied that he knew this to be incorrect and that he knew for a fact that other children had been allowed to leave just that day. The counselor then stated that children with parents or relatives could go, but not Itka.

Why? Because she is already miserable as an orphan, you make her more unhappy? If you give her a few days' leave she'll spend time with her closest friend, Ziva. But the counselor replied, "Absolutely not." And poor Itka stood by in tears, for she knew she would not be able to go. The counselor said that Itka's friend should come to him so he can look her over, to make sure she won't be a bad influence on Itka if she spends several days with her. . . .
Is this how you counter external influence, by forcing a child to accept religion! She is crying, she is suffering! I left, accompanied partway by Itka. She was in tears, and finally said: 'Poor me, they think I am religious."

Although the kibbutz members stayed in close touch with Itka, her greatest support came from someone no longer at Afikim—Yechezkel Tydor. Tydor visited the Youth Village frequently, and sent letters between visits. As Itka recalled, "Each letter recharged my batteries. He visited often, always bringing chocolate for everyone. But the others did not understand me or what I had experienced. They were very impressed with my tattooed number from Auschwitz, and used to say: 'Show us what they did to your hand.' "[73]

Despite the members' expectations to the contrary, most of the youth did not rejoin the kibbutz upon completing their studies. Like other Youth Aliyah members throughout the Yishuv, they were drafted, fought in Israel's wars, and built their own lives elsewhere in the emerging state. One exception was Naomi Applebaum, who studied at Ahavah, but who, in her own words, "always thought of myself as a child of the kibbutz." Upon concluding her army service in 1949, Naomi made Kibbutz Buchenwald her home.[74]

Another aspect of collective concern was expressed by intensive discussion of how to enhance group cohesiveness and prevent loss of membership on social grounds. The Active frequently addressed this problem, whose roots were apparent to all: The Buchenwalders had begun to resemble the Afikim members, in that they had lost their sense of family loyalty and now put personal concerns first. Among the proposal suggested to counteract this trend were the institution of more classes, the renewal of the lapsed Oneg Shabbat party, and the transformation of the cultural club into the focus of the of the social life of the chalutzim. Each suggestion met with a negative response: There were no funds for additional classes; the Oneg Shabbat had been discontinued because of linguistic difficulties ("We had abandoned our former languages, but were still not proficient in Hebrew."[75]) and the dependence on a set program. As for the club, not everyone, especially not the newly formed couples, wished to spend every bit of free time in the cultural club.

The Active refused to be deterred and, these objections notwithstanding, implemented a recovery program. It incorporated elements of each of the outlined proposals. First of all, the Oneg Shabbat was renewed. With the consent of the chaverim, the evening opened with a candlelighting ceremony in the cultural club, aimed at creating a sense of family among the participants. Second, in order to overcome the language problem, part of the program was now devoted to musical selections. With regard to additional classes, the members were asked to submit a list of suggested topics of interest. The suggestion reflected the members' thirst for culture as well as their need for practical instruction. Among the topics proposed were: Zionism and the history of the workers' movement, socialism, political economics, agriculture, political geography, and the Middle East. Two practical topics were of overriding interest: sexology and women's role in society. The kibbutz members keenly felt their lack of knowledge and experience in the realm of male–female relationships. As one member wrote openly in the kibbutz diary, "We should not overlook the fact that for years we were isolated from the normal framework where these problems find expression, the years that determine one's identity in that respect. Now they play an important part in out lives."[76]

One result of the intense concern with the intimate social sphere— marriages between members—also ensured increased social cohesion and population growth. Hasty marriages and a high birthrate were characteristic of the she'erit hapletah, both in Germany and the Yishuv. During the hachsharah's first year at Afikim, thirteen couples were married. Some found their spouses within the group; others brought their partners to Afikim. This phenomenon found humorous expression in the kibbutz diary:

ENOUGH AND TO SPARE

A state within a state—Buchenwald at Afikim.
We know what to do. Always. Get married. Get married.
One or another chaver inquires:
Tell me, when will this business end?
No single women are left! Not a one!
You answer him:
Have no fear, we are still going strong.
You guess in vain, in vain. Do not despair!
Is that all? In our kibbutz there are enough and to spare.[77]

The formation of the first kibbutz families comprised but one means of ensuring the group's continuity. Two additional groups also had an interest in maintaining the collective—the chalutzim at Geringshof and Gersfeld, as well as those among them who had tried to reach Palestine illegally and had been deported to Cyprus. Because they were well aware of how eagerly the Diaspora members awaited news from the Yishuv, the members of the Afikim contingent made a concerted effort to maintain constant contact. This letter was written by Benny Applebaum, an Afikim member and supporter of the Nocham unity concept, who was in Germany at that time:

I was greatly pleased to learn that Kibbutz Buchenwald has been accepted for training at Afikim, and that preparations have been made to meet the group's religious members' special needs. I informed Kibbutz Buchenwald's Diaspora branch when I visited Geringshof yesterday. They expressed their deep gratification. Rumors had spread here to the effect that Kibbutz Buchenwald's members had scattered upon reaching Palestine—which would have undermined the unity of the pioneering movement established here with such great effort. The fact that the kibbutz members have surmounted the evil divisive winds that blow in the Yishuv and continue their collective existence is very encouraging.[78]

Close contact was also maintained with chalutzim who ended up in Cyprus, as seen from the following letter to the Yishuv that was published in the Afikim newsletter:

Greetings, friends! We were glad to receive your letter dated October 25 on November 8 and read it at the Shabbat party held that evening. Your letter made a vivid impression on us; it was as if we could see everything with our own eyes.

We had to read it twice in order to get everything. I found it difficult to believe that new immigrants could already write Hebrew so well. . . . We had two reasons to rejoice: First, we await letters daily; and second, that we have loyal friends in Palestine who take an interest in us, who identify with our plight.[79]

A common theme recurs in letters from Geringshof, Gersfeld, and Cyprus alike: "We are pleased to learn that you have found your place in the Yishuv, that the unity concept has gained acceptance, and that you are successfully realizing this ideal." Whether this actually was the case can be seen in the third and final phase of Kibbutz Buchenwald's collective absorption—the group's perception of life in the Yishuv.

Upon their arrival, Kibbutz Buchenwald's members resembled the majority of immigrants who had succeeded in reaching Palestine. On the one hand they were enthusiastically prepared to work hard in order to fulfill their role in the Zionist endeavor; on the other, they were somewhat apprehensive of the host society that they had visualized to themselves while still in the Diaspora. How did the chalutzim react to the sociopolitical reality of the Yishuv? Did Yishuv society as a whole, and Afikim in particular, meet their expectations?

By and large, Kibbutz Buchenwald's members reached Afikim with but a hazy impression of life in the Yishuv, or even none at all.[80] This did not interfere with their social absorption, which proceeded rapidly. The initial months of hachsharah saw the development of friendly relations between the Buchenwalders and Afikim's adult population, a relationship grounded in mutual respect and joint pioneering effort. As one of the Buchenwalders put it: "Relations with Afikim members were good . . . they helped us learn the language, organize the nucleus's institutions . . . and with everything necessary for starting a new settlement."[81] In contrast, contacts with youth at Afikim—a Palmach (part of the pre-State army) group, a group of Syrian youth, and Afikim's younger members—were tenuous. The latter found the Buchenwalders too Diaspora-oriented in dress and behavior. Throughout the hachsharah period, almost no significant relationships developed between the chalutzim and Afikim's youth.[82]

Adjustment by the chalutzim to the Yishuv's political climate was slower. For an entire year, Kibbutz Buchenwald's members nurtured the illusion that its institutions would tolerate the unity concept, that it would be feasible to establish a nation-wide branch of Nocham's settlement movement in the Yishuv. During 1946, several Nocham nucleii were founded in the Yishuv, of which Kibbutz Buchenwald remained the largest and strongest. Nocham's decline in the Diaspora, and its subsequent transformation into a Mapai-supported movement, tabled plans to found a separate Nocham settlement in the Yishuv.

Consequently, Kibbutz Buchenwald had to plan its political future independently. The issue was first explicitly raised at a meeting held by the chalutzim to summarize their initial year at Afikim, during preparations for Rosh Hashanah in 1946: "Thus, we must prepare ourselves. In what way? We already have foundations. We must build upon them. How? . . . In the ideological sense. We cannot remain a lone kibbutz. We will have to join one of the national kibbutz movement frameworks, since Nocham no longer wishes to found a national kibbutz movement in the Yishuv. We shall have to define ourselves. Therefore, we must now study the kibbutz movement."83

Although they were aware that inevitably they would have to conform to the Yishuv's political reality, Kibbutz Buchenwald's members tried to preserve a measure of pluralism by allowing each member to determine freely a personal political loyalty.

To whom did Kibbutz Buchenwald turn? Their experiences during their first year at Afikim helped shape Kibbutz Buchenwald's future political mold. Dating from their arrival at Afikim, the Kibbutz Hameuchad secretariat had stayed in touch with the group, noting the hachsharah's progress in its ongoing reports.84 In the fall of 1946, Hakibbutz Hameuchad also made contact with Nocham, Kibbutz Buchenwald's parent organization. At a meeting in October of that year, the two secretariats agreed in principle that the existing settlement nucleii in the Yishuv would join one of the already established settlement movements.85 In light of their inability to found an independent settlement within the Nocham framework, Kibbutz Buchenwald decided to turn to the movement with which it was most familiar—Hakibbutz Hameuchad, Afikim's parent organization. In early winter 1946, Kibbutz Buchenwald's representatives approached the Hakibbutz Hameuchad agriculture center and its secretariat with a request to found an independent settlement under their aegis. A positive response came a few weeks later; it was only necessary to decide what type of temporary settlement to establish. Ideologically and practically speaking, this step signified a dual change. On the one hand, it opened the door to a pioneering future within the framework of an established settlement movement; on the other, it marked the final abandonment of the broad unity concept and of the dream of a network of Nocham settlements in the Yishuv.

In spite of having to abandon their dream of a unity kibbutz, members of Kibbutz Buchenwald could attribute their generally successful assimilation into a new society to the fact that they had been absorbed by a kibbutz framework in general and by Kibbutz Afikim in particular. Indeed, as early as 1943, the Yishuv leadership became aware that absorption would be the make-or-break issue in their relationship with the survivors who would later reach Palestine. The arrival of the first refugees in the summer of 1945 intensified the debate over that matter. Yitzhak Zukerman and Abba Kovner, acknowledged heroes of ghetto uprisings, tendered suggestions at the November 1945 meeting of the Hashomer Hatza'ir Executive. On that occasion, Abba Kovner articulated the chasm dividing Yishuv mentality from that of the survivors: "Despair is not a doctrine; it is inherent in the psyche of the masses. . . . It is unnecessary to blow this out of proportion. But we must seek a bridge to the soul of the masses. Where is the link between those seated here and the person from there, who is so different, so incomprehensible, so demoralizing?"[86]

From the outset, the ability of "those seated here" to understand the person "from there" was circumscribed. Consequently, efforts to find an effective means for absorbing survivors were hampered. In her study of she'erit hapletah's integration into the Yishuv, Hannah Yablonka distinguishes between two types of absorption offered to adult survivors— ordinary institutionalized absorption and kibbutz movement absorption. In her estimation, Yishuv institutions in general generally failed to integrate the survivors. No specific consideration was given to their special needs, nor were steps taken to provide professional guidance or rehabilitation. In contrast, the kibbutz movement structured an orderly, well-planned absorption process for adult survivors.[87]

Despite active campaigning by settlement movements, however, only a small minority of the survivors opted for collective existence. From 1946 to 1947, only some 8 to 10 percent of the new immigrants sought to join kibbutzim. Of these, half left the kibbutz during their final year in Palestine. Although, as Yablonka has put it, the "kibbutz absorbed the newcomer into a home, into the fabric of life," the survivors experienced difficulty in adjusting to a cooperative existence and avoided collectivism in general. Several factors contributed to this trend: negative associations with closed places; lack of opportunity to learn a trade; and the inability to harness energy for national causes. Other problems were intrinsically related to kibbutz structure. Survivors found it difficult to feel at home in the insular kibbutz society with its conflict between the polarities of ideal equality opposed to the privileges granted in reality to veteran kibbutz members.[88]

Despite these impediments, between 1945 and 1949, the kibbutz movement continued its massive effort to attract and integrate the she'erit hapletah. Their contribution went far beyond paying lip service to an ideal. While these steps can be viewed as but one aspect of the national effort to cultivate potentially useful sectors of the survivor population, it must be noted nevertheless that many kibbutz members made a personal commitment to the task of absorption. It is well known that when theory metamorphoses into reality, even the bravest have been known to fall by the wayside.

While Kibbutz Buchenwald groped to define its future, voices from the past made themselves heard. They belonged to contingents from the Diaspora hachsharot who had now reached the Yishuv. In March 1946, more than sixty chalutzim from Geringshof and Gersfeld arrived on the SS *Tel Chai;* in July 1946, a dozen arrived on the *Biriya;* in August 1946, nineteen sailed on the *Catriel Yaffeh.* An additional sixty sailed on the *Mordei Hagetaot* in May 1947, and on the *Aliyah* in November of that year. While some immigrants arrived in Palestine directly, others were deported to Cyprus and reached the Yishuv following a few months' delay. Apart from the *Tel Chai* group, some fifty-three members reached Afikim. Of the last groups of illegal immigrants, only a handful joined the hachsharah at Afikim. Conflicts emerged between these groups, which ostensibly adhered to a uniform ideological platform. In reality, they represented different offshoots of the original nonpartisan unity movement. Each new group that tied its destiny to Kibbutz Buchenwald added a new dimension to the flavor of the kibbutz. Gradually the group was transformed from a covenantal assembly into a community, to employ Yonina Talmon-Garber's sociological definition.[89] This change was marked by the loss of homogeneity characteristic of the covenantal stage and by a redefinition of collective goals. Kibbutz Buchenwald would subsequently acquire the status of a community, based upon both collaboration between families that insisted on maintaining their privacy, and the pluralistic principle.

Kibbutz Buchenwald's subsequent history, in both its covenantal and communal aspects, exemplified the statement made at a reception for newly arrived immigrants: "Kibbutz Buchenwald represents the history of Zionism in the postwar era."[90] This Zionism was simultaneously strongly ideological but pragmatic, visionary but practical, ready to embrace all opportunities but uncompromising with regard to its ultimate aims, a Zionism that hovered between hope and despair. This picture was true for the Diaspora as well as for the Yishuv. In letter to a European member, one Kibbutz Buchenwalder summed up her first year in Afikim and the metamorphosis she had undergone since her aliyah:

I am aware that you fear for the experiment's success, whether the flower plucked from its roots and cruelly broken can take root in the soil. . . . Sometimes, at dusk, I wonder: Who is happier? You with your shiny rose-tinted glasses, or I who have had a chance to remove them, or more accurately, that reality has removed. . . . I recall now those moments just a year ago when with dreamy eyes I absorbed from ship's deck the outlines of a land slowly emerging from the mist. . . . My heart pounded, and I was engulfed by an otherworldly sensation. . . . My gaze met the sky, then the waves rolling in the water. I felt as if I hovered between heaven and earth, even without wings. Today this appears dreamlike, for I stand firmly on the ground.

If you wish to discover what has really changed me—look in my eyes. My eyes have seen another world. . . . Here I can live with the knowledge that I will often find disappointment. Here the ideal can be transformed overnight into dull reality, and dull reality can become the realization of an ideal. Yes, such are our lives. . . . I have begun to understand what lies ahead, how much we have yet to learn, to know, to take—and to give. . . . Even if our path is difficult and fraught with unexpected dangers, we shall not be deterred, for we remember that you and many others among our brothers and sisters look to us, pinning their hopes on us. We remember that you are many believers. Your gaze lends strength to our struggle and chosen path, a difficult but correct one.[91]

How did their "brothers and sisters" in Europe continue to build their collective existence after learning of the breakup of unity among the founding group in Palestine? How did they react to the news that Kibbutz Buchenwald had joined Hakibbutz Hameuchad's settlement framework? How did the changes in Nocham affect Kibbutz Buchenwald in the Diaspora? Finally, in the conflict between the real and the ideal, how long did the European hachsharat retain their "rose-tinted" view of life in the Yishuv in general and of immigrants from among the she'erit hapletah in particular? These questions bring us back to Kibbutz Buchenwald's other arena in the American sector in Germany—Geringshof and Gersfeld.

The Kibbutz in the Diaspora: The Hachsharot at Geringshof and Gersfeld, 1945–1948

"We had only the vaguest notion
of what Palestine was like."

SEPTEMBER 1945. Late summer in liberated Germany. The DP centers were overflowing with Jews desperately seeking to leave Europe; the majority—for Palestine. Every evening, former camp inmates, partisans, underground fighters, and those who had spent the war in hiding—paced the narrow paths between the buildings—talking and debating, spinning dreams of the future. The twin training farms at Geringshof and Gersfeld were filled with young Jews: at first, liberated camp inmates; later, underground fighters and repatriates from the Soviet Union. Unceasingly, chalutzim bound for Palestine arrived at the farms; sooner or later they would reach their goal. The immigrants who left Europe in spring 1946 through Aliyah Bet (illegal immigration) were sent to Atlit; those who tried to reach Palestine after this date found themselves deported by the British to Cyprus.

KIBBUTZ BUCHENWALD'S MEMBERSHIP IN AUTUMN 1945

In September 1945, Kibbutz Buchenwald's two hachsharot in Germany numbered some forty chalutzim. The majority belonged to one of three groups that have arrived at the kibbutz just before the fall. First were some twenty people sent to the kibbutz in mid-August by the Hechalutz center in Bergen-Belsen. They included center activists (Pize Simcha and Herbert Growald), young survivors from various movements (Shlomo Schiff—General Progressive Zionists; Bella Shtaub—Hashomer Hatza'ir; Gusta Ziegler—Hashomer Hadati), and unaffiliated members as well (Manci Onhaus; Anna Adler).

Many had belonged to the wartime hachsharot at Padaborn and Neuendorf, both in Germany.[1] The second cluster, approximately a dozen young women and two young men, also belonged to the Beth Jacob center, organized at Bergen-Belsen shortly before liberation. The Beth Jacob contingent was led by Rachel Shantzer and Rivka England, two young teachers who had taught in the Beth Jacob school system in Poland before the war.[2] The third and remaining group, some ten in number, reached the hachsharah after hearing about it from Jewish Brigade members, army chaplains, or Jewish soldiers in the American armed forces.[3]

These three groups had several things in common. The first of these was the intense desire to reach Palestine with all due haste. For this reason alone the young women from Beth Jacob were willing even to risk the "danger" of joining a hachsharah with secular members. Other young people walked long distances at great risk to reach Geringshof, in hopes of expediting their aliyah. The living link between all the groups at the kibbutz, both incoming and outgoing, was Arthur Poznansky, the hachsharah's coordinator of external affairs. Poznansky had chosen not to exercise his right to go to Palestine with the founding group to which he belonged; rather, he preferred to remain in Germany as the farms' administrator. Ostensibly, it appeared that Poznansky had decided to remain with his group of wartime chalutzim who had been liberated in Bergen-Belsen and only joined Geringshof in late summer 1945. In truth, his decision had been made for more personal reasons. Poznansky had resolved not to leave Germany until he learned the fate of his wartime sweetheart. Eventually, he discovered that his girlfriend had been shot and had died in Hanover.[4] In early September, he was joined by Isidore Juker, who was to assume the leading role in the kubbutz's agricultural endeavors. Juker, or Papa as everyone called him, a mature farmer from Biale and a survivor of Buchenwald, remained at the hachsharah until the fall of 1947, when he immigrated to Palestine using one of the rare certificates granted to the kibbutz following the summer of 1945.[5]

The second group of chalutzim at Geringshof (and later at Gersfeld) differed radically from the founding members—not by virtue of their makeup, as the majority were still former concentration camp inmates, but by virtue of their self-image and their relationship with outside agencies. These differences found a dual outlet. Internally, their distinct self-image was expressed in the lifestyle that evolved at the hachsharah. Externally, their patterns of interaction with the movements, organizations, and institutions that had connections with the hachsharah also underwent a change. Nonetheless, the changes on both levels were the function of a single process—the second group's transformation from displaced persons into chalutzim.

The transition from prisoner to survivor as experienced by the founding group primarily affected two spheres—the physical and the psychological.

Physical recovery began with liberation; psychological rehabilitation was more gradual, characterized by sharp mood swings—from depression to euphoria, from despair to hope. For the original group, all other issues, including preparation of the farm for hachsharah purposes, seemed peripheral. Consequently, the endeavor had a transient atmosphere that assumed concrete form in midsummer 1945. The founding group was packed and ready to go for several weeks prior to its aliyah; in this respect, the second group differed radically from the first. Its initial rehabilitation had already begun during its four-month stay in DP centers. Upon their arrival at Geringshof, the group's members already exhibited the defining characteristics of DPs—increased egocentricity and an almost morbid interest in the past. Both characteristics were tempered by an acute awareness of the group's present circumstances as well as an acknowledgment of the need to plan ahead.[6] From the autumn of 1945 onward, these were major factors in institutionalizing the kibbutz in the Diaspora, in both structural and conceptual terms.

The differences between the first and second groups of chalutzim at Kibbutz Buchenwald mirrored the demographic changes then taking place among the she'erit hapletah in Germany. By September 1945, a majority of the Jewish DPs were located in the American zone in Germany and Austria. Upon liberation, this group had originally numbered some thirty to fifty thousand Jews, but according to Yehudah Bauer, with the transfer of the majority of survivors to dozens of DP camps in the American sector in the summer of 1945, Germany became "the haven for hundreds of thousands of Jews, a vast transit camp into which the Brichah (illegal immigration network) was to lead the survivors of Eastern European Jewry."[7] As a result of this mass infiltration, by the summer of 1947, the Jewish population in the American zone would swell to a quarter of a million.[8]

Within months of liberation, the survivors liberated on the spot in Germany were joined by Jews from Poland and so-called Asiatics, Jews who had fled to the USSR during the war and had now been repatriated to Poland. From autumn 1945 on, Jews from Poland—partisans, camp internees, and Jews who had spent the war in hiding—infiltrated the American zone. Joined by the Asiatics by late 1946, more than 65 percent of the survivors in Germany were repatriates who had reached that country through the Brichah network. Following the closing of Balkan escape routes in 1945, and Ben-Gurion's decision to concentrate the survivors in Bavaria, its agents shunted Jews to the American zone, thus creating a tool to be used in pressuring world public opinion on the Palestine issue.[9]

In his study of Jews in postwar Poland, Yisrael Gutman cites three major reasons underlying the Jewish reluctance to remain in that country, which generated this massive exit of Jews from Poland. First, the personal and national lessons of the Holocaust were still fresh in their minds. Second, attempts to renew contacts with Poles were characteristically greeted by hostility, even open hatred, and by a refusal to return or make restitution for Jewish property. Third, many Jews felt strong antipathy against residing in a country saturated with Jewish blood.[10] Consequently, by late 1946, the American Zone had been flooded by more than one hundred forty thousand Jews, most of whom made their way to the DP camps scattered throughout the area.

The arrival of Polish Jews and Asiatics transformed the demographic composition of the she'erit hapletah in Germany. The survivors liberated in Germany itself were largely young, aged fifteen to forty, and in extremely poor physical condition. Almost no babies or children had survived. Furthermore, although their numbers included some religious Jews, their influence was imperceptible. The Polish contingent had a different profile. Since many had been partisans, ghetto fighters, or people who had been liberated in 1944, their physical condition was superior to that of the Jews liberated on German soil. This group included some children, and observant Jews as well. It was the Asiatics whose age span and sociological makeup most closely approached normality. Their physical health was good; they included entire families; the orthodox Jews among them were prepared to take a firm stand for their religious rights. Thus by 1947, the composition of the she'erit hapletah had been radically altered, a fact expressing itself in both the demands and the lifestyle of the Jewish DPs in Germany and Austria.[11]

DAILY LIFE IN GERINGSHOF AND GERSFELD

One consequence of the demographic changes among the DP population was a form of normalization, a realization that this "temporary" state might continue for months, if not years, to come. On Kibbutz Buchenwald, the agricultural sphere was the first to become officially normalized. During the fall months, the operational aspects of the pioneering venture began to take shape. The laissez-faire attitude that had characterized the founders dissipated, to be replaced by organized wake-up calls, intensive preparations of the farm for winter, and the sense that the hachsharot were an ongoing venture, the first group's departure notwithstanding. Consequently, the agricultural sphere was now characterized by an organized routine. Upon their arrival, new members were immediately assigned to work—in the fields, the cowshed, or the orchards, or at general household tasks.

In practice, the hachsharah now functioned as a fully operating agricultural concern. Romek (Avraham) Mor, a former Bergen-Belsen inmate who reached Geringshof in the autumn of 1945, recalled how the young people worked hard in the fields under Papa Juker's supervision, plowing and caring for the horses. "I did a lot of building with bricks, and all sorts of jobs. We did everything that was called for at the training farm."[12] This description was corroborated by Yocheved Schwimmer, who also joined the Geringshof hachsharah in fall 1945. Noting how the kibbutz was effectively organized like any other, with work rosters and committees, she described her work on the farm: "We worked very hard, especially those who worked with the cows. They had no prior training for that type of work."[13]

Henia Traube reached Geringshof with the Beth Jacob group at that time and was assigned to the cowshed, where she was immediately taught how to milk a cow.

> I was scared to death. I went into the shed and they told me that the cows are milked by hand. They sat me by a girl who already knew what to do. I saw her milking the cow with no effort, and then she revealed the secret: You have to squeeze and pull at the same time. How can one squeeze and pull simultaneously? That was something I could not yet grasp. In time I acquired the knack, but meanwhile I lost all feeling in my fingertips. For six months I couldn't hold a needle. I couldn't even tie shoelaces. I thought I was handicapped for life.[14]

Parallel to the development and organization of Geringshof, the situation at Gersfeld was also undergoing a change. Yitzchak Handler, an observant Jew from Bendin and a survivor of Bergen-Belsen, who was the new hachsharah's first kibbutz leader, recalled his arrival at Gersfeld on Yom Kippur eve, 1945. Prior to that time, there had been almost no hachsharah at the center. "My first job was to arrange for supplies, which I accomplished through the committee at Bergen-Belsen and the Joint [Distribution Committee]. My next task was to organize work. Gersfeld had no fields, or chicken coops, but it had orchards. Whoever took part in agricultural work did so at Geringshof."[15]

The training farms' successes in the agricultural realm were reported in the many articles that appeared in both the American and the Yishuv press between 1945 and 1947. For example, in spring 1946, The *Cotton Baler* devoted an entire page to the hachsharah. Under the headline—"They Returned from the Dead," the reporter described life at Geringhof and Gersfeld in early 1946. Awakening every day at six, the chalutzim would eat at six thirty, and begin working at seven o'clock. The workday would end at four thirty, and during the next four hours the members would engage in sports and go to classes in various language and cultural subjects. "A committee of six is their governing body. And every Saturday night the whole community meets to talk over problems and to learn and discuss the world news of the week."[16]

The writer continued, portraying the chalutzim and describing the physical conditions on the hachsharah, but what merited a second glance was not simply the intriguing text, but the eleven centerfold photographs. Each photograph illustrated a different aspect of postwar chalutz life: folk dancing to the accompaniment of an accordion; chalutzim-survivors tanning themselves outside the cowshed; a typical, rather spartan room; a two-week-old calf; and public singing. Prominently featured were two pictures considered wholly evocative of the kibbutz's spirit—first, a picture of the kibbutz flag flying from the same flagpole where but a year before the Hitler Youth flag had hung; second, the Sefer Torah hidden at Geringshof in 1943 by the Bachad chalutzim before their deportation, found after the war. The members used this scroll, written in Belgium in the early nineteenth century, to read the scriptural portion on Shabbat and holidays.

The kibbutz's primary articles of faith—Jewish religious pluralism and nonpartisan pioneering Zionism—still held sway in fall 1945, when the second group arrived at the hachsharot in Germany, but these two credos, which embodied Kubbutz Buchenwald's innovative bent, were to undergo trial by fire during their tenure at the hachsharah. This test of principles shaped the kibbutz's long-term image, and ultimately contributed to the sense of permanence that characterized the hachsharot from that point on.

Apart from the farming sector, other realms at the kibbutz began to take on institutionalized form as well. If the agricultural sector was being fleshed out, organizationally the kibbutz had reached full flower. When the groups at Geringshof switched over, a new va'ad (committee) was chosen to oversee administration, social integration, work assignments, and contacts with the authorities. Among the committee's active members were Arthur Poznansky, Herbert Growald, Aharon Batzia, Yisrael Lerner, and Rivka Englard, each of whom represented one of the subgroups now populating the hachsharah. A similar pattern emerged at Gersfeld. Different individuals filled administrative roles, both officially and unofficially, including Yitzchak Handler, Gersfeld's kibbutz leader. A second person who made a central contribution to the realm of social integration at Gersfeld was Rachel Shantzer, who was in her late twenties when she arrived at Geringshof with the Bergen-Belsen Beth Jacob group in August 1945. Rochka, as her friends called her, was a former student of Sarah Schenierer, the founder of the Beth Jacob school system, and had taught in its schools prior to the war.[17] The attractive blue-eyed woman, with the "soul-penetrating glance,"[18] endowed the hachsharah at Gersfeld with a homelike feeling, and participated in its initial organizational steps. Her activity was described by American GI Akiva Skidell in a letter to his wife, written in September 1945:

> The woman, who is the leader of the place, used to be a teacher in the orthodox Bet Yaakov [Beth Jacob] school in Cracow. . . . She is a woman of about 30 or so, I should say. Her husband is missing. Her influence in the place is felt all over, and it is an influence in the direction of refinement. . . . She has ambi-

tions to extend this idea of groups like this one further. There is a little argument going on between her and a few others and the bulk of the younger people in Geringshof as is the character of these places: Shall they be restricted to chalutz elements alone, or shall an attempt be made to get broader circles of the Polish Jews in Germany interested in them? . . . It is, of course, also a question of possibilities, of the availability of leadership material, but she maintains, with a great deal of justice, that those will arise once there is the determination to do the job."[19]

Rachel Shantzer's stay at Gersfeld lasted but a few brief weeks, but her guiding philosophy—concern for all survivors, not just those with pioneering potential—became a fundamental principle at Kibbutz Buchenwald-Gersfeld. In this it differed from Geringshof, where efforts were made to recruit members with Zionist pioneering backgrounds. This affected the relationship between the two hachsharot. Yocheved Schwimmer noted that at Geringshof there was a high concentration of individuals with a prior background in the Zionist movement. "Somehow, the feeling emerged that they were the real chalutzim. At Gersfeld, all sorts of people joined for all sorts of reasons. Ideological background was of no importance. While I wouldn't say that we were treated as 'second-rate' chalutzim, it was clear that the chaverim at Gersfeld could not fully symbolize chalutz existence."[20]

Scholarly opinion is divided as to the degree of independent Zionist leanings found among the she'erit hapletah.[21] Despite the overwhelming Zionist orientation so often cited in studies of the DP camps, evidence does exist for other trends. For example, Eliezer Rabinowitz, a Hashomer Hatza'ir emissary, related that when he reached Bergen-Belsen in 1946, he found a not inconsiderable number of Jews engaged in "business-dealings" with Germans. Upon inquiring, "What would you do if Uncle Bevin [Ernest Bevin, the British foreign secretary] granted you an entry permit to Palestine tomorrow?" he received the following evasive reply: "First I have to put together a bit of capital, and then perhaps learn a trade. Anyway, Palestine is not some type of mirage, it won't disappear; we're in no rush."[22] Even in the absence of unequivocal data for the number of survivors that saw aliyah as their only option, it appears that in the 1946–47 period a considerable number of Jews could conceive of no other practical solution to their situation. Moreover, with the exception of the communists and a small ultra-orthodox minority (located near Pocking, Germany), no militantly anti-Zionist stands were taken against the representative Zionist body, Hahistadrut Hazionit Haachidah Shel She'erit Hapletah Begermania (The United Zionist Organization of the DPs in Germany), that emerged in Germany.

Whether they were Zionist out of conviction or Zionist from expediency, almost no potential members turning either to the hachsharah at Geringshof or to that at Gersfeld were rejected. The distinction between the Zionist background of the chalutzim at the two hachsharot explains the different pace at which they developed. The kibbutz at Geringshof was always perceived as more innovative and active, while its younger twin at Gersfeld reacted more slowly to changing situations. The hachsharot also differed in their attitude toward the pioneering endeavor. Anna Adler, who arrived at Gersfeld in September 1945, recalled that immediately upon arrival, she was assigned to the kitchen. "My prior experiences had taught me nothing about a kibbutz, and even less about how to manage in a kibbutz kitchen. But things worked out once I discovered the secret. We worked, but only to the required minimum. That's how things were at Gersfeld in general."[23]

Adler's description applies to all realms of endeavor at Gersfeld. Its status as a "semi-hachsharah" was reminiscent of the atmosphere at Geringshof just before the first group's departure—people worked, but not too hard, and while the general atmosphere was one of pioneering endeavor, idleness often prevailed. What enabled Gersfeld to continue to function was first of all, its organization; second, the realization that certain jobs had to be done to ensure the farm's existence; third, increased contact with emissaries from the Yishuv from spring 1946 onward, which were to have a great impact on life at the hachsharah; and finally, the intense desire to belong to a framework that would expedite their aliyah.

Although they differed in population and in their attitude toward work, politically and organizationally the two hachsharot were in concord. Both nucleii belonged to the Nocham movement, and functioned fully as training farms. Sarah (Hollander) Bar'am, who was at Gersfeld from fall 1945 to spring 1947, summarized the situation succinctly: "There were committees, there were disagreements, it was a real kibbutz."[24] More importantly, throughout their existence, the two hachsharot maintained such a close relationship that they were considered of one unit: Kibbutz Buchenwald-Geringshof and Kibbutz Buchenwald-Gersfeld. Another indication that life on the kibbutz was becoming settled appeared on the personal level. In fall and winter 1945, many young members were moved by the impulse to marry and raise families. This mirrored the next stage in the normalization of the she'erit hapletah, following its initial physical rehabilitation.[25] By and large, these marriages were inspired more by the desire to escape loneliness and to have children than by love and emotional intimacy. A description of a DP camp, dating from the summer of 1946, noted that the majority of the young women were either pregnant or pushing baby carriages. Indeed, the high birthrate among the she'erit hapletah (35.8 per 1,000 in 1948) bore witness to the survivors' strong desire to rectify swiftly the Jewish demographic curve.[26]

The couples at Geringshof and Gersfeld differed from their fellow survivors in one respect. The knowledge that they might be leaving for Palestine by illegal means at any time led the majority of the couples in the second group of chalutzim to postpone marriage until after their aliyah. Only those unable to join the "second wave" in December 1945 were married during the spring and summer of 1946. American army chaplains, who maintained constant contact with the survivors, officiated at the ceremonies.[27] This wave of weddings was noted in May 1946, in a short entry in the diary kept by the third group at Geringshof:

> Everything is flowering. Intoxicating smells fill the air. The days are delightful, so are the evenings and nights. We go for walks whenever we have free time. We have become even more closely knit. We are always cheerful. We have become romantic. Everything is in flower, not just outside, but within. We are beginning to understand what it means to be a free person.[28]

And in June: "Our society has become consolidated and united. Couples are forming. The wedding season is beginning."[29]

The wedding season opened, but not the season of procreation. The chalutzim were reluctant to sanction their Diaspora existence. Although dozens of couples were married at Geringshof and Gersfeld, only one child was born.[30] The general consensus agreed with Sarah (Hollander) Bar'am, who met her husband at Gersfeld and married him in spring 1946 but waited four years before starting a family: "Many couples got married on the hachsharah, but no one considered having children then. Why? We believed that we would be leaving for Palestine any day, and did not want to bring children along on the journey."[31]

Finally, the kibbutz became established in terms of its psychological framework. At its inception, the hachsharah at Geringshof was a singular lone venture, with no movement or institutional affiliation. Accordingly, its founders tended to perceive their venture as an avant-garde, original experiment. At the same time, they developed a somewhat egocentric psychological approach, ascribing central importance to the kibbutz and only secondary helping status to the external agencies with which it had contact. Political developments among the she'erit hapletah in the summer of 1945 changed this picture, however, radically altering the second group's perceptions of the hachsharah in general and their own future in particular. Fundamentally aware that the hachsharah was an ongoing concern that would continue to function after their aliyah, they felt themselves part of a larger enterprise. This perception was affirmed by their psychological relationship with the outside agencies that assisted the kibbutz, in the emergence of close ties with Nocham, with the Hechalutz and Beth Jacob centers in Bergen-Belsen, with representatives from the Joint Distribution Committee and other welfare agencies, as well as with emissaries from the Yishuv, Jewish Brigade members, and Brichah activists.

KIBBUTZ BUCHENWALD AS MAINSTAY OF THE SURVIVORS' UNITY MOVEMENT

A major factor in understanding the significance of Kibbutz Buchenwald against the background of the she'erit hapletah in general is its role as a linchpin of the unity movement in Germany. Between 1944 and 1946, various unity movements emerged among the she'erit hapletah. Several were offshoots of organizations founded during the war; others were formed at the war's conclusion.[32] The two largest organizations of this kind emerged in Germany in late summer 1945—the Zionist Organization of the DPs and, within its framework, the Nocham pioneering movement.[33] Although Nocham espoused a pluralistic outlook, it adopted a consistent stand on major issues confronting the Zionist movement. Nocham endorsed the necessity for a Jewish state, and encouraged illegal immigration and settlement in Palestine. Moreover, it promoted a strong Zionist orientation among the she'erit hapletah in general, uniting various Zionist factions under its auspices.

Five bodies had cooperated in founding the Zionist Organization of the DPs and Nocham, the two main unity organizations in Germany. The first were members of Kibbutz Lochamei Hageta'ot (Ghetto Fighters' Kibbutz) who reached Germany through the Brichah network. Second were members of Irgun Brit Zion, an organization formed during the war in the Kovno ghetto, which had called for unity as early as 1941. Third was the Bergen-Belsen Hechalutz center, which maintained close contact with the hachsharah at Geringshof, and had encouraged unity from its inception. Fourth were soldiers from the Jewish Brigade—Zvi Langsam (Shiloah), Yosef Benkover, Ben-Zion Yisraeli, and Chaim Ben-Asher—who nurtured the survivors along with their incipient unity movements.[34] The final participants were Zionist youth movement members whose organizations had already called for unity during the twenties and thirties.[35] Wartime reality had brought home the harmful effects of divisiveness, thus intensifying this trend. Not surprisingly, these youth groups served as an unfailing prop of unity in the postwar era as well.[36]

Its broad base notwithstanding, the unity trend did not go unopposed. Some opponents raised objections to what they viewed as a renewed Mapai (labor party) attempt to achieve supremacy following the failure of its Unified Hechalutz plan. Nor was opposition restricted to Europe; Yishuv bodies expressed antagonism as well. Of these, the left-wing Hashomer Hatza'ir was the most vocal. Its members received instructions from the Yishuv parent body to guard party particularism zealously. It was on this basis that the separatist Hashomer Hatza'ir consistently refused, in the words of Ze'ev Mankowitz, "to grant normative standing to the world of the dead over and above the world of the living and their current obligation to it."[37] In September 1945, Hashomer Hatza'ir took steps to disband a unity organization that had been organized in Poland, following which the movement withdrew totally from Nocham.

Despite the departure of the left-wing Zionists, Nocham remained the single largest organization among the she'erit hapletah in Germany. Some six thousand members attended the Nocham Congress held at the Nili farm in February 1946. At that juncture, Nocham's official membership numbered more than 3,370 members in Bavaria, of whom 1,731 were kibbutz affiliated and 1,643 were not.[38] Nonetheless, despite Nocham's ostensible strength, Hashomer Hatza'ir's separationist model set a precedent. During 1946, other movements withdrew from Nocham. Over the course of that year, Nocham, once the symbol of the demise of extreme political particularism, slowly disintegrated, becoming in the final analysis what its opponents had feared from its inception that it would become—a Mapai-sponsored unity movement.

No scholarly consensus exists about what caused the breakup of the unity movements in general, and of Nocham in particular. Leaders of the left such as Meir Ya'ari and Ya'akov Hazzan attribute the disintegration to directives issued by party leaders in the Yishuv.[39] Others note the existence of factionalism within the European she'erit hapletah, citing as evidence Hungarian Zionist youth leaders, and groups that feared Mapai domination.[40] Finally, there are those who seek the seeds of separatism in the composition of the groups comprising the she'erit hepletah. They differentiate between the "direct" survivors of the camps, who endorsed the unity trend, and the leaders of the partisans and Asiatics, whose perception of the role played by the party in their survival led them to maintain greater party loyalty.[41] It should be noted, however, that the founders of one of the major unity movements, Chativat Seridei Mizrach Eiropah (The Division of Eastern European Survivors), had been partisans and ghetto fighters.

These explanations relate only to the motivation of the leadership of various groups in bowing out of the unity movements. They do not explain the behavior of the rank and file, who, although they had personally suffered the negative effects of factionalism, seemed to experience no qualms about disbanding the eight-month-old unity movement. The explanation lies both in the state of the she'erit hapletah in 1946, as well as in the nature of post-Holocaust political affiliation. During 1946, life in the DP camps achieved stability and established patterns. Concomitantly, enthusiasm for new trends, and for movements in general, dissipated. Second, the vital role played by the idea of "movement" in the survivors' lives must be noted. For many, ideological shadings aside, the movement conferred a sense of belonging, a substitute home and family. Loyalty to youth movements and their leaders was the prime factor behind the willingness of their members to leave the unity movements they had formed only a few months earlier. In the battle between unity and loyalty to party particularism, the movements scored nearly a total victory.

Kibbutz Buchenwald's hachsharot at Geringshof and Gersfeld are atypical when viewed against this background of demographic change and political ferment. Although beginning with the summer of 1945, dozens of kibbutzim were founded by survivors, agricultural training farms were the exception, not the rule. Formed in the DP camps, these collectives served to ameliorate the difficult camp conditions while simultaneously fulfilling the survivors' need to organize.

In contrast, Kibbutz Buchenwald was the first Nocham hachsharah founded in Germany, its special status determining the nature of the kibbutz's relationship to the Bergen-Belsen Hechalutz center, which had fluctuated from paternalism to a desire to participate actively in Kibbutz Buchenwald's dream. Now the hachsharah had achieved independent status, which in turn allowed it to serve as a patron for the new hachsharot that were being founded. Kibbutz Buchenwald became a model for all those who sought to establish similar frameworks in or near DP camps. Moreover, the link to Nocham transformed Kibbutz Buchenwald into a component of a kibbutz movement, with all its attendant implications. No longer were the hachsharot at Geringshof and Gersfeld isolated kibbutzim; rather, they were now part of a well-developed movement machine that exercised substantial influence among the she'erit hapletah.[42]

THE ULTRAORTHODOX CONTINGENT

The link between the kibbutz and the Beth Jacob center was more problematical in nature. Founded a few weeks after liberation, the Beth Jacob center served as a home and mentor for hundreds of its former students who survived the camps.[43] In summer 1945, the center leaders agreed to send a group of young women to Geringshof in order to expedite their aliyah. For their part, the members of the hachsharah acceded to the demand that the religious status quo be maintained: Sabbath observance in the public domain and a kosher kitchen for those who observed dietary laws. With the kibbutz's expansion, the Beth Jacob group split. Eight girls remained at Geringshof under Rivka England's supervision, while the remainder joined the new hachsharah at Gersfeld under Rachel Shantzer. At the same time, the young women remained in close contact with the leaders of the Beth Jacob center at Bergen-Belsen, keeping up to date with developments in their movement.

Mid-September saw the first disagreement over religious matters. Friction emerged mainly over the nature of the Oneg Shabbat parties held at Geringshof. During Kibbutz Buchenwald's founding period, on Friday nights religious tenets had been strictly observed in public, but things changed with the arrival of the chalutzim from Bergen-Belsen. Musical selections had been added to the program, which angered the ultraorthodox members. The first to voice her objections was Rivka Englard, who also served on the culture committee. Her opposition came against the background of a prior incident in which some chalutzim had smoked at the Shabbat table in flagrant disregard of the "gentleman's agreement" between themselves and the religious members.[44] The rift widened on Yom Kippur 1945, following an announcement that a discussion of the Book of Jonah would take place the next day. As Rivka Englard recalled, "Nu, what could be more appropriate than to discuss Jonah on Yom Kippur? But when I got there, I couldn't believe my ears. What blasphemy, what *apikorsut* [heresy]! I was in shock." Then it was Englard's turn to speak as a member of the culture committee. "I talked about Divine Providence in history. Then they were furious. We appeared to have reached an impasse."[45]

The story does not end here. Englard called an urgent meeting of the committee heads at which she tendered several conditions for continued coexistence. The meeting, and its consequences, were described in a letter written by Akiva Skidell in September 1945. Shedding light on the intergroup interaction at the hachsharah, as well as on the nature of the link between the ultraorthodox young women and the Beth Jacob center at Bergen-Belsen, Skidell's letter succinctly sums up a major problem then plaguing Kibbutz Buchenwald: the lack of tolerance.

Until very recently there was no friction between the two groups [religious and freethinking]. There was a little heartache, caused to the orthodox by a few *shkotzim* [Yiddish for, literally, non-Jews; here, militantly nonreligious], and a little annoyance caused to these by the orthodox, but in the atmosphere of toleration all this passed. Then, it seems, this teacher came out with some demands, which sounded like an ultimatum: If they are not granted, she and her group will have to leave. There are two specific ones: 1) that there be no smoking at the table on Friday night: and 2) that there be no playing of music on Shabbat. It is not likely that the demands will be granted, certainly not the second one, and there is a tenseness as a result of it. . . .

Now, I had a long talk with one of the finest fellows in the place last night on this business. He is himself a member of Mizrachi [the religious Zionist party], I believe, but this is not important. . . . He placed the blame squarely on the shoulders of this teacher, though he could understand her motives. She didn't actually come alone. She and the group were in a sense delegated to the place by a much larger group of Bet Yaakov [Beth Jacob] people in Bergen-Belsen, and consequently they feel that they have a mission—the propagation of the faith. This, and not too much gray matter, he says, have combined to create the situation. It puts him, and the others in his group, in a very difficult position. If an open break comes, he will be forced to leave with the girls, though he has found his place here, likes it and feels that he belongs there. But if the break is on a matter of principle, as between the religious and the others, his conscience won't let him stay on. . . . They hope that perhaps at the time of the congress in Bergen-Belsen next week the question will be raised privately with the big-wigs of the Bet Yaakov group and will be straightened out.[46]

Skidell was not aware that the Beth Jacob functionaries had other plans for the group. During that period, the question of the feasibility of founding a Po'alei Agudah [ultraorthodox pioneering movement] kibbutz near the Zeilsheim DP camp was under discussion. The young women at Geringshof were counted upon as an important component of this kibbutz's population base. Several days later, emissaries from Zeilsheim ordered the young women at Kibbutz Buchenwald to pack their bags and join the new kibbutz, Chafetz Chaim. This call elicited an immediate positive response.[47]

Hilda Gruenwald recalled now the Hechalutz center leaders at Bergen-Belsen responded to this development, immediately dispatching to Geringshof emissaries who sat and talked with the girls all night. "We suggested various compromises, but they were determined to leave. Finally, we gave up and discussed continued cooperation following their relocation to the new hachsharah."[48]

The Agudah contingent left Kibbutz Buchenwald in early October. Despite the discord that had led to a split, parting was difficult. Rivka Englard recalled with nostalgic irony that many stood by, weeping. "You're taking our best people away," they cried. "Finally they brought horses and wagons, loaded our bundles, and gave us a beautiful 'funeral' procession."[49]

Surprisingly, the Mizrachi contingent elected to stay at Geringshof, rather than join the departing faction, but even more unexpectedly, some of the Beth Jacob group stayed in contact with Kibbutz Buchenwald members after the split. A few individuals even made aliyah in company with Geringshof's second contingent, which sailed on the the illegal immigration ship *Tel Chai*.

The Beth Jacob affair illustrates the complex nature of the ties between the Kibbutz and the external bodies that assisted it. Whereas the founding group reached Geringshof with no movement or other formal affiliation, many in the second contingent had ties to a center, movement, or party active among the survivors. Once dual loyalty—to the kibbutz and to an external group— came into play, it fostered the possibility for conflict. Problems of this nature could be resolved only in those cases in which the kibbutz members submitted to Nocham movement discipline, accepting its broad framework as the binding authority.

CONTACTS WITH THE WELFARE AGENCIES

Welfare agencies, especially the Joint Distribution Committee, comprised another type of external link for the kibbutz. In summer 1945, the kibbutz founders received aid from all available agencies, including the U.S. Armed Forces, UNRRA, the Jewish Brigade, and the JDC. Although these agencies were certainly generous, provisions arrived sporadically and often represented only ad hoc solutions to problems. In order to ensure the effective functioning of the hachsharah, the second contingent at Geringshof sought to institute a more regular arrangement, so they turned to the JDC with a request to establish fixed procedures. The JDC responded favorably, and sent delegates to investigate the members' requests at first hand. One such visit, which occurred during the fall holiday season, was documented by Akiva Skidell, who was at Geringshof during that time:

> The news of the day was a visit of some Joint dame and friends, a couple of Jewish civilian employees of the army, from the States, and the *shikse* [Yiddish for non-Jewish woman] wife of one of them, herself in UNRRA. The *chava* [farm] expected them and put on a good show. The place was *yom-tov-dick* [Yiddish for clean and ready] anyhow, though the guest didn't know what the occasion was, and thought, in her modesty, that it was all for her. They went around the farm, then had supper, and she enjoyed some of the *kreplach* [Yiddish for stuffed dumplings] they had. So did I. Then there was some "spontaneous," though somewhat prepared, singing, a little skit, some solo singing, the fiddler, and a little speech by the leader of the group. And then the group dancing, and they certainly dragged everybody into it, and, like good social workers that they all no doubt are, they were very good sports about it, I must say. The kids certainly did the job well, you could see that it was all prepared with some "*sechel*" [Hebrew for sense] probably by someone with a little experience in relations with "seniors."[50]

The kibbutz members had planned their steps carefully. Winter was approaching, and they needed warm clothing and heaters. Supplies from the U.S. Army had virtually ceased, but even when they had no specific needs, the chalutzim always made certain to treat visits from JDC representatives as a special occasion. Naturally, they sought to create a pleasant atmosphere conducive to fulfillment of their request in general. They differed from the founding group in this respect. The founders directly benefited from the wave of enthusiasm created by their pioneering venture, so they had no need to solicit contributions, but by the fall of 1945, the hachsharah's members were well aware that they were but one group among many within the she'erit hapletah, and that many claims were being made upon the welfare agencies' limited resources. Pragmatically speaking, they knew that their economic survival depended upon their access to the various welfare agencies and upon their ability to charm their representatives. The relationship that developed between the chalutzim and the JDC constituted another step in Kibbutz Buchenwald's maturation. It also represented another stage in the enhancement of their sense of belonging to the broader framework of the she'erit hapletah.

CONTACTS WITH ILLEGAL IMMIGRATION AGENTS

Finally, the chalutzim had contacts with agents of Aliyah Bet. Since the kibbutz's move to Geringshof, it had maintained regular contact with Jewish Brigade members, who also acted as agents for the Brichah network. The latter were aided by Jewish GIs in the American armed forces, who supplied the Brichah agents with the forged border passes so essential to their work.[51] A third agency instrumental in *ha'apalah* (illegal immigration) was the Mossad Le'aliyah Bet (Institution for Second [illegal] Immigration) headed by Shaul Meirov (Avigur), headquartered in Paris.[52]

The ha'apalah from Germany, even as a clandestine illegal organization, had its set procedures. Brichah agents or representatives of the Mossad Le'aliyah Bet entered the picture whenever a ship was secured, or alternately, whenever a decision was reached to send a group of DPs to Palestine illegally. Both arms cooperated fully. While the Mossad's agents searched for ships and acquired the necessary papers, members of the Jewish Brigade scouted among the DP camps and hachsharot in Germany for suitable candidates for aliyah. In early winter 1945, it was decided to transfer five hundred candidates for Aliyah Bet from Germany to Belgium. The potential immigrants were carefully chosen from various groups at DP camps and hachsharot. They included a contingent of chalutzim from Geringshof.

The delegation's activities had practical as well as psychological import. At that juncture, for most of the she'erit hapletah in Germany, escape routes through Italy were no longer accessible. The delegation's arrival aroused the DPs' first hopes that reaching Palestine actually was within their grasp. The timing of the visit was also significant. Its appearance encouraged the Jews remaining in Germany and strengthened their Zionist convictions in preparation for the anticipated UNSCOP (United Nations Special Committee on Palestine) commission visit in early 1946.[53]

On November 28, Jewish Brigade members instructed Kibbutz Buchenwald to select a group of candidates for aliyah, to be transferred to Bergen-Belsen prior to their departure for Palestine. Despite its euphoric reception, the announcement placed the hachsharah in a double dilemma: first, how to choose the candidates for aliyah; second, how to recruit new members to ensure the hachsharah's continued functioning. As in the past, hasty decisions were made. Since the number of potential immigrants was not linked to a specific quota of certificates, the entire group, with the addition of a few individuals from Gersfeld, could embark for Palestine.[54] Those who remained at Geringshof did so for personal reasons. Once again, Arthur delayed his departure in hopes for locating his sweetheart. He was joined by other chalutzim who preferred to wait for a legal means of making aliyah, or who were still searching for relatives. Now the hachsharah had to address the question of future reserves. When the founding group's aliyah had been in the offing, the Hechalutz center in Bergen-Belsen had provided assistance. Now that Kibbutz Buchenwald belonged to the Nocham framework, its members turned to the party center with a request to ensure the hachsharah's continuity. In consultation with the center, a decision was reached to send delegations to several DP camps to recruit new members. A visit by one such delegation and the response by Nocham members was documented in the diary of the third contingent at Geringshof: "Landsberg am Lech: December 1945. Emissaries from Kibbutz Buchenwald-Geringshof—Hilda Gruenwald, Rivka Kopferberg—have brought good news. Their aliyah to Palestine (Aliyah Bet) is imminent, and it is imperative that a large group from Nocham ranks be sent immediately to replace them. We are organizing to depart for Geringshof in a few days time, generously provisioned by the committee at Landsberg."[55]

Preparations for departure were well under way when the kibbutz leader and Brichah activists were faced with an unanticipated problem—the Chaim Meyers affair. Meyers, an American GI who belonged to Hashomer Hatza'ir, had become friendly with the chalutzim and was a fairly frequent visitor at Geringshof. One rainy night in mid-December, he arrived at the farm bearing essential equipment for the chalutzim. Under the cover of darkness, they informed him of the group's impending illegal departure for Palestine. Meyers was captivated by the idea and requested permission to join the immigrants. The Jewish Brigade members were in a quandary. After all, this was a member of the U.S. Armed Forces who as about to go AWOL. Should they allow Meyers to attempt aliyah with the Kibbutz Buchenwald group, thereby putting himself and the entire contingent at risk? Pize recalled how the contingent's leaders had but one thought uppermost: how great a danger Meyers would pose to the entire group's aliyah if he were caught. "So we consulted with the Jewish Brigade members, and they advised us to allow him to come on aliyah even though he was a deserter. What could we do? First we had to effect a transformation. We gave him a *musselman*'s [starving concentration camp inmate] haircut, found him pants, and buried his gun at Geringshof. That's how he came to Palestine with us.[56]

Matters were not quite so simple from Meyers's point of view. After having him change his clothes in the dining room, ridding him of his uniform, and taking away his gun, they decided to change his name, calling him Weiss, since that was the only name he could pronounce without an American accent. "We left several hours later in trucks supplied by the Jewish Brigade; we all hid under the canvas. In back, someone sat in a British soldier's coat, as if guarding prisoners of war. Then I suddenly realized that I was a deserter, and that we were still in the American zone. I almost made in my pants."[57]

The chaverim had only been informed that they were bound for Bergen-Belsen, that they would make aliyah from there, but they had not been told that they would spend approximately two months in a Jewish Brigade center for immigrants in Antwerp. At Bergen-Belsen, Meyers met an emissary named Gershon, who told him not to worry, that in twelve days he would be in Palestine. "I knew that a soldier was declared a deserter after twenty-one days. I remembered the case of an American soldier who had been declared a deserter during World War Two, was caught, and shot. I began to get worried."[58]

After a week at Bergen-Belsen, the illegal immigrants were assembled in preparation for the continuation of their journey. Once again they were informed that they were bound directly for the ship. Meyers recalled that the Brigade's commanders instructed them to inform anyone who inquired that they were en route to Argentina. At Bergen-Belsen, the group was again assembled by Gershon from the Brigade, who said that they were bound directly for the ship. Then he changed his tune. "There will be a slight delay," he said. Meyers recalled how Gershon then turned to him and asked, "If you reach Israel in twenty days they can't catch you for deserting, can they?" Now it was no longer twelve days, but twenty. "I was no longer slightly concerned. I was very worried, but it was too late."[59]

The chalutzim departed for Antwerp, where they were housed in two residences for *olim* (immigrants to Palestine) until early March. A detailed diary logged the varied activities in which they participated during their stay. A typical week included a Shabbat party, dancing and singing, Hebrew classes, writing a wall newspaper, classes about Palestine and the Bible, lectures on Zionist history, a trip to the opera, and lectures on Labor Federation history.[60] What this record does not reflect was the growing political polarization of the chaverim, particularly Hashomer Hatza'ir members from Geringshof. During the months at Antwerp, Jewish Brigade members affiliated with Hashomer Hatza'ir engaged in an intensive indoctrination campaign, unceasingly reiterating that it would be impossible to found Nocham kibbutzim in the Yishuv, that upon their arrival they would have to renew their allegiance to their former movement. Gusta Ziegler recalled how the Jewish Brigade members injected a great deal of Yishuv spirit into the group. "We learned Hebrew systematically. There were lively political debates. We spoke about partition, the Biltmore program, the Labor Federation, and how to organize a farm. There were endless debates about Ben-Gurion's ideas, about the political parties, and about our role in the dream of the future state."[61]

Bluma Rosenstein recalled how one day the emissaries came to the group and began to talk to them about the concept of Nocham. One approached her and said, "Bluma, the Yishuv is built on Mapai, and this [party] and that [party]. Each has its own kibbutz movement, whereas you have nothing in the Yishuv, and will be unable to found a new kibbutz." When she mentioned Nocham, he replied, "There is no such thing. You will have to undergo hachsharah and then choose a movement." From that moment on, it was plain to every person with a prior movement background that it would be necessary to seek out a movement following aliyah.[62]

According to Meyers, the corrosive effects of movement factionalism made themselves felt only after their departure from Antwerp, while they were on their way to Palestine. In Antwerp, the group talked about Nocham incessantly, stating categorically how they were all going to join a kibbutz in Palestine. "Then, while we were on our way, Hashomer Hatza'ir delegates grabbed and assembled us in order to explain that once we reached the Yishuv, we would be transferred to a Hashomer Hatza'ir kibbutz, Kibbutz Mesilot."[63]

The growing politicalization of Kibbutz Buchenwald's members in Antwerp echoes the prevalent trend among the Jewish DPs in Germany a year after the liberation: an abstract desire for unity over which a concrete understanding of its unfeasability was slowly being superimposed. Similar to the encounter of Kibbutz Buchenwald's members with the separatist tendencies of Hashomer Hatza'ir, by spring 1946 the left-wing Zionist party had spearheaded the breakup of unity movements throughout both Germany and Poland. This was yet another nail in the coffin of Zionist unity, the last bastion of utopian illusion during the postwar era.

Life in the residences for olim was run on a collective basis, with supplies largely provided by the Antwerp Jewish community. In this setting as well, Chaim Meyers was forced to keep his identity a secret. Meyers recalled that the group lived in two buildings with a dentist living next door. "One day I went to him, and when I opened my mouth, he said, 'That's an American mouth.' I prayed that I would need no outside dental care. Once they took us out to a soccer game during the day. Suddenly I shrank two feet. Opposite me stood two soldiers from my unit." That episode also passed without incident.[64]

The stay at the residence for olim, under "conditions of confinement," in the words of one female member, lasted for nearly two months.[65] In early March, the illegal immigrants were transferred from Antwerp to Marseilles in a convoy organized by the Jewish Brigade. In the dead of night, the convoy reached a field near Marseilles, where it rendezvoused with Brichah and Mossad Le'aliyah Bet agents. After instructions were received, the trucks entered the city and deposited the emmigrants in a French DP camp. From there, they were transported in French naval vessels to the port of La Siata, where they boarded the SS *Tel Chai*. The ship sailed on the evening of March

17, 1946, with 743 persons on board, of whom 736 were illegal immigrants. This number included some seventy members of Kibbutz Buchenwald.[66]

How did the illegal immigrants experience their journey? One woman recalled seeing a luxurious passenger liner at the dock. "I was certain that it was waiting for us. Next to it was docked a small, miserable-looking ship. I could not believe that all of us, some six hundred people, could be compressed inside. Later, they brought even more people."[67]

Further hardships awaited them on the high seas. The trip on the *Tel Chai* differed radically from the experiences of the founding group on the *Mataroa* only six months earlier. Here, sanitary conditions were intolerable. "It was possible to contract typhoid fever," recalled one immigrant. "There was hardly any food, and worst of all was the water shortage. During the final days we were rationed one cup of water [each] daily. We washed our hands with seawater."[68]

One rainy night near Crete stands out in the memory of the entire group. Yisrael Lerner recounted that a terrible storm blew up one night, just as the ship neared Crete. "The ship was tossed about, and all the engines failed. The captain wanted to radio for help, but the Haganah commanding officer on board refused to give his consent. When dawn came and we saw where we were stranded, we all recited '*Shema Yisrael*' [Hear O Israel]. It wouldn't have taken much for the ship to break up entirely."[69]

Ten days after it set sail, the *Tel Chai* was intercepted by British naval vessels and towed to Haifa. Chaim Meyers, who was in charge of the ship's generator, recalled that the crew took steps to cover their mission. First they threw the wireless radio overboard. Meyers tossed away all the tools except for a pair of pliers, which the British confiscated at Atlit. After reaching Haifa, the British took the Greek crew aside so that they could point out the Jewish crewmembers. "We knew in advance that we would have to change our appearance. I gave my eyeglasses to someone else; another shaved off his beard. The arrangement was that everyone would board the buses, and they they would disappear. And that's what happened. The British loaded us onto buses, and the Palyam [Naval Palmach (pre-State army)] members exited through the driver's door, and did not reach Atlit with us."[70]

The illegal immigrants spent a week at Atlit and were released as part of the immigration quota. Some twenty chaverim repaired to Kibbutz Afikim to continue their training; a handful of Hashomer Hatza'ir members made their way to Kibbutz Mesilot; while the rest scattered throughout the Yishuv, where they were reunited with friends and relatives. The *Tel Chai*'s passengers were the last to be released under the quota, following a brief stay at Atlit. There was a three-month hiatus in sailings from Western Europe following the *Tel Chai*'s embarkation. During this interim period, logistical problems that had delayed the departure of additional groups of illegals were resolved.[71]

COMPARISON OF FIRST AND SECOND WAVES OF CHALUTZIM
FROM KIBBUTZ BUCHENWALD

Both before and after they reached Palestine, the difference between the first and second waves of chalutzim from Geringshof was noted in three main spheres. The first was the absence of friction between Polish-born and German-born Jews. Some of the leaders, like Arthur Poznansky, Herbert Growald, and Pize, were Yekkim (Yiddish term for Jews of German origin); others, like Yisrael Lerner and Aharon Batzia, were of Polish origin. German, Yiddish, and Polish as well were spoken, but the prevailing culture was "chalutz culture," in Hilda Gruenwald's words.[72] How did these different groups interact? Yocheved Schwimmer recalled that the members had little time to dwell on differences. "Actually, our life at Geringshof quickly took on a normal pattern. As if we had bypassed the years of atrocities, as if this were the natural sequel to what should have been before the war."[73]

The same lack of conflict characterized relations among chalutzim who represented different movements, as well as between movement-oriented chalutzim and unaffiliated ones. Gusta Ziegler, a product of a very religious family, had come to Geringshof with no prior movement experience. Arriving with the Bergen-Belsen group, she had been brought to Zionism by a friend from Hashomer Hatza'ir. "My connection was to its Polish sector. I remember that there were members from Betar [a right-wing Zionist group], as well as from all the other movements, that I had a sense of 'a tiger shall dwell with the lamb' [paraphrase of Isaiah 11:6]. Certainly there were cliques based on national origin or movement membership, but their existence disturbed no one, and they did not interfere with the administration of the hachsharah in any way. Actually, even the 'nonaffiliated' were ardent Zionists. That was what bound the entire group. Besides, we were simply too busy to waste time on altercations."[74]

A third distinguishing factor was the group's attitude toward the hachsharah diary. The founding members enthusiastically recorded every event in kibbutz life, and many individuals made entries in the kibbutz diary. In contrast, the members of the second group evinced no interest in keeping a diary, nor in leaving behind historical records to document their activity. Even the diary kept at Antwerp was the work of outsiders who joined the potential immigrants from Geringshof, not of hachsharah members. Did this reflect a trend of sorts, or, perhaps, did the second group's historical consciousness fall short of that of the founders?

Opinion is divided on this question. Pize cited tradition as the main reason for the lack of a diary. The first group had kept a diary, which they took to Palestine. The second group had brought no diary from Bergen-Belsen, and therefore did not think of starting their own at the hachsharah.[75] Yocheved

Schwimmer had a different view of the situation: "Perhaps some individuals kept personal diaries, but there was no kibbutz diary. Why not? After all, some of those who came from Bergen-Belsen had lived with the founding group and were aware of the existence of a kibbutz diary. But our group did not lean toward collective writing, despite the example set by the founders."[76]

They did concur in one respect; both reported that their contingent was "work-oriented," with no time to make detailed entries in a hachsharah diary. Pize summed up this feeling: "We were too involved in daily living and Nocham affairs to find time each day to write in a diary."[77]

This simplistic explanation recurs regarding each of the second contingent's previously mentioned distinguishing characteristics, but the claim "We were too busy" to argue about national origins or movement affiliation, or to write a diary, reflects but a partial picture. A fuller explanation comes from a key factor nonexistent before the second contingent's arrival—the twin hachsharah at Gersfeld. Innate differences had developed between the hachsharah at Gersfeld and the one at Geringshof. Many of its members had no prior movement background, and leaders and members alike were mostly of Polish origin. Over time, these selective criteria became entrenched. Sarah (Hollander) Bar'am, who arrived at Gersfeld during Sukkot 1945, recalled how the Hechalutz leadership at Bergen-Belsen decided who would be sent to Geringshof and who to Gersfeld. "Chalutzim went to Geringshof; everyone else went to Gersfeld. Those of German origin to Geringshof; of Polish origin to Gersfeld."[78]

Evidently, the key to the lack of friction in areas that afflicted the founders lay in the creation of more homogeneous groups. Sarah Bar'am's comment, "At Gersfeld the Yekkim were not in charge,"[79] was corroborated by another Gersfeld member, Gavriel Rosenbaum. "We were all Polish [Jews] from observant homes. Therefore, there were no arguments about maintaining a kosher kitchen or holiday observance, unlike at Geringshof."[80] Concerning movement affiliation, by absorbing most of the "unaffiliated," the hachsharah at Gersfeld eliminated additional tension on that score. Indeed, creating an alternative farmstead for all those who did not toe the Geringshof pioneering line, or whose background was otherwise unsuitable, was an ideal solution to the discord that had plagued the initial group. This was not a case of "divide and conquer"; rather, it represented the creation of an appropriate framework for those without movement background, or a lack of motivation for the hard labor at Geringshof for those in need of a massive infusion of Zionist guidance. Indeed, emissaries from the Yishuv became involved in running the Gersfeld hachsharah as early as the beginning of 1946, which far predated their administration of Geringshof.

The second contingent avoided specific areas of friction that afflicted the founders. However, a serious rift did emerge in a sphere that barely touched the most veteran group during their stay in Geringshof—a split over religious issues. We have already noted one explanatory factor—loyalty to a center outside the Nocham framework. Two additional factors, human and chronological, also had bearing on this problem. The founding group contained many observant Jews who adopted a tolerant attitude toward their partners, the chalutzim. Two of them—Tydor and Zauderer—held key positions and set the normative standards for religious—nonreligious coexistence on the hachsharah. This was hardly the case for the second group; only one religious individual, Rivka Englard, regarded as a hard-liner on religious questions and as rigid in her dealings with secular members, held a key position. Time was another significant factor. The founding group emerged shortly after liberation, when the survivors were moved by overwhelming feelings of solidarity, but the second contingent had had time to reenter the world of movement factionalism and religious rivalry. This development directly affected the relationship between the ultraorthodox and secular wings of the hachsharah, a relationship that deteriorated into hostility and, eventually, an open rift. Evidently, each of these three factors—loyalty to an external framework, the absence of religious members in key positions, and the dissipation of postliberation brotherly solidarity—contributed significantly to the ultimate outcome of the Beth Jacob affair in the fall of 1945.

THE THIRD WAVE OF PIONEERS AT GERINGSHOF AND GERSFELD

Life on the hachsharot continued even after the departure of the "second aliyah," as the chalutzim termed it. The nucleus of the third group at Geringshof was comprised of those Nocham members who answered the appeal for volunteers made at the Landsberg DP camp. Unlike its predecessor, this contingent did keep a diary, albeit of limited scope. Nonetheless, it provides a record of essential features of life on the hachsharah. A December 1945 entry describes the new group's reception at Geringshof:

> The trip to Geringshof was extremely difficult. Trains do not run regularly, and the coaches are crammed to the limit. A large organized group cannot travel as a unit. We progressed by means of various ploys and reached Fulda several days later. We notified Geringshof, and they came to fetch us with a car and several wagons. We are at Geringshof. The prior group is already gone, with the exception of a few individuals, and the members of Kibbutz Buchenwald-Gersfeld. They come to give us instructions and go off to Gersfeld. Backbreaking work begins. We must tackle the cowshed, the pigpen, the water cistern that is acting up. . . . We do not have enough people. A large vehicle is going to Bergen-Belsen to recruit more. New chalutzim are on their way.[81]

The key sentence that describes the relationship that now developed between the two hachsharot is: "They come to give us instructions and go off to Gersfeld." No longer twin sisters enthusiastically cooperating in a joint venture, they were two independent entities, Geringshof and Gersfeld, under one rubric—Kibbutz Buchenwald. During this period, the first emissaries from the Yishuv reached Gersfeld, taking management of the hachsharah their wing. At a later date, this would pertain to Geringshof as well. This arrangement lasted until the last chalutzim made aliyah in 1948.[82]

From this point on, the pattern of life on the hachsharot diverged from that of the two initial groups. It was obvious that the sole means of reaching Palestine was through Aliyah Bet; therefore, the stay at the farm could last for months. As a result, the third group decided to renovate the living quarters at Geringshof, and to acquire supplies essential to improving the quality of life on the hachsharah. An entry in the kibbutz diary dated January 1946 reflects the extent of these activities: "We are renovating our living quarters. . . . The house is extremely neglected. We are installing central heating and exchanging the bunk beds that remind us òf the concentration camps for ordinary ones. We study Hebrew, discuss topics of interest, learn Hebrew songs, dance the hora, grow accustomed to kibbutz life."[83]

Two individuals in particular assisted the kibbutz in its efforts at consolidation. One was Rabbi Mayer Abramowitz, an American army chaplain whose ties to the hachsharah dated from winter 1945. He was instrumental in supplying the "third aliyah" with the forged pass that enabled the group to move freely across Germany en route to Palestine.[84] The second was Yishuv emissary Shaul Netter, a former native of Mannheim and a member of Kibbutz Deganyah. Upon his discharge from the Jewish Brigade, he was assigned to direct the hachsharot at Geringshof and Gersfeld. Netter, who was killed during the battles for Tzemach (near the Sea of Galilee in northern Palestine) in the War of Independence, mediated between the kibbutz and the Palestinian Welfare Units. He also injected the spirit of the Yishuv at the hachsharah.[85] One kibbutz member recalled the attitude of the young kibbutz member as being totally different from what they were used to from other emissaries:

He tried to broaden our horizons, to expose us to a world of beauty, of art. I recall that he brought books about Michelangelo, reproductions of Van Gogh and other artists. He did not engage in cheap propaganda. He only tried to instill in us a love of nature in general, and of our homeland in particular. He lived with and by the poems he taught us. Often he sat with one individual member or another. He understood each and every one, and gave friendly fatherly advice. We never felt divided by a gap in status or age.[86]

A noteworthy event in the lives of the chalutzim was the day they found the Sefer Torah. Toward winter's end, the chaverim had begun to organize various workshops—shoemaking, sewing, and carpentry. The latter was to be located in a loft above the barn. As they began to clear it, they found a large box lying in the corner of the room. To their amazement, they found in it a Torah scroll. Above the box, the following words were written on the wall: "*Sie werden noch manchmal an uns denken*" (German for "Think of us on occasion"). This was another memento left by the members of the Bachad hachsharah who had been deported to their deaths in 1943.[87] The group now faced a dilemma. Should they turn the Torah scroll over to the nearest Jewish community or keep it at the farm? Following a brief debate, they decided to start a library that would also house a synagogue and an ark for the Torah scroll. The kibbutz woodworking shop prepared a commemorative plaque for victims of the Holocaust, which was hung over the entrance. Books were obtained from the Rothschild Library in Frankfurt.[88] The founding of the library and synagogue represented a further stage in the kibbutz's institution-alization during 1946.

The demographic changes that affected the She'erit hapletah as a whole during 1946 left their mark on the composition of the hachsharot as well. Whereas the first groups at Geringshof and Gersfeld were composed almost exclusively of concentration camp survivors, from 1946, the members who arrived at the hachsharot were largely repatriates who had reached Germany from Russia by way of Poland. One of these was Shimon Fleishon. Fleishon, born in Poland and a Hashomer Hatza'ir trainee, was exiled to Russia during the war and had been drafted into the Red Army. After the war, he returned to Poland with the wave of repatriates. Aided by the Brichah network, he reached Czechoslovakia. From there he made his way to Austria, and then to Germany. Fleishon oversaw the work roster at Geringshof for nearly a year. He recalled there being approximately twenty chalutzim at Geringshof upon his arrival, including Arthur Poznansky and Papa Juker. "During the day, the chaverim worked on the farm, in the cowshed, with the horses, and in the pigpen. The kitchen no longer served kosher food, as no religious members remained on the kibbutz."[89]

The changes in the composition of the hachsharot brought two conse-quences in their wake. First, they effected a change in the members' attitude toward the idea of hachsharah; over the year, it lost its idealistic visionary tone and became an "industry," a necessary evil to be endured in order to join Aliyah Bet. Second, relations with the surrounding German society, previ-ously characterized by frosty aloofness, were now thawed. This change cer-tainly resulted from the fact that by 1946, the kibbutz roster did not contain members who had spent the war years in German camps. Shimon Fleishon recalled how relations developed with the Germans in the nearby village of

Hattenhof. Members of the kibbutz used to go to the local tavern to drink beer. "We were used to drinking vodka from our days in Russia. . . . Our relationship with the locals was extremely friendly. The Germans were hungry for bread. A non-Jewish barber used to come from Fulda and give us all haircuts by appointment. In return, he got bread from the kibbutz."[90]

Dolik Bergman, another repatriate, recounted how bread was their passport to German stores: "With bread, one could buy the entire village. A famous photographer resided in Fulda. Whenever we went there, we brought along bread and other provisions for her, and she would photograph us. One guy even took a chocolate bar in hopes of finding a chance sexual encounter in the nearby village."[91]

Other kibbutz members from that period corroborated this description. Measured against the criterion of the she'erit hapletah in Germany, a process of normalization took place in all spheres. Regardless of this, and in direct contradiction to this trend, idealized descriptions of life on the hachsharah continued to appear in *Nitzotz* and in other she'erit hapletah organs. A report, "At Kibbutz Buchenwald Geringshof," appeared in the 1946 issue of *Nitzotz:* "I spoke with a new arrival from Gauting. . . . He assured me that he has never felt so at ease as in the few days he has been at the Geringhof *hachsharah*. The chaverim do not work for the Germans; they know that they work for themselves—for us. The healthy impulse for renewal among the surviving remnant through work and self-realization led to the creation of the first nucleus immediately after liberation; the initial sign of the rise of a productive she'erit hapletah."[92]

The reference to the founding group and the exaggerated use of idealized terminology are but two indications that reality in the hachsharot had already begun to diverge widely from the ideal.

Concurrently, relations between Arthur Poznansky and the few Yekkim left on the farm, and the new chalutzim, worsened. Shimon Fleishon recalled how antagonism emerged between the German-born members, such as Poznansky, and the others. "They were concentration camp survivors and spoke German among themselves. We spoke Yiddish or German. We felt condescension on their part. Numerically, the Polish-born members outnumbered him; we no longer needed him. The group began to become successful workers, each in his own field."[93]

This is an example of a different kind of polarization—no longer veteran Zionists versus newcomers to the fold, as few of the new members of Kibbutz Buchenwald had previous Zionist training; no longer was the line of demarcation drawn between orthodox and freethinking, as both the ultraorthodox and religious Zionists had already found pioneering homes elsewhere. Now the chalutzim were back to square one—country of origin, a traditional bone of contention for Jews long before the war. It was a sad reminder of how quickly the utopian society could falter, fail, and disintegrate as the Jewish DPs in Germany progressed further and further away from the time of liberation, when dreams of unity had not seemed impossible.

THE LAST GROUPS OF KIBBUTZ BUCHENWALD IN EUROPE

Four additional groups of chalutzim left Geringshof and Gersfeld in the course of 1946–1947. In March 1946, a small group from Geringshof reached France. In June, it sailed to Haifa with the *Biriya*'s 999 immigrants. This contingent included several people who had been slated to sail on the *Tel Chai* but whose departure had been delayed due to ill health. Following their release from Atlit, only a few joined the hachsharah at Afikim. In early April, a second group left Gersfeld, this time for Italy. After a three-month stay in Milan and Bari, its members joined the *Catriel Yaffeh*'s 604 immigrants. The ship, which reached the shores of Palestine on August 13, was intercepted by the British, and its passengers were deported to Cyprus.[94]

The *Catriel Yaffeh* episode marked a watershed for Kibbutz Buchenwald. Up to that point, all illegal immigrants had been sent to Atlit, where they stayed for an interim period until they could be released under the current immigration quota. In July 1946, the British government decided to implement a long-standing plan—to deport all illegal immigrants caught trying to enter Palestine in response to the worsened relationship between the British and the underground organizations. From August 1946 onward, all illegal immigrants intercepted were deported to detention camps set up on Cyprus. Release from the Cyprus camps proceeded slowly, creating a bottleneck for the fifty-two thousand deportees detained there.[95]

The potential illegal immigrants from Geringshof-Gersfeld were aware that from that point on they would probably end up in Cyprus. A combined group of some forty chalutzim from both hachsharot left for Palestine via Italy in spring 1947. Following several weeks in Rome and Bari, the contingent reached Palestine on May 24, on the *Mordei Hagetaot*. Its passengers were immediately deported to Cyprus. Another group of some sixty olim, mainly from Geringshof, sailed on the *Aliyah* and reached Nahariyah on November 15, 1947, without being caught. Part of this contingent chose to join Kibbutz Tel Yosef.[96]

On Cyprus, Kibbutz Buchenwald continued to function as an autonomous unit, thanks to the camps' unique sociological structure, which was in Nachum Bogner's words, "a rare social phenomenon."[97] Over 90 percent of the deportees on Cyprus were politically identified with one of the wings of the Zionist movement. The Nocham movement held a high status among the survivors on Cyprus; consequently, Kibbutz Buchenwald's members were able to remain together and to benefit from movement support. In a letter to

Nocham leaders in the Yishuv, Eliezer Lapid described the Kibbutz Buchenwald members on Cyprus: "They are young and extremely pleasant. They
greeted the New Year sentimentally, exchanging kisses while wishing each
other a good New Year. On Yom Kippur they all went to pray, both young
and old; these are solitary individuals, the sole members of entire families, a
saved remnant. The need to pray to God beats in their hearts."[98]

There were also instances of individual chalutzim who reached Palestine
legally, by means of an entry permit. One such individual was Papa Juker,
who arrived in the Yishuv in fall 1947. Others chose to leave the kibbutz and
to relocate in various German cities in order to enhance their economic
standing in the meantime. Many of these individuals made aliyah immediately following the founding of the State.[99]

The final group at Geringshof was unique in both its composition and
behavior. Its members were Romanian Jews, almost totally lacking in Zionist
background, who reached Vienna and then Germany through the Brichah
network. The group belonged to a large contingent of nineteen thousand Jews
smuggled out of Romania by the Brichah network in 1947.[100] Their arrival
transformed the atmosphere on the hachsharah. According to Dolik Bergman,
a repatriate who left Geringshof in summer 1948, by later 1947, hardly any
emissaries from the Yishuv visited the farm, and no lectures were given.
Interest in Zionist affairs was virtually nonexistent. The few Polish Jews
remaining on the hachsharah regarded the Romanians as a bunch of provincials
whose behavioral standards set a new low in the hachsharah's history. One
example was an incident concerning the barber from the neighboring village.
One day the Romanians discovered that some wheat was missing. This continued to happen periodically. Suspicion fell on the barber, and they laid a trap for
him. Dolik Bergman recalled how the Romanians decided to lie in ambush for
him above the cowshed near the stable, where he used to leave his motorcycle.
"Then they saw him stealing food. They put him in a sack, gave a signal,
caught him, and beat him up. Then someone got cut by a knife and was
arrested. They called in the American military police and they came to take
him away. They returned two or three times to investigate everyone."[101]

Bergman was not alone in his negative evaluation of the group. In their
discussions of the Romanians, the leaders of the Brichah network expressed
the opinion that they comprised "a group with low moral standards . . . poor
human material for settlement in Palestine, if they get there at all."[102]

"Low moral standards" characterized the Romanian group at Geringshof
as well. According to Bergman, one of the last to leave the hachsharah, the
Romanians tried to persuade him to sign on a deed as the "owner" of the farm
so they could sell the hachsharah to some Germans. Bergman thwarted this
plot, and brought it to the attention of the pair of emissaries from Giv'at
Brenner who were in charge of the hachsharah. In late summer 1948, the

episode of Kibbutz Buchenwald in the Diaspora came to a close. Dolik Bergman and his comrades traveled to Munich and reached Palestine several months later. The Romanians also went on their way, some to Palestine and some to other countries. Arthur Poznansky assembled goods belonging to the kibbutz and shipped them to Kibbutz Buchenwald in Palestine.

In early 1949, the hachsharot at Geringshof and Gersfeld reverted to the administration of Southern Hessen. In 1950, they were converted into a rest home for workers. From 1950 to 1956 they also served as an agricultural school for local students. In 1956, the former hachsharah at Geringshof became a residential center for Czechoslovakian refugees. From 1960 until the present, it has functioned as a home for the aged.[103]

In his study of the she'erit hapletah in the American zone in Germany, historian Ze'ev Mankowitz cites a unique feature of this population: its highly developed collective consciousness. This awareness was grounded in two elements: its experience of the Holocaust and the desire to realize Zionist aims. In Mankowitz's words, "She'erit hapletah perceived itself simultaneously as the final remnant of a world that had been destroyed and as the active nucleus that would contribute to future rehabilitation, as a living bridge from the Holocaust to the task of revival."[104]

Kibbutz Buchenwald in the Diaspora played a central role as a bridge between destruction and rebirth, but like its components, upon its transfer to the Yishuv, Kibbutz Buchenwald lost its organizational structure, its political uniqueness, and its leadership ability. Upon arrival, the immigrants in the second, third, and fourth aliyot scattered among the towns and the various kibbutz movements. Leaders and members alike became workers, petit bourgeoisie, or anonymous chalutzim learning Zionist tasks in the field or shops of host kibbutzim. The latter held fast to a single hope—that some day they would be able to found their own kibbutz, where they could implement the ideals they had imported from the Diaspora. Perhaps then, when the first kibbutz founded by the she'erit hapletah came into existence, the visionary spirit that had disappeared on the way from Geringshof to Afikim could be revived.

CHAPTER SIX

The Road to Independence

"On our own two feet."

By SPRING 1947, the members of Kibbutz Buchenwald at Afikim had concluded that the time was ripe to advance to the next stage. After eighteen
months of hachsharah, they felt physically and emotionally ready to operate
their own autonomous farm community. Already consolidated socially, the
group decided that it would no longer accept new arrivals from Geringshof or
Gersfeld automatically, but would require them to go before an admissions
committee. Actually this was a formal decision only, as almost no reinforcements from the European hachsharot were arriving in Palestine at that point.
The remaining groups had been deported to Cyprus, where they awaited
permission to enter Palestine.[1]

Kibbutz Buchenwald's members now sought to establish an independent
farm community. Generally, prior to occupying permanent sites, many
hachsharot spent time in a temporary *moshavah* (cooperative settlement, less
communal than a kibbutz), for continued training, but as autonomous units.
The Buchenwalders, however, intended to skip the moshavah stage and to
proceed directly to a permanent settlement. Two factors underlay this plan.
First, by expediting the path to autonomy, the Buchenwalders hoped to make
up for the lost war years. Second, they wished to ensure the group's unity,
since as a rule only part of the hachsharah was transferred to the moshavah at
any one time. Concern for group integrity dominated all discussions between
Kibbutz Buchenwald representatives and the Afikim secretariat regarding the
colony issue. "If we leave, then everyone [goes], and if we stay, this means
our entire group," they declared.[2] An additional problem was the need for
equipment. The Buchenwalders proposed that a member be delegated to
travel to Germany in order to ship supplies from the hachsharot there to
Palestine. The Afikim secretariat promised to consider this request.

In late June, the request for a settlement site was forwarded to the agricultural center, and the possibility of granting the group a site in the Galilee was
immediately raised, but, as the Jewish Agency's financial state did not then

permit practical implementation of this matter, its consideration was postponed until the summer's end. Thus, six weeks intervened between the time the proposal was raised and its discussion, six weeks during which the Buchenwalders—now numbering over seventy members—speculated about their future. The kibbutz diary reflects how the Buchenwalders reacted to this moratorium:

> We knew that summer 1947 was our last at Afikim. This knowledge was subsumed in the general feeling that we were too "ripe" to continue as a body within a body, in the decision to move on to a fully autonomous state. We intended to skip the "independence in a colony" stage and to settle immediately on our own land, which was hazily visible somewhere in the Upper Galilee. But objective factors forced us to proceed step by step without shortcuts.[3]

Throughout the summer's heat, the chaverim waited, making preparations for the future and completing their training in such essential tasks as operating a tractor and running a children's house (Kibbutz building where all children lived). In late July, the die was cast. The agricultural center announced that the Galilee site was available, but that only thirty chalutzim could settle there. Now the group faced a dilemma: Should it split and settle the Galilee site, or reject the proposal and leave for autonomy in a moshavah? Or perhaps the veterans should settle in the Galilee, leaving the new arrivals to complete their year of hachsharah at Afikim? After a stormy debate, the group decided to maintain its integrity and to move to a moshavah. The next problem the group faced was: In which moshava should it settle? The proposed sites included Petach Tikvah, Kfar Saba, and Rishon Lezion. Following initial inquiries, the group opted for the third choice, Rishon Lezion, where it had been promised work in factories, construction, road-building, electricity, the orchards, and the bakery. The kibbutz's advance party— fifteen men and five women—was carefully selected. The potential candidates' names were announced, and individually approved by the secretariat following public debate. The remaining members were to follow within two months' time.

The decision to strike out independently was an important milestone in the history of Kibbutz Buchenwald. This was the true test of adulthood for this group, which had been the first representative of the She'erit hapletah with whom many local kibbutz movement members had contact. This was the litmus test for the continued existence of an ideological trailblazer, the vanguard of the European Nocham movement, which had brought the tidings of unity to the Yishuv. Unlike other cases of hachsharot that had finished a training period and prepared to found their own settlement, Kibbutz Buchenwald faced a double, if not triple dilemma. The first was an issue facing all hachsharot at that time: the need to succeed in forming and developing an independent settlement, in view of the uncertain security and economic status of the Yishuv prior to the establishment of the State. The second dilemma was one particular to the she'erit hapletah: how to convince the kibbutz movement that survivors could establish an independent kibbutz without needing the guiding hand and stabilizing influence of a local *gar'in* (nucleus group). Finally, the third issue was one inherent solely to Kibbutz Buchenwald: how to maintain their unique principles of unity in the face of tacit party disapproval and pressure.

On Sunday, September 7, an initial group of sixteen members from the Kibbutz Buchenwald nucleus left Afikim for "autonomy" in Rishon Lezion. They were warmly received both by the neighboring kibbutz, Revivim, and by the secretary of the Rishon workers' council, Comrade Goldman. The group described its first day in the diary begun in its new residence:

> We are in Beit Bernstein, which is well organized with all the amenities. We reached Rishon Lezion at twelve noon in a good mood, and immediately fell asleep on the floor from exhaustion. At 2:30 we were awakened by the noise and shouts of the chaverim who had arrived by car with our belongings. We got up and enthusiastically but quietly unloaded the beds, closets, trunks, various parcels, and, most important—the tents and the refrigerator. The girls were especially glad about the refrigerator—it is new, large, and impressive. We immediately began to get organized; we cleaned, put things away, got the kitchen organized. At seven in the evening, we bathed, shaved, and set up the radio. The girls decorated the porch table with a white tablecloth and flowers. The new teapots, spoons, and forks sparkled on the tables.[4]

The festive meal was delayed for hours, until the return of two chaverim who had gone to town to look for work. They brought with them discouraging tidings: There were jobs, but not enough for everyone. It quickly became apparent that the promises the group had received before leaving Afikim were empty ones. In a humorous but ironic tone, Avraham (who had already changed his family name from Gottlieb to Ahuvia) described the job-hunting process. The account opened with a dialogue between the secretary of the Rishon workers' council and a delegation of Buchenwalders:

> COUNCIL SECRETARY: The main thing is, do you have skilled workers?
> DELEGATION MEMBER (LAUGHINGLY): That's a trifling matter! Each and every member of our society is an expert in his field.
> That's good, that's wonderful—says the council secretary—what skills did you acquire during your hachsharah? Do you have drivers?
> —Drivers? That's nonsense! I have! We have nine drivers!
> He continued to ask: Do you have metalworkers?

—Metalworkers? answers the chaver with a scoffing laugh. We excel at that.
—Do you have carpenters?
—We're a little weak in that. We have only four carpenters.

The meeting continued in this fashion.

Someone to run the kitchen? Someone to supervise work in the orchards?
—We have these and more.

The council secretary made a note and asked: How many are you? Eighty. Eighty chaverim and 122 skilled workers. Hmmm . . . but pardon me. Yes, we will help you job hunt. I'll pay you a short visit in a few days.

When the delegation returned, they gleefully reported: Gang, there is work for 122 people, and we are only eighty chaverim.

One evening the Rishonites paid a visit. It just so happened that all the drivers were out and had not yet returned home. Most of the metalworkers were on vacation. Three carpenters had taken on outside jobs, and the fourth had been injured. With great effort, the Rishonites managed to get hold of Drora, who was in charge of the kitchen, and Yisrael, the construction worker. The conversations were brief.

CONVERSATION NO. 1: Are you Drora? Nice to meet you. Well, you'll have to supervise the cooking in a Histadrut [workers'] Day Care Center. Washing up and cleaning will be done by others.
—But that's just what I know, says Drora—I don't know a thing about cooking.
—Hmm . . . Excuse us. . . .

CONVERSATION NO. 2:
—You're a construction worker, Yisrael? What do you know about building?
—I can carry cement on a high roof. Did you see the new depot roof? I know how to mix cement with sand and help the climber climb.
—Hmm . . . Excuse us. . . . In the meantime the group became noisy. What was to be? What a mess. . . . We were down in the dumps until Siniya came and rid us of our depression with one speech. He told us what independence meant, what Rishon Lezion was like. He repeatedly stressed: It's hard to be autonomous; we shouldn't delude ourselves on that score. He told us how difficult it was to stand in the corridors of different institutions and to be a *nudnik* [Yiddish term for pest] (otherwise, nothing is accomplished). And how hard it is to be a nudnik every evening in the colony's employment office, but once again, it's impossible to find work otherwise. "Yes, friends, the most important thing is to be a nudnik. And from what I've seen of this delegation's members, I rest easy on that score," Siniya concluded his talk.

And we rejoiced. We have many many skilled workers.[5]

This humorous little piece provides but a partial reflection of the reality. Although there were skilled workers among the chalutzim, no jobs were available in Rishon. During their first days in the colony, only four members found work: in roadbuilding, in construction, in sanitation, and in fertilization of orchards. The employment picture improved gradually, but for a lengthy period, many had to seek jobs outside the colony.

Rosh Hashanah fell about a week after the transfer to Rishon. The chaverim declared a day off, switched off guard duty every two hours, freed the women from kitchen duty, danced, sang, ate, and longed for their comrades at Afikim. Yom Kippur was the same. A few members fasted and attended services locally. Others attended meetings, but all missed friends and family at Afikim.

Now the countdown to reunification of the nucleus began. By the fall holidays, Beit Bernstein had already acquired a homey atmosphere, and there was talk of transferring the entire group to the moshavah. Some individuals at Afikim became impatient and made their way to Rishon, without waiting for the official move. The nucleus in Rishon was expanding, and it looked like the long-awaited day of unification was near, but in mid-November these plans went awry. The fall rains turned the yard into mud, and flooded the tents. Beit Bernstein was becoming overcrowded, and the Jewish Agency had not yet built the promised camp for the chalutzim. Consequently, in early December, a decision was made to move the group to an existing camp in Nachalat Yehudah, near Rishon Lezion, previously occupied by Emunim members, a Hapo'el Hamizrachi kibbutz that had left to settle Ein Hanatziv in the Beit She'an Valley.

The transfer from Afikim to Nachalat Yehudah was completed on Tuesday, December 23. As tension ran high in this pre–War of Independence period, the women and children were transported in an armored ambulance. Upon completion of the transfer, the group numbered some seventy members, including six babies born at Afikim. Now the entire group faced the job shortage problem. Left with no other alternative, the chaverim opted to open independent ventures, including a tailor shop and a metalworking shop. Others cultivated the vegetable garden, and built coops for the three hundred chickens that had been a gift from Kibbutz Afikim. An American benefactor, Sam Rothberg, gave the group its first tractor-bulldozer, a significantly lucrative tool. A truck purchased was from the British Army.[6]

Unemployment was not the sole obstacle facing the chaverim. Three additional tasks were on the agenda: organizational, social, and cultural consolidation, for which three committees—administrative, social, and cultural—were formed. The committee members quickly discovered that social integration was proceeding no more smoothly at Nachalat Yehudah than it had at Afikim. Its shared sense of commitment and vision notwithstanding, organizationally the group did not act in concert. The cultural sphere presented a brighter picture. Hebrew classes were renewed and parties were held—Oneg Shabbat parties on Friday nights, a Chanukkah celebration, a housewarming, and a party to mark the declaration of the State. The camp began to acquire an air of permanence.

The War of Independence broke out while the chalutzim were at Nachalat Yehudah, but claimed only one victim from the group. The kibbutz treasurer, Yehuda Luxembourg, lost his life in the Egyptian bombing of the Tel Aviv Central Bus Station in May 1948. Early in the war, a number of chaverim were drafted into the army and were sent, along with members of the neighboring hachsharah, Zikim, to a joint task—guarding the nearby Schiffon farm from the Jordanian Legion, which had halted some three kilometers away. Established in 1889 by Theodore Shneller, the founder of the Syrian orphanage in Jerusalem, the farm had housed an agricultural school under the direction of Baron Von Schiffon. The site's Arabic appellation, Bir Salim, reflects the name then assigned to the farm's well—the "well of peace and salvation." During World War I, the farm was a center of activity in its capacity as General Allenby's headquarters, but political upheavals notwithstanding, non-Jewish German settlers remained at the site until World War II. When the war broke out, first the adult men, and later the women, children, and the elderly, were moved. In 1942, they were deported to Australia, with the option to return to Germany at the war's end.

Members of Kibbutz Buchenwald arrived at the Schiffon farm to serve as its defenders during the War of Independence. In addition, the Buchenwalders began to work the abandoned farm. This in turn gave birth to the resolve to found their kibbutz at this site. The group forwarded a request to the settlement agencies to receive the farm, in their words, as a "permanent possession." This request was acceded to following the location of an alternative holding for the Zikim nucleus along the southern coast of the new state. In accord with the then standard practice, the group was advised to occupy the farm first as soldiers, and later as settlers. Three days before the move, the members underwent military training to prepare them to guard their lives and the property for which they were responsible. On June 20, 1948, an initial group of sixteen Kibbutz Buchenwald members, armed with Czech rifles, moved to the Schiffon farm. This event was noted by the Voice of Israel in its evening radio broadcast, and some of the kibbutz's unique history was recounted. The report closed with the information that the kibbutz numbered some one hundred members, and would be absorbing additional members from its European hachsharot presently detained on Cyprus.[7]

The chaverim found at the Schiffon farm more than a square mile of land, composed of orchards, eucalyptus groves, and irrigated fields. They also possessed eleven heads of cattle and two wells—Bir Salim and a well near Nes Zionah. In addition there were cisterns and irrigation ditches.[8] This preexisting agricultural substructure, which seemed advantageous at first, would later become a disadvantage, as it compelled the kibbutz to adjust to a given situation not necessarily compatible with the concepts or needs of modern kibbutz farming, but at that moment, the chaverim imagined that they had acquired a gold mine. They brought their tractor to the farm and work animals as well. A metalworking shop was opened, along with a factory to produce iron bars. The chaverim began to adjust to life on the farm. They expanded the chicken run and named the cows; Ditzah, Rinah, Chedvah, Gilah (synonyms for joy), Shalvah (tranquillity), Yaffah (pretty), Adumah (red), and Chamudah (sweetheart). The initial settlers retained their military standing for three months, but following the conquest of the Arab enclaves of Ramla and Lod, they were joined by the women and children. A new stage began—Kibbutz Buchenwald at its permanent site.⁹

During 1948, the nucleus settled down in its new home. The diary became a kibbutz newsletter, and the debates that had previously been noted on activity lists were now recorded separately as the protocols of secretariat or other committee meetings. The kibbutz's male members continued to develop the ventures they had started earlier, and the female members were sent to learn how to wrap citrus fruit. Avraham Ahuvia, who due to injury to his hand at Afikim had been sent to a teachers' seminary, began to teach regularly scheduled Bible classes. Aharon Batzia was given a two-month leave to work at the Mapai center. Members who had been detained on Cyprus were trickling into Palestine, and several joined the kibbutz.

The time had come to formalize the kibbutz's relationship with the kibbutz movement. On April 10, 1949, Kibbutz Buchenwald formally applied to the Kibbutz Hameuchad secretariat for membership. Interestingly, the application sheds light on the members' continued adherence to the Nocham ideal of pluralism despite their recognition that Yishuv reality dictated conformity to the party line.

We join the Kibbutz Hameuchad framework firm in the knowledge that this step strengthens the kibbutz movement. We identify in the main with this movement's path as it has developed in the course of its existence: we will work to direct the masses to kibbutz life. We will do our utmost to develop all branches of our collective farm, and to foster our social values. Thus will we build a home for ourselves as well as for those who as yet are homeless. We shall strive to shape and stabilize the chalutz way within our ranks and lend a hand to making it the possession of the masses. We will join in the struggle to better mankind, and fight alongside the entire proletariat to secure the victory of socialism in our land and the world.

We are convinced that the values shared by all members of Hakibbutz Hameuchad will unify and strengthen our kibbutz. We are convinced that the differences between the various branches of the kibbutz settlement movements have been largely blurred, and the time is ripe to unite the entire movement.

Hakibbutz Hameuchad should lead the way by demonstrating its desire to move in this direction.

We believe, that with our entry to the kibbutz, we will make a contribution to the above-mentioned guiding principles.[10]

Less than a month later, at a metting held at Kibbutz Dafnah on May 7, 1949, the Kibbutz Hameuchad Council accepted thirteen settlement bodies to its movement's ranks. Together, these bodies numbered 1,260 members. Representatives of the thirteen settlements appeared before the Council and unfolded the individual stories of the paths traversed from nucleus to kibbutz. In more than one instance, the Holocaust appeared as a significant crossroads in this journey. Naturally, this was the case for Kibbutz Buchenwald.[11]

A final matter remained to be settled before Kibbutz Buchenwald could be considered a "real" kibbutz: A new name had to be chosen. Despite their nostalgic attachment to the name that had accompanied them from the kibbutz's inception, its members were aware that the Yishuv found this name unacceptable. The foreign word "Buchenwald" set the Israeli ear on edge; moreover, the name of a concentration camp hardly seemed appropriate for an Israeli kibbutz. The search was on for a Hebrew name that would reflect the kibbutz's uniqueness as an autonomous venture by the she'erit hapletah, and at the same time secure approval by the Names Committee. Initially, three names were proposed: Alonei Yachel (Oaks of Hope), Miflat (Shelter), and Gerofit (Shoot), to which Pedut (Redemption), Pelet (Refuge), and Chosen (Strength) were added. Another suggested name was Segev, an acronym for Seridei Golat Buchenwald (The Buchenwald Remnant). None of these proposals evoked an enthusiastic response, and the search continued. Finally, Mordechai Dekel, an Afikim member, suggested Netzarim (Shoots). Subsequently, he proposed the shorter name Netzer. At its general meeting on June 11, 1949, the National Fund's Names Committee approved the latter name. This official stamp of approval notwithstanding, the kibbutz retained its former name, and in the early fifties, it was referred to both by its members, and in official movement documents, as Netzer-Buchenwald.[12]

From that point on, Kibbutz Netzer's development did not differ substantially from the path normally followed by new collective farms in the early State era. The kibbutz newsletter reflects the members' current concerns in those years. In June 1949, the newsletter reported the interaction with the neighboring *ma'abarah* (transit settlement for new immigrants) following the theft of six crates of cucumbers from the kibbutz's fields. One thief was apprehended, and two crates were recovered. In July of that year, the members implemented an Environmental Improvement Committee resolution and placed garbage cans in the corners of the yard. In September, the kibbutz faced physical danger: A fire in the eucalyptus grove had threatened the settlement with severe damage. The item noted that mobilization to fight the fire proceeded swiftly and was crowned with success. In February 1950, an era of "luxury" (by contemporary standards) began when a hot shower was built for general use. In June, the kibbutz took steps to establish its long-term presence: A cornerstone was laid, as were foundations for the first three permanent structures on the settlement. August saw the first evidence of "materialism"—each kibbutz member was presented with a clock, and it was agreed that teapots and cups would be purchased for everyone. At long last, in January 1951, two and a half years after they had first moved to the Schiffon farm, the members occupied the just-completed permanent housing, which consisted of three large buildings and a new baby nursery.[13]

Examination of the kibbutz newsletter does indicate one area where Kibbutz Netzer diverged significantly from the usual kibbutz pattern—the family. Sociologically speaking, the family unit is perceived as having been a central building block of kibbutz society, but the family-building process generally proceeded in stages. The early years of a new kibbutz were devoted to realizing the ideal, building the kibbutz's economy, and, at most, to the creation of couples. Only in the second stage were families formed, with childbirth becoming a factor in the kibbutz's growth, in addition to the recruiting of new adult members.[14] At Netzer, a different pattern emerged. The first newsletters contained items about kibbutz children and babies; childbirth had begun as early as the group's first year at Afikim. Why did Netzer's members seemingly skip the initial stage, or at least shorten it radically? The explanation lies in the composition of the kibbutz's population, in the fact that an overwhelming majority were Holocaust survivors. We have already noted that as a group, the she'erit hapletah was characterized by high birthrate in the postwar years, a sign of its normalization. This was certainly true of Netzer's members. Moreover, Netzer's population was somewhat older than that of most hachsharot in the Yishuv. Its distinctive reproductive pattern is but one factor indicating Netzer's unique status as an autonomous she'erit hapletah venture in Israel.

In 1951, the chaverim were already in permanent housing, and the kibbutz's economic ventures had begun to take shape, but did Netzer's members feel that they had reached "their allotted haven"? The answer is an unequivocal no. The attempts to stabilize the kibbutz were accompanied by economic and social distress. Its members were in despair. In mid- to late July 1951, a committee was formed to examine the existing situation and to make proposals for change. This committee dealt mainly with the problem's organizational and social aspects; a separate committee was assigned the task of examining its economic implications. In mid-September, the committee published its findings as culled from a poll taken among the kibbutz's members: twenty-five, a quarter of the total membership, were disillusioned with the kibbutz framework and favored disbanding it for a *moshav shitufi* (cooperative settlement of small, individually owned farms); sixty-nine chaverim wished to retain the kibbutz framework but suggested changes in personal allocations, sleeping arrangements for children, reduction of work hours for female members, and the function of the dining hall. Now the kibbutz members split into two groups—kibbutz enthusiasts versus those who desired a moshav system. At first glance, it appeared that Kibbutz Netzer, which had experienced so many vicissitudes in its brief history, would finish its fourth year by splitting in two, but at this crucial juncture, the kibbutz movement intervened in order to restore order to the kibbutz. It decided to devote intense discussion to the issues raised by the members in the poll.[15]

The year 1951 was also decisive for the Kibbutz Hameuchad movement itself, it was a year that saw the culmination of an ideological struggle that had begun almost a decade earlier. In a nutshell, the issue at stake was jurisdictional. Did Hakibbutz Hameuchad possess autonomous authority, or was it obligated to bow to party dictates, or alternatively, to the Labor Federation? This issue, rooted in the thirties, had deepened when Mapai split in 1944. Four years later, in 1948, the dissenting faction (the Achdut Ha'avodah movement) united with Hashomer Hatza'ir to form the left-wing Mapam (United Workers') Party. As a result, the members of Hakibbutz Hameuchad were now forced to choose between the option of remaining in the labor-oriented Mapai or of joining the newly created left-wing party. In some kibbutzim, unanimity reigned; in others, both parties were represented, leading to constant friction and open clashes. It was clear that this situation could not be allowed to continue. Kibbutzim which divided membership would either have to split into two, or exchange population, with other kibbutzim in a similar position.

The consequences were clear. During the first half of 1951, Hakibbutz Hameuchad split, and decided to expel Mapai members from its ranks. In July 1951, the kibbutzim that had withdrawn from Hakibbutz Hameuchad founded a kibbutz movement along their own ideological lines—Ichud Hakevutzot VehaKibbutzim (Union of Collective Settlements). Kibbutz Netzer joined the dissidents.[16]

The split in Hakibbutz Hameuchad sent severe shock waves through broad sectors of Israeli society. Most affected, naturally, were the members of kibbutzim that split, who were now forced to leave settlements they themselves had founded and built. Such was the case at Giv'at Brenner, which chose to remain within the Hakibbutz Hameuchad movement, and asked members who remained loyal to Mapai to leave the kibbutz. As noted, concurrently, at Kibbutz Netzer, an economic and social crisis dictated the introduction of new blood in order to prevent the breakup of the kibbutz. Following the split in Hakibbutz Hameuchad, Ichud Hakevutzot Vehakibbutzim proposed that

Netzer absorb the dissenting group from Giv'at Brenner. The decision to unite was not easily made. On one hand, Netzer's members saw the potential chaverim as a real chance to lift the kibbutz out of stagnation, or worse. On the other, the Giv'at Brennerites were strangers. They were without any Nocham background; nor did they belong to the she'erit hapletah. As such, they could prove to be a foreign body in the future. There was also an age gap to consider; The Giv'at Brennerites were mainly between forty and fifty, while Netzer's members were younger. Finally, the two groups differed in training and experience. The Giv'at Brennerites were old hands at running a kibbutz, while the Netzer members had taken their initial steps toward autonomy barely three years earlier.

Deliberations regarding unification continued into the autumn of 1951. Not until October of that year was a decision finally reached to accept the Giv'at Brennerites. The merger process was accompanied by intense consultations that lasted nearly a year. As at many other kibbutzim during that period, the initial merger proceeded fairly rapidly, but full integration of the new members into the fabric of kibbutz life was a process that lasted for months, and even years.

A unique episode—with broader social, psychological, and political implications—emerged on the fringes of the merger, sparked by the attempt to change the kibbutz's name. Following unification, the Giv'at Brennerites expressed the desire to have the new reality reflected in the name of the kibbutz that they had joined. Their proposal was to perpetuate the memory of Enzo (Chaim) Sereni, an early Hakibbutz Hameuchad leader and a founder of Giv'at Brenner, who had died parachuting into Europe in 1944. For their part, the Netzerites found this proposal acceptable. They saw Sereni as a Holocaust victim, and in their opinion, the proposed name further emphasized the kibbutz's uniqueness. In 1954, the members tendered a request to the National Names Committee to change the kibbutz's name from Netzer to Netzer Sereni. The request was rejected on the grounds that foreign names were unacceptable for any settlement in Israel. In its response, the committee suggested the name Netzer Chaim, for Sereni's Hebrew name. Three letters to this effect were dispatched to the kibbutz, which refused to reply, giving rise to the suspicion that its members intended to defy the committee and to announce their chosen name anyway. The battle lines were clearly drawn. Netzer's chaverim assertively demanded that their kibbutz be called Sereni in order to avoid confusion, as Chaim was a common name. For its part, the National Names Committee saw Kibbutz Netzer's behavior as an attempt to detract from its absolute authority and to undermine the principle forbidding the use of non-Hebrew names for settlements in Israel.

Naturally, the debate surrounding the kibbutz's name did not take place in a vacuum. Its significance must be assessed in light of the contemporary political-psychological context. At that time, Israeli society was marking the decade anniversary of the parachutists' mission in which seven volunteers lost their lives: Sereni, Chavivah Reik, Hannah Szenesz, Abba Berdiczev, Peretz Goldstein, Rafi Reiss, and Zvi Ben-Ya'akov. As part of the decennial events, a public committee was formed to memorialize Sereni, headed by Prime Minister Moshe Sharett, with the participation of Sereni's friends, cabinet ministers, and members of the Labor Federation Executive, Ichud Hakibbutzim, the Jewish Agency Executive, and the Knesset. As part of the campaign, Kibbutz Netzer's members proposed that the philatelic service issue a first-day cover with a special postmark to commemorate Sereni. Plans were also made to hold a special convocation at the kibbutz. The highlight of the program was to be the renaming of the kibbutz as Netzer Sereni.[17]

In this strong desire to commemorate Sereni, clearly more was at stake than simply the desire to recognize the Giv'at Brenner presence within the Netzer context. It was primarily a desperate political attempt by the Mapai party, which felt that it had been deprived of its heroes in the wake of the Kastner trial of the 1950s, to regain legitimacy in the public eye. Yisrael Kastner, who had been a Mapai activist in Hungary during the Holocaust, was accused publicly in 1952 of collaborating with the Nazis in order to save his family and associates at the expense of the rest of Hungarian Jewry. In response, the Israeli government instituted a libel suit against his accuser, which soon became the major political trial of the decade. Shortly after the trial began, the de jure libel suit became a de facto trial of the Mapai apparatus's wartime behavior in general, and that of Yisrael Kastner in particular. They were accused of appeasing the enemy (the Nazis, or in Mapai's case, also the British) for personal or political gain. Consequently, the trial served as a Pandora's box of ammunition for Mapai's rivals on both the right and the left, supplying them with claims against the party that had held almost absolute hegemony over the Yishuv's political system for over three decades.

By renaming Kibbutz Netzer after a Mapai hero, the party was attempting to adopt a Holocaust figure equal in stature to Mordechai Anielewicz, Hannah Szenesz, and others, who had been co-opted by the rival leftist party Mapam. Although Sereni himself had no opportunity to declare his stand officially on the Kibbutz Hameuchad split before his departure for Europe in 1944, his pro-Mapai sentiments on this matter were known, and consequently, Mapai claimed him as one of its own. Thus, the idea was born to give a Mapai-identified kibbutz a name to counterbalance Yad Mordechai, Lehavot Chavivah, or even Yad Hannah (Szenesz). This was also a way to counteract accusations leveled against Mapai leaders for their "traitorous" behavior during the Holocaust. The entire episode reveals the extent to which the concept of heroism dominated the Israeli political scene in the fifties, a factor influencing both the self-image of Netzer's members and the means by which they projected themselves to the Israeli public.

In whose hands should the final decision regarding Kibbutz Netzer's new name be vested? This question, which started as a dialogue between Netzer and the Names Committee, quickly became a matter of public interest. When negotiations reached an impasse, the debate moved to the public political arena. In late 1954, the issue reached the Knesset in the form of the proposed Netzer Sereni Law. Led by Chaim Ben-Asher, a Mapai member from the Giv'at Brenner contingent at Netzer, the proponents of the law had the backing of thirty-three Knesset members from all factions. Thus the matter developed into a complicated and charged public issue, which indirectly touched upon one of Israeli society's sacred cows—its attitude toward the Holocaust and heroism.[18] The press commented on the issue as well. In his poem "Seventh Column," Nathan Alterman addressed the problem with his characteristic irony:

> How shall we respond to the Names Committee decision?
> We will say Netzer Chaim is a lovely, natural name
> It wholly fulfills two essential requirements
> Its content is true
> Its sound is Hebrew.
> A lovely clear name, it is well justified
> Symbolism and reality within are united
> have disappeared from it, been hidden.
> From the map of Israel it will silently peer out
> To thousands of passersby it will actively recall
> Everything necessary but the memory of the man
> Whose name it is intended to inculcate and remember. . . .[19]

The Netzer Sereni Law came up for its first reading in early January 1955. In the plenum, Chaim Ben-Asher reviewed the circumstances that had instigated the law's proposal. In referring to the rationale offered by the Names Committee, Ben-Asher delicately suggested that at times special considerations could allow divergence from the accepted rules: "The Names Committee has rich experience and primary authority in this matter. But as we have suggested in our proposal, the problem of giving or changing a name is not always exhausted by checking its musical sound or its antiquity. Sometimes the special needs of a generation, which deviate from the path of these principles, must be considered."[20]

During the session, speakers from Mapai, Mapam, Herut, the Progressives, the Sephardim (Eastern Jews, of Spanish and Portuguese origin), and Hapo'el Hamizrachi addressed the arguments tendered against the name Sereni. Time and again it was noted that the name had a Hebrew ring, and ancient Hebrew roots as well. In addition, it was argued that the name Netzer Chaim was too vague, leaving room for doubt as to which Chaim was meant. Moreover, during his lifetime, neither Sereni nor his friends had used his Hebrew name. Other speakers indicated that in the struggle over the name, practically speaking, the kibbutz held the upper hand. In illustration of this point, examples of other settlements that had refused to accept the Names Committee decision were cited. These settlements, mainly founded by the right-wing Irgun Tzva'i Leumi, continued to use their chosen names until the establishment knuckled under. Finally, the claim was made that due to the appeal of the name Sereni to youthful immigrants from the Diaspora, its adoption would serve a national purpose. The essence of the debate—whether to transfer the right to determine names of settlements to the Knesset's Internal Affairs Committee—was occasionally forgotten in the heat of the moment, but none of the speakers deluded themselves that the question at stake was restricted to the Hebrew-cultural nature of the State, or to the mere question of a name. It was eminently clear that this was a political move by Mapai to elevate its chosen hero to the pantheon of Israeli heroes, to combat accusations leveled against its leadership of indifference, cowardice, or collaboration during the Holocaust.[21]

The debate closed with a decision to send the proposed law to the Knesset's Internal Affairs Committee for a final ruling. Many Knesset members feared that the proposed law would set a precedent for the transfer of jurisdiction from one national body to another. In light of this potential danger, the Names Committee found it expedient to accede to Netzer's request, thereby removing the law from the calendar. The episode ended in a compromise: The Names Committee would approve the proposed change to Netzer Sereni, but would retain its jurisdiction. Following the debate in the Internal Affairs Committee, the following announcement was published in *Divrei Haknesset* (The Knesset record):

> The Names Committee is convinced of the merit of its principle to assign Hebrew names only, and not to allow foreign place names in Israel. It will continue to guard vigilantly the place of Hebrew on the map of Israel. But upon consideration of the Knesset's opinion, and its request, its view that Chaim Enzo Sereni's martyrdom was exceptional, and in consideration of the fact that the name is not far from Hebrew-sounding, the Names Committee grants its approval to Netzer-Buchenwald's request to change its name to Netzer-Sereni.
>
> The Internal Affairs Committee is satisfied that this decision by the Names Committee fulfills the strong desire to memorialize on Israeli soil the envoy-parachutist Chaim Enzo Sereni, who sacrificed his life for the honor of Israel and humankind during World War II, and ended his life in the Dachau crematorium.

The Internal Affairs Committee therefore recommends that no further debate be devoted to the abovementioned law. It is satisfied with the publication of this announcement in *Divrei Haknesset*.[22]

Thus the name-changing chapter came to an end, closing a circle opened a decade earlier, in the summer of 1945. At that time, a Jewish Brigade member who visited Kibbutz Buchenwald in Germany expressed his overwhelming enthusiasm for this venture. At the conclusion of his visit, the Kibbutz decided to allow him to be the first "outsider" to make an entry in the kibbutz diary. On the eleventh day of the month of Av (July 21), 1945, the soldier wrote: "Our visit to the first kibbutz founded on the defiled soil of Germany will be preserved in our hearts on our way to the Yishuv and in it. *Lehitra'ot* ("*Au revoir*") within the venture shared by Israeli fighters and freed prisoners of death, which will enlarge the borders of our land, improve our productivity, and provide future seed."[23] That soldier certainly did not envision that a few years later he would find himself a member of that very same kibbutz founded by survivors in the Diaspora, nor that he would lead the struggle to change the kibbutz's name. The entry was signed "A Brigade member from Giv'at Brenner, Chaim Ben-Asher."

Ben-Asher's comments are part of an intrinsic element of Kibbutz Buchenwald from its founding—the kibbutz diary. The very concept of keeping a diary indicates the presence of kibbutz members with a highly developed historical consciousness. Their intent—that the diary reflect both their lives and the general atmosphere as it related to kibbutz events—found expression in the earliest entries. Open to all members alike, by its very nature the diary reflected the members' desire for intellectual openness and pluralistic thought. Moreover, frequent relocations notwithstanding—Eggendorf, Geringshof, Afikim, Rishon Lezion, Nachalat Yehudah, and the Schiffon farm—the diary continued to be kept. Kibbutz Buchenwald's members felt impelled to create a continuous documentary record of their kibbutz's unique experiences.

The official kibbutz diary, in its various permutations, is a historical and literary treasure trove. its contributors adhered to no set pattern, and entries in different languages and literary genres appeared in conjunction. (From mid-1946 on, the diary was kept in Hebrew only). The diary contains straightforward reports, letters to friends in the Diaspora, short prose pieces, poems, plays, and censorious comments, alongside a factual chronicle of the kibbutz's history and development. At first glance, the reader assumes that the diary includes all possible genres suitable for this type of record, but closer analysis reveals that an essential contextual, rather than textual, feature is missing. Throughout the diary's hundreds of pages, there are scarcely any explicit references to either the historical context or the major events against which Kibbutz Buchenwald's saga unfolded. The DP problem in occupied

Germany, American army policy, Aliyah Bet, political upheaval in the Yishuv, the Anglo-American Commission, deportations to Cyprus, underground activity in the Yishuv, the 1947 U.N. vote on partition, even the founding of the State of Israel received but passing mention in the kibbutz diary. While oblique references to the general setting did appear, there were only three explicit references to the broader contemporary historical context. The first appeared in a letter to members on Cyprus. The split in Nocham was its topic:

> Here in the Yishuv we have become aware of the split's true dimensions, especially now, just before elections for the [Zionist] Congress. At a time when the Jewish nation in general, and the workers' movement with its special national obligation in particular, should be united in light of the difficult situation, each party runs separately. As a result, the Jewish nation's strength is dissipated in different channels instead of making waves for our goal.[24]

In actuality, this split was a matter of grave concern to the chaverim and the subject of intense debate during their first year in the Yishuv, but this entry represents the sole written reference to the topic in the diary. Moreover, it appeared simply as one of many issues that the hachsharah's members at Afikim wished to share with the Cyprus detainees.

A second, much briefer entry unveils a fraction of the tension that prevailed between the Yishuv and the British authorities. The entry for March 10, 1947, reads: "We have received the distressing news that our member Ze'ev Lustiger, granted leave by the secretariat a few months ago due to his failure to adjust to our society, who went to Tel Aviv, where he found a job in construction, was shot in Tel Aviv by British soldiers on Saturday night while innocently crossing the street. He died of his wounds the next day, the 17th of Adar."[25]

Although certainly it would have been contextually relevant, the entry made no references to the Yishuv's current political problems or to life under the British Mandate, a new concern for Kibbutz Buchenwald that dated only from its arrival in the Yishuv. Similarly, other issues directly related to the hachsharah and its future—Aliyah Bet, the deportations to Cyprus, and the like—found no expression in the diary.

The third entry, a short piece entitled "Dialogue," was written shortly after the November 29, 1947, U.N. vote on the Partition Plan. The author of this unusual entry chose to treat humorously the pressing problem of the future state's borders:

> EITAN: Nu, Menachem, are you pleased? . . . A Jewish state at last, borders, an army, a Jewish national home. Bring wine and we'll drink a toast—Long live the Jewish State!

MENACHEM: What are you carrying on about, you fool? What's the celebration? A home indeed—a home that is only corridors with no rooms . . . and furthermore, the corridors are surrounded on all sides by seas, and are so narrow that if you do not watch your step, you'll slip and fall, and drown in the sea.

EITAN: Hey, man, what are you talking about? Where do you see oceans on all sides? Here's the Chulah and the Sea of Galilee, which are about as big as swimming pools in my eyes, about one eighth of the Dead Sea. Access to the Red Sea is not even worth mentioning. So, that leaves the Mediterranean. Where are your seas on all sides?

MENACHEM: Now I see more clearly. On one side we have the Mediterranean Sea, and on the other, the Arab Sea.

EITAN: Ha, ha, ha! The Arab Sea—have you reached the Indian Ocean already? . . . You either never studied geography or have forgotten everything.

MENACHEM: The sea . . . I forgot, I forgot. What's the difference—an Arab Sea or a sea of Arabs?

EITAN: And I'm telling you that this is actually for the best. We have many seas, I agree, but not all are the same, so we'll proceed thusly: Whoever showers in the first corridor in the Dead Sea will proceed to the second to rinse the salt off in the Mediterranean. From there he will proceed to the third to rinse off the salty water in the Sea of Galilee or Lake Chulah. And then he'll go to . . .

MENAHEM: To, to, to . . .

EITAN: Then, from the Sea of Galilee or Lake Chulah he'll go to Safed to rest a little.

MENACHEM: And then what? And after that?

EITAN: And then: prepare yourself in the corridor to enter the parlor [Ethics of the Fathers 4:16] . . . ha, ha, ha.[26]

This skit is the only written reference to one of the major political events that shaped the Yishuv's future.

Why did the members avoid writing about the current events that shaped the political, military, social, cultural, and economic context of their lives? Did this phenomenon reflect any open or hidden agenda? Was it the result of political or security consciousness, or was it simply accidental?

The various explanations for this phenomenon are complementary; each relates to a different stratum in the group's life and awareness. The first explanation lies in the inherent nature of the kibbutz diary. Intended to serve a dual function—to chronicle the kibbutz's development and to provide its members with a means of expression by which any topic of interest could be freely raised—the diary's focus on the group's internal development did not leave room for profound consideration of the broader context into which the kibbutz was born and functioned.

The second explanation is related to security. Perhaps the kibbutz members practiced self-censorship at the time, avoiding direct references to the events related to the Yishuv's political climate, lest the material fall into the wrong hands and be used against them. However, this explanation does not apply to the earlier parts of the diary written in Europe, which nonetheless failed to relate to the DP question or other burning political issues in postliberation Germany.

The third explanation, which complements the first two, lies in the psychological realm, in the survivors' emotional profile. In his article "Jewish Life in Liberated Germany," historian Koppel Pinson notes the survivors' self-centeredness and extreme egocentricity. "The interest of the Jewish DP in Germany revolves almost entirely around himself. . . . It is but natural that after such suffering in the past . . . that preoccupation of the DP should be with himself."[27] At Kibbutz Buchenwald, this tendency was diluted by a sense of mission, of belonging to the Zionist endeavor. The constant debates on current issues also indicate how far the group's behavioral lifestyle deviated from the egocentric tendencies noted by Pinson. Nonetheless, Kibbutz Buchenwald's members were not entirely immune to the defining psychological characteristics displayed by the she'erit hapletah. The inclination to self-absorption found expression elsewhere—in the kibbutz diary. Here it was possible to depict a world where the kibbutz members played a center-stage, if not exclusive, role, where every external event could be viewed through the prism of the kibbutz's development, if it was considered at all. In that world, the group's social integration, admissions policies, or naming the kibbutz's cows took precedence over the implications of Black Saturday in 1946 (when the leaders of the Yishuv were arrested by the British) or of the hanging of two British sergeants by the Irgun Tzva'i Leumi. The kibbutz diary was the sole venue where the members could give free rein to their natural self-absorption, against which they tenaciously struggled in their daily lives.

This struggle reflects but one aspect of the kibbutz's dual identity. On one hand, the kibbutz, as part of Nocham, was a unique autonomous venture by the she'erit hapletah in the Yishuv. On the other hand, it later became part of the settlement plan of Hakibbutz Hameuchad, thus joining with a preexisting movement. When the kibbutz tried to take its place in each of the two frameworks to which it belonged, this duality led to heightened friction. It was necessary for the members to cope with their dual identity and its concomitant tension.

CHAPTER SEVEN

Kibbutz Buchenwald in Historical Perspective

Though our kibbutz is but a small place, to us it is very precious.
May it not disappear in the coming days. Perhaps it is no idle dream
to imagine that many years hence a grandfather, now one of our
young members, will live in a Hebrew village in Palestine that we
founded. Perhaps that grandfather will sit at the table and thumb
through these pages, and remark, with a smile, "It was worth it! It
was worth the effort, the hard work—because we founded
something, we built a home for you and for ourselves!" That
grandfather will find recorded in those pages our former
[celebratory] parties, our meetings, our committee work, the training
in the cowshed, the banana grove, the chicken run, and, while he is
driving his wagon, will long for those days, will quietly whisper,
"Those were the days!"[1]

WITH THIS ENTRY, Avraham Ahuvia opened part 2 of the Kibbutz
Buchenwald diary, begun at the conclusion of the group's first year of
hachsharah at Afikim. Indeed, those years for which the future grandfather
would nostalgically long were filled with activity. With time, Kibbutz Netzer
Sereni became one of the most successful kibbutzim in its chosen kibbutz
movement affiliation, and was privileged to host the founding convention of
the United Kibbutz Movement in 1979. Concurrently, the kibbutz continued
to foster the other aspect of its identity—its origins as an independent venture
started by the she'erit hapletah in Israel. From its founding, kibbutz members
employed various means to integrate the two halves of the kibbutz's dual
identity. Its Holocaust origins were reflected by its erecting of a memorial
building; centrally placing an impressive bronze statue by Batya Lishansky,
From Holocaust to Redemption, in its large grassy plaza, and hosting the World
Congress of Holocaust Survivors in summer 1981. The very concept of such a

convention emerged from talks held at Netzer, and several kibbutz members were actively involved in its organization.

A new level of inquiry emerges from the issue of Kibbutz Buchenwald's dual identity. If up to this point, the starting point of each discussion has concentrated primarily on the micro level—studying the kibbutz's operative, instrumental, and integrative patterns in largely chronological order—it will now revolve about the macro level, as represented by three conceptual frameworks: Kibbutz Buchenwald's role within the broader concept of communes as utopian frameworks; the ideological and practical implications of its being the first hachsharah kibbutz to be created in postwar Germany; and, finally, the expression of its dual identity as compared to other kibbutzim similarly initiated by the She'erit Hapletah.

THE KIBBUTZ AS A UTOPIAN FRAMEWORK

What prompts individuals to choose communal life, a form that requires strict discipline and far-reaching concessions in the realm of personal freedom? Two different theories, one instrumental and the other conceptual, address this phenomenon, providing insight into the workings of the human psyche. The instrumental approach attributes the communal phenomenon to environmental factors, arguing that communal living often becomes a preferred lifestyle in times of crisis and revolution. In such circumstances, adopting a collective system may solve the individual's plight at no greater personal sacrifice than abandoning a former lifestyle. This thesis fails to explain, however, why communes emerge in certain settings, while no communes are founded in others settings of similar upheaval. The second explanation ascribes the drive for collectivism to the human need to belong, to the unceasing search for utopia. Here the phenomenon is sparked by human rather than environmental factors—a charismatic leader, a religious revelation that engulfs the masses, the birth of a new doctrine. However, both approaches share a common denominator: the yearning for communal life—in one case termed "escapism" and in the other "vision"—that appears when prior social forms become irrelevant.[2]

Communal life has several distinctive features and is characterized, first and foremost, by voluntarism. Communes emerge as acts of free will on the part of their founders and members, without coercion by any political, religious, military, or economic body. Second, communes share the desire to build a better society. Most communes find fault with the existing order, and aspire to plant the seeds of the future. Third, communes generally espouse the desire to create a separate and autonomous way of life and to build unique educational, cultural, and ritual patterns. Finally, communes almost always face a dichotomy between their own way of life, principles, and ideology and that of the outside world.[3]

Despite superficial similarities in matters of framework, several important factors distinguish the commune from the kibbutz, including the role each has played in the history of their nations or states. As communal scholar David Cana'ani has observed the existence or disappearance of communes has not affected national history, while the kibbutz has been a pivotal factor in the national history of Palestine and, later, Israel. Generally, it appears that throughout history, the mergers of sects into communes were one-time acts, while in Eretz Israel the individual kibbutz groups merged into a movement. "With their founding, the 'messianic element' in religious (or secular) communes abated," states Cana'ani. "In Palestine, the forward-looking element was strengthened. Older communes isolated themselves from the world; the kibbutz saw the world as its arena and living space. And unlike sectarian communes, the kibbutz displayed flexibility, adaptability, and pliancy."[4] This set the basis for a kibbutz movement that incorporated various settlements into one ideological framework.

Kibbutz Buchenwald epitomizes two major factors evident on the broad spectrum of the communal idea. Initially, the kibbutz was formed in response to a crisis, in order to enable the individual to survive on the most basic level and to continue to function in the most elementary sense. Indeed, this appears to be the rationale behind the establishment of dozens of kibbutzim both inside and outside the DP camps in Germany and Austria. Kibbutz Buchenwald exemplifies elements of the second thesis as as well, of the unceasing human utopian aspiration. More than half of Kibbutz Buchenwald's founding members were graduates of prewar or wartime Zionist youth movements, some even having lived on hachsharot. For these pioneers, life on Kibbutz Buchenwald was a continuation of a previous lifestyle that had abruptly been terminated by war and devastation.

KIBBUTZ BUCHENWALD'S ROLE WITHIN THE SHE'ERIT HAPLETAH

Can Kibbutz Buchenwald, seen against the background of the she'erit hapletah in Europe and in comparison with the nature and activity of that group, be considered a representative microcosm of the she'erit hapletah? With regard to Kibbutz Buchenwald's European aspect, the answer is definitely affirmative. Studies of the she'erit hapletah in Europe, and in the lands where it was absorbed from the war's end to the founding of the State of Israel, reveal certain defining characteristics that Kibbutz Buchenwald's story reflects: the impulse to form collective frameworks, demographic changes in the composition of the she'erit hapletah, the Zionist leanings of that body as well as its attempts to combat idleness, and the growing egocentric tendency that developed in the DP camps.[5] The survivors' outstanding feature, as embodied by Kibbutz Buchenwald, was their attitude towards the concept of unity. In the immediate postwar era, the she'erit hapletah displayed a strong negative orientation toward the now seemingly irrelevant prewar movement and ideological barriers. This tendency was particularly pronounced among Kibbutz Buchenwald's founders, who aspired to create a unified collective framework for all Zionist settlement movements. During the first year after liberation, this trend weakened and eventually disintegrated both at Kibbutz Buchenwald and among the she'erit hapletah, as the sectarianism characteristic of prewar Jewish society reasserted itself.

Anthropological concepts based upon examination of the functional territory of the group in question further elucidate this trend. According to this thesis, a group forced to function in foreign, hostile territory will adopt functional patterns of behavior, eliminating barriers between subgroups in the interest of enhanced protection and efficiency. In contrast, groups operating in safe territory tend to factionalism, as subgroups feel secure enough to express their individuality and to press for their own interests. This thesis also accounts for the discord among the various branches of the Jewish underground in the Warsaw Ghetto, which can be termed as isolated Jewish arena. This conceptual framework applies to the she'erit hapletah in general, and even more strongly to Kibbutz Buchenwald. Regarding the immediate postliberation period, Jews found themselves in a foreign, non-Jewish, hostile arena—the DP camps that held Jews together with other nationalities. Those circumstances lent force to the need for unity, eliminating barriers that had formerly divided the various factions. In Jewish spheres of action—DP camps populated entirely by Jews, for example—the need for unity declined, and separatist tendencies reemerged more strongly.

Kibbutz Buchenwald as well was directly affected by these processes, but in stages. When they left the Buchenwald camp, the kibbutz members found themselves in an entirely Jewish environment, a state of affairs that should have enhanced factionalism. Nonetheless, by dint of their very strength, their wartime experiences continued to direct the members' actions even in the postliberation period. On the other hand, the second group, which came from the Jewish environment of the Bergen-Belsen DP camp, already showed separatist and factional divisions. Among the original founders, sectarianism took root only after their arrival in the Yishuv, an all-Jewish arena characterized by extreme movement partisanship.[6] It is in this light that we must consider Elik Gruenbaum's remark regarding the kibbutz's long-range chances for success: "A kibbutz like we had there could exist only among non-Jews, in the Diaspora. It had not even the slightest chance of surviving here, among Jews in the land of Israel."[7]

KIBBUTZ BUCHENWALD AS A UNIQUE SHE'ERIT HAPLETAH SETTLEMENT IN ERETZ ISRAEL

Kibbutz Buchenwald expressed its dual identity differently than did other autonomous settlements and kibbutzim formed by the she'erit hapletah in the Yishuv. From 1947 to 1949, more than a dozen kibbutzim were founded by nucleii composed of Holocaust survivors, including: Baram, Revadim, Megiddo, Safiach, Magen, Zikim, Barkai, Lehavot Chavivah, Reshafim, Hayotzrim, Yas'ur, Lochamei Hagetaot, and Kibbutz Buchenwald.[8] The first two settlements were founded by mixed nucleii of survivors and natives of the Yishuv; the remainder were independent ventures by the she'erit hapletah in the broad sense of the word.[9] During that period, survivors also founded *moshavim*, including: Beit Elazari, Yavneh, Zarnogah, Kerem Maharal, Kefar Hanagid, Udim, and Sitriah. The attitude of the settlement movements in the Yishuv to these ventures' very existence comprises a separate issue in and of itself, which, according to Hannah Yablonka, can serve as "a gauge of the amount of trust vested by the kibbutz movement in members of the she'erit hapletah as a qualitative dynamic base for realization of chalutz ideals."[10] In Yablonka's estimation, emotional and ideational rather than ideological factors underlay support for the survivors' aspirations to autonomy. The settlement movements feared that their failure to back autonomous she'erit hapletah ventures would create bitterness and discontent among the immigrants, leading to a crisis in their relationship. In any event, the settlement movements had little faith in the ability of the she'erit hapletah nucleii to function independently. This led in turn to the idea of augmenting them with local nucleii, a suggestion that was not implemented in many cases until the 1950s.

Individual European nucleii reacted differently to this proposal of a merger. Some sought to unite with local nucleii on their own initiative. For example, the nucleus that underwent hachsharah at Ma'anit forwarded this request to the kibbutz's social and cultural division: "We wish to unit with a body that knows Hebrew. Socially, we require that our partners in this venture not be concentration camp survivors."[11] Other nucleii, like Kibbutz Buchenwald, wished, at least initially, to start their settlement experience independently, without partners. In Kibbutz Buchenwald's case, due to the nucleus's size and nature, and the continued arrival of reinforcements from its European hachsharot, the settlement agencies acceded to this request.

Of all the kibbutzim founded by the she'erit hapletah during the period, only one chose the Holocaust as its focus, its raison d'être—Kibbutz Lochamei Hagetaot. Founded in April 1949, this kibbutz united three nucleii of Holocaust survivors: Lochamei Hagetaot, which reached Palestine in 1946 and received hachsharah at Yagur; Hama'avak from Wroczlaw, which made aliyah from Austria and joined the first nucleus; and Dror-Hama'apilim from Germany, which received hachsharah at Beit Hashittah and Ginnosar following its arrival from Cyprus.[12] The idea of founding a kibbutz devoted to the Holocaust had already been raised in Poland in 1946, during the Lochamei Hagetaot nucleus's planning stages. Led by Yitzchak (Antek) Zuckerman and Tzivia Lubetkin, the group decided to turn its future kibbutz into a documentation center and memorial to the Holocaust.[13]

Hakibbutz Hameuchad's response to this proposal was not overly enthusiastic. Apparently fearful that the nucleus would be unable to succeed on its own, the movement's leaders decided to complement it with a local nucleus, due to technical reasons, this decision was never implemented. Nonetheless, two additional she'erit hapletah nuclei joined the group, and together the three settled in 1948, first in the German Templar village of Waldheim, and subsequently in Samariah in the western Galilee.

A crucial episode in the history of Kibbutz Lochamei Hagetaot, in its struggle to establish its identity, was the issue of choosing a name. Initially several proposals were made, including: Vilna (suggested by Yitzchak Tabenkin); Irgun Yehudi Lochem (Jewish Fighters' Organization) Hachoma al Shem Lochamei Hagetaot (The Wall Named for Ghetto Fighters) Chai-Ad (Living Forever); Nes-Ad (symbol Forever); and Giv'at Yitzchak, in memoriam for Yitzchak Katznelson. Following intense debate, the name Kibbutz al Shem Lochamei Hagetaot (Kibbutz Named for the Ghetto Fighters) was chosen. The Dror Nucleus for Cooperative Settlement, Ltd., and the kibbutz secretariat forwarded a request to the National Names Committee for official recognition of the name.

The Names Committee rejected the kibbutz's request, and proffered several counterproposals of its own, including Morag (Mordei Hagetaot—Ghetto Insurgents) DegeL (Degel Getaot Lochamim—Flag of Fighting Ghettos), and PeleG (Pelitat Lochamei Hagetaot—Surviving Remnant of the Ghetto Fighters). The kibbutz's members refused to back down, however, and were finally allowed to choose between Mordei Hagetaot and Lochamei Hagetaot. In a letter to the kibbutz secretariat, the committee voiced its opinion that the first name, which "embodied the spirit and act of rebellion, was preferable to the second, which only specified the war."[14] For their part, the kibbutz members insisted on the latter choice, as it was the name of one of the founding nuclei in Poland.

At first glance, the development of Netzer Sereni and Lochamei Hagetaot appears similar. Both were autonomous ventures initiated by the she'erit hapletah under the aegis of Hakibbutz Hameuchad. Both were founded by nuclei that had espoused the Zionist idea in Europe, and had undergone consolidation in Europe. Both saw themselves as the heirs of their brothers and sisters who perished in the Holocaust. Finally, both engaged with the National

Names Committee in a semantic or ideological struggle that was directly rooted in the question of how to commemorate the Holocaust and the Diaspora. Nevertheless, these two kibbutzim differed both structurally and programmatically. Analysis of these differences sheds light on a central issue for Israeli society from the 1940s on: the commemoration of the Holocaust.

First, the two kibbutzim differed by dint of the composition of their founding nucleii. While Netzer's founders were largely concentration camp survivors, Lochamei Hagetaot's founders were partisans and underground fighters. Each group's wartime experiences affected its postwar social and political orientation.

The two groups differed both in self-image and in the eyes of the surrounding society as well. The overwhelming heterogeneity of the entity termed she'erit hapletah led to the creation of a number of internal hierarchies, each according to its own individual criteria. One criterion was that of active resistance. For a long period, partisans and participants in armed uprisings tended to keep aloof from other survivors, perceiving themselves as a separate elite distinguished by leadership, bravery, and initiative. Lochamei Hagetaot's founders belonged to this circle. A second operative hierarchical criterion was marked by the degree of suffering. Because concentration camp survivors stood at the pinnacle of this hierarchy, they also were endowed with special status among the she'erit hapletah. Kibbutz Buchenwald's founders belonged to this second elite.[15] Thus, in effect, the nucleii of these two kibbutzim, Netzer and Lochamei Hagetaot, belonged to competing elites. At a later date these contending elites would compete to establish the image of she'erit hapletah in the eyes of the Yishuv, but the odds were against Netzer from the outset. The Yishuv's initial contacts with survivors were with partisans and underground fighters, all members of Zionist youth movements. Ruzka Korchak reached the Yishuv toward the end of 1944; Abba Kovner made contact with Jewish Brigade members in Italy in July 1945; Antek Zuckerman and Chaika Grosman participated in August 1945, in the London Conference, where they conferred with Ben-Gurion, left-wing Zionist leaders Meir Ya'ari and Ya'akov Hazzan, and other members of the Zionist leadership. The Yishuv viewed these individuals as a source of pride, as a model to be emulated. For the Yishuv, the partisans and underground fighters personified Zionist bravery under frightful conditions, the realization of the Zionist vision in wartime. Against this image, even the most Zionistically-oriented concentration camp survivors were reflected in a more negative light. More often than not, they even aroused feelings of revulsion. The shame of the Diaspora adhered to them, as they had not succeeded in arming or defending themselves. These conflicting images in the eyes of the Yishuv had direct bearing on each group's future status in Israeli society. During the forties and fifties, leadership and initiative conferred prestige; suffering conferred no status, although their ordeal was recognized. Consequently, Netzer's members struggled far longer for full acceptance as equals by Israeli society than did the members of Kibbutz Lochamei Hagetaot.

Not only did the two kibbutzim differ in their status in the eyes of the Israeli public, they differed in their attitude toward the Holocaust as well. On the personal level, for decades the Holocaust was a persistent note in the lives of Netzer and Lochamei Hagetaot members, as it was for survivors worldwide, but on the collective level, a significant distinction existed. Whereas Netzer's members emphasized the aspect of redemption and downplayed the Holocaust, at Lochamei Hagetaot the Holocaust was their raison d'être. This distinction was expressed on many levels, beginning with the names chosen by each kibbutz and ending with the nature of their Holocaust-related activities. Kibbutz Buchenwald chose the name Netzer, which symbolized redemption; the name Lochamei Hagetaot drew attention to its members' unique role during the Holocaust. With respect to commemorative activities, at Netzer the Holocaust was marked by a memorial building, the Lishansky statue, and the organization of the Holocaust survivors' conference, but none of this comprised a major aspect of daily kibbutz life. In this context, it also is of note that Netzer, unlike many other settlements founded by the She'erit hapletah, has yet to publish a book of eyewitness accounts by survivors.[16] In contrast, Lochamei Hagetaot's members had already decided in Poland to devote themselves to forming an official body to commemorate the Holocaust, a decision that charted the kibbutz's future course. In addition to its Holocaust museum and its sponsoring of manifold scholarly and documentary studies, Kibbutz Lochamei Hagetaot engages in Holocaust-related educational and cultural activities.[17]

How is it possible to account for the gap between the approach of these two kibbutzim to Holocaust commemoration? Why did two Holocaust-derived nucleii, who shared the slogan "Remember, Do Not Forget" in Europe, treat the subject so differently? The answer lies on two planes: first, in the internal dynamics of each kibbutz, and second, in the interactive plane between the kibbutzim and the surrounding society. Kibbutz Netzer and Lochamei Hagetaot differed radically on the internal plane. Lochamei Hagetaot was created when three nucleii composed of Holocaust survivors of differing backgrounds united. Adopting Holocaust memorialization as its raison d'être served to unify the kibbutz. On the other hand, Kibbutz Netzer's members were already bound by a shared framework. All had belonged to the kibbutz in Europe, and had received hachsharah (albeit at different times) at Geringshof or Gersfeld. Consequently, this group required no further common denominator beyond a united framework in Palestine/Israel.

On the external interactive plane, the two kibbutzim differed in status in

Israeli public regard. As concentration camp survivors, Netzer's members were "second-class" survivors. In order to gain acceptance as equals in Israeli society, its members understood, they would need to express public endorsement of societal norms. Although they continued to commemorate the Holocaust at the kibbutz, at the same time they avoided making the Holocaust a focal part of their public identity. By contrast, at Kibbutz Lochamei Hagetaot, whose members were "first-class" survivors—partisans and members of the armed resistance—the kibbutz could allow itself to espouse openly the cause of Holocaust remembrance. This difference in status also explains the tolerant attitude displayed by Israeli society, which sought to downplay remembrance of the Holocaust on principle, toward the aspirations of Kibbutz Lochamei Hagetaot. Its members personified the only aspect of the Holocaust with which Israel society was then capable of identifying—heroism. The Kibbutz Hameuchad movement even welcomed the opportunity to highlight its heroes, and to establish an official commemorative body. An additional advantage ensured from this arrangement: By this means the Holocaust could be compartmentalized at one site, thus obviating the need to deal with it generally everywhere.

Kibbutz Buchenwald's members maintained a low profile. Only in the mid-fifties did they approach the status of their compatriots at Lochamei Hagetaot with the adoption of the name Netzer Sereni, which linked the bravery exhibited by the parachutists with the vision of redemption. Nevertheless, the kibbutz continued to refrain from drawing public attention to its singularity within Israeli society. Only in the mid-sixties, in the wake of the Eichmann trial, did kibbutz members proudly march through Jerusalem as Holocaust survivors to mark the twentieth anniversary of the kibbutz's founding. It took until the late seventies, with the growing awareness of the Holocaust in Israel and the world, for the kibbutz to be ready to host the world conference of Holocaust survivors, an act that highlighted its origins as a she'erit hapletah kibbutz. Apparently, decades of proven Zionist activity were required before concentration camp survivors could allow themselves a retrospective look at their past in public without fear of stigma.

How do the founders and members of this unique enterprise sum up the era of Kibbutz Buchenwald?

ELIK GRUENBAUM: It was a singular phenomenon that could have been established only in the Diaspora. There was no chance to continue in the same fashion after we reached Eretz Israel.[18]

ARTHUR POZNANSKY: It's true that interpersonal relationships between the members were not always smooth, but look at the wonderful youth that we produced. Yes, it was certainly worthwhile.[19]

YECHEZKEL TYDOR: For us, Kibbutz Buchenwald symbolized our chosen path, our decision not to live in the past, but also not to forget it while preparing ourselves for the future. From Buchenwald to Kibbutz Buchenwald—from darkness to light; from slavery to redemption.[20]

ITKA (HARASH) BERKOWITZ: For me, the members of Kibbutz Buchenwald represented the height of perfection. Mature enough to make decisions, and strong enough not to fear the obstacles that lay in the path to realization of their chosen ideal.[21]

HENIA TRAUBE: After the war, everyone wanted to judge himself and God. We had nothing, we had to start from nothing. But on the kibbutz we did not think of that; therefore, we were able to move on and to achieve what we did.[22]

PIZE SIMCHA: After liberation, we knew that we had to unite on our initiative in order to succeed in reaching Palestine. Reality dictated that we join forces in order to inject the pioneering ideal among the youth. We had no alternative.[23]

ONI ONHAUS: We were naïve idealists. I, for example, had an affidavit to travel to America. Instead, I came to the kibbutz in Germany and decided to come build a land, and not just the land but a kibbutz. Crazy, wasn't it?![24]

RACHEL (SHANTZER) TELLER: Kibbutz Buchenwald was united by the hope of founding a new Jewish society after the war, where all Jews would live as equals. It was naïve on our part to believe that it would succeed, but for a while, it did.[25]

AVRAHAM AHUVIA: We had something special there. We no longer had homes, or parents. And finally, following years of atrocities, we succeeded in realizing at the kibbutz the idyll we had created in our imaginations. The dream became a reality. And today, looking back forty years later, the reality appears to us to have been a dream.[26]

The retrospective process that began in the late 1970s has continued to gain strength. As the kibbutz's past and present membership approaches the so-called third stage in human existence, that natural urge to examine their lives and come to grips with the past has been enhanced. This trend has been encouraged by additional factors, first and foremost by the ever-increasing interest in the Holocaust among younger Israelis, and scholarly interest in the history of the she'erit hapletah in general and of Kibbutz Buchenwald in particular. During the 1980s, kibbutz members continued to confront their past, both in the public eye, and within the more restricted private kibbutz forum. Some of these events formed the basis for this book. There were individuals who welcomed the opportunity to document the history of a Zionist venture initiated by the she'erit hapletah. Others expressed surprise that anyone could take an interest in their life stories or in the history of their kibbutz. Without exception, however, all those who were approached willingly shared unique episodes from their past—whether painful, hopeful, or amusing. They—along with the tens of thousands of other Jews who rebuilt their lives after the Holocaust—are the true heroes of this turbulent and traumatic period in history.

Afterword: Where Are They Now?

RABBI MAYER ABRAMOWITZ—U.S. Army chaplain. Returned to the United States in 1947. Served as rabbi in various Jewish communities. Presently the rabbi of the Menorah Synagogue in Miami Beach, Florida.

AVRAHAM (GOTTLIEB) AHUVIA—founding member of Kibbutz Netzer. Lecturer, writer, and biblical scholar. Married, with two children. Lives on Kibbutz Netzer Sereni.

CHAIM-MEIR (GOTTLIEB) AHUVIA—founding member of Kibbutz Netzer. Left the kibbutz in the fifties. Taught Yiddish at Ben-Gurion University. Married. Lives in Ramat Aviv.

LOLA (SULTANIK) AHUVIA—founding member of Kibbutz Netzer. Works in the kibbutz clothing warehouse. Married to Avraham Ahuvia, mother of two children. Lives on Kibbutz Netzer Sereni.

SHMUEL (GOTTLIEB) AHUVIA—founding member of Kibbutz Netzer. Left the kibbutz in the sixties. Worked in the aviation industry. Married, with three children.

SARAH (HOLLANDER) BAR'AM—joined Kibbutz Na'an upon aliyah. Widow, mother of two children. Lives on Kibbutz Naan.

AHARON BATZIA—founding member of Kibbutz Netzer. An economist, he is the director of the kibbutz's industrial plant. Married, with three children. Lives on Kibbutz Netzer Sereni.

YEHUDIT (ITKA HARASH) BERKOWITZ—arts and crafts teacher. Married, with two children. Lives in Kiryat Ata.

SHIMON FLEISCHON—police officer, now retired. Married with children. Lives in Givataim.

ELIYAHU (ELIK) GRUENBAUM—storeowner in Tel Aviv, married, father of children. Died in 1988.

RIVKA (ENGLARD) HOFFMAN—former director of the dormitory at the Rabbi Wolff Beth Jacob Seminary in Bnei Brak. Widow and mother.

YISRAEL LERNER—founding member of Kibbutz Netzer. Industrial entrepreneur. Married, with three children. Lives on Kibbutz Netzer Sereni.

ALIYA (EVYASAF) LEVI—aliyah and absorption activist. Lives on Kibbutz Afikim.

RABBI ROBERT MARCUS—returned to the United States in 1946. Served in the rabbinate. Died in the fifties.

CHAIM MEYERS—following aliyah received hachsharah at Kibbutz Mesilot. Lives on Kibbutz Shoval.

ARTHUR POZNANSKY—works for the International Reparations Committee. Married. Lives in Yad Eliyahu.

RABBI HERSCHEL SCHACTER—rabbi emeritus of the Mosholu Jewish Center in New York. Lectures at Yeshiva University; former president of the Conference of Presidents of Major American Jewish Organizations. Married, with two children.

CHAIM SHULMAN—entertainer. Married. Presently resides in Miami, Florida.

AZRIEL (PIZE) SIMCHA—founding member of Kibbutz Netzer. Chief buyer for the kibbutz industrial plant. Married, with two children. Lives on Kibbutz Netzer Sereni.

HILDA (GRUENWALD) SIMCHA—founding member of Kibbutz Netzer. Works in the kibbutz clothing store. Married to Pize Simcha, with two children. Lives on Kibbutz Netzer Sereni.

RACHEL (SHANTZER) TELLER—after aliyah moved to Tel Aviv and later to Bnei Brak. Married with children. Died in 1992.

YECHEZKEL TYDOR—left Kibbutz Buchenwald after his aliyah. Succeeded in locating his two older children in the United States after the war. Moved to America in the 1950s; resided in the New York until 1974, when he moved back to Israel with his second wife and third child. Lived in Givataim. Died in 1993.

MOSHE ZAUDERER—director of Religious Youth Village. Died in the sixties.

Glossary

All terms are in Hebrew unless otherwise indicated.

Akiva—Zionist youth movement connected with the General Zionists
aliyah—immigration to Palestine/Israel; literally: ascent. See also *olim*.
Aliyah Bet—illegal immigration to Palestine
Bachad—acronym for Brit Chalutzim Datiyim—League of Religious Pioneers
Beit Ya'akov—Beth Jacob ultraorthodox girls' school movement
Brichah—network in postwar Europe that organized illegal immigration to Palestine
chalutz—Zionist pioneer (plural: *chalutzim*); *Hechalutz*—umbrella organization for several pioneering movements primarily affiliated with Labor Zionisim
Chanukkah—Festival of Lights
chaver—kibbutz member (literally: friend, plural: *chaverim*)
Dror—pioneering Zionist youth movement associated with Labor Zionism
Eretz Israel—Land of Israel
gar'in—nucleus of a pioneering group (literally: seed)
Gordonia—pioneering Zionist youth movement based on the pacifist principles of A. D. Gordon
ha'apalah—illegal immigration. See also *ma'apilim*.
Habonim—The Builders; Zionist political movement
hachsharah—kibbutz training farm; pioneering preparation for emigration (plural: *hachsharot*)
Hakibbutz Haartzi—left-wing pioneering kibbutz movement
Hakibbutz Hadati—religious kibbutz movement
Hakibbutz Hameuchad—Unified Kibbutz; kibbutz movement originally associated with Labor Zionism
Hapo'el Hamizrachi—Religious Zionist pioneering movement

Hashomer Hatza'ir—Young Guard; left-wing Zionist pioneering youth movement
Herut—right-wing revisionist Zionist party
Histadrut—Organization; workers' federation
ichud—unity
Ichud Hakevutzot Vehakibbutzim—Union of Collective Settlements
Irgun Brit Zion—Zionist Organization; wartime Zionist unity movement
Irgun Tzva'i Leumi—right-wing pre-state underground movement with revisionist leanings
kashrut—Jewish dietary laws
kibbutz—collective settlement (plural: *kibbutzim*)
ma'abarah—transit settlement for new immigrants
ma'apilim—illegal immigrants. See also *ha'apalah*.
Mapai—Israeli Labor Party
Mapam—left-wing United Workers' Party
Mizrachi—modern religious Zionist political party
moshav, moshavah—cooperative settlement; less communal than a kibbutz (plural: *moshavim*)
moshav shitufi—cooperative settlement of small, individually owned farms
Netzach—acronym for No'ar Tzofi Chalutzi—Young Pioneering Scouts; part of Hakibbutz Hameuchad
Nocham—acronym for No'ar Chalutzi Meuchad—United Pioneering Youth; postwar unity movement
olim—immigrants to Palestine/Israel. See also *aliyah*.
Oneg Shabbat—Friday night party welcoming the Sabbath
Po'alei Agudat Israel—ultraorthodox pioneering movement
Po'alei Zion—Workers of Zion; left-wing pioneering movement
Rosh Hashanah—the Jewish New Year
Sabbat—the Sabbath; Saturday
Sefer Torah—Torah scroll
Selichot—penitential prayers
Sephardim—Eastern Jews, of post-Inquisition Spanish and Portuguese origin
Shavuot—Pentecost festival
she'erit hapletah—Holocaust survivors (literally: the surviving remnant)
shlichim—emissaries
Sukkot—Feast of Tabernacles
Tu Bishevat—holiday marking the beginning of spring
va'ad—committee; secretariat
Yekke—Yiddish term for a Jew of German origin (plural: *Yekkim*)
Yishuv—Jewish settlement in pre-state Israel
Youth Aliyah—Immigration framework for children and teenagers

Notes

Introduction: The Founders

1. The slow recuperation of the survivors is noted in the majority of recent studies on this topic, which largely relate to external agencies, their policies, and their rehabilitation efforts among the she'erit hapletah, rather than to the survivors themselves L. Dinnerstein, *America and the Survivors of the Holocaust* (New York: Columbia University Press, 1982); A. Grobman, "American Jewish Chaplains and the Remnant of European Jewry, 1944–1948" (Ph.D. diss., Hebrew University, Jerusalem, 1981); H. Genizi, *Yo'etz Umekim: Hayo'etz Latzava Haamerikani Veleshe'erit Hapletah, 1945–1949* (The advisor on Jewish affairs to the American army and the Displaced Persons, 1945–1949) (Tel Aviv: Sifriyat Hapo'alim, 1987); Y. Weitz, "Reshit Hakesher Beyn Chayalei Habrigadah Levein She'erit Hapletah" (First contacts between the soldiers of the Jewish Brigade and the Jewish survivors), *Yahadut Zemanenu* 3 (1986): 227–247. Two works are exceptional in this regard—Y. Bauer's pioneering work, *Flight and Rescue: Brichah* (New York: Random House, 1970), and Z. Mankowitz, "Idiologiah Upolitikah Beshe'erit Hapletah Beezor Hakibbush Haamerikai Begermaniah, 1945–1946" (The politics and ideology of survivors of the Holocaust in the American zone of Occupied Germany, 1945–1946 (Ph.D. diss., Hebrew University, Jerusalem, 1987)—in that they also address the internal affairs and initiatives taken by the survivors.

Chapter One: From Death March to Liberation

1. S. Krakowski, "Machanot Hanazim Beaviv 1945—Pinui, Tza'adot Hamavet Haachronot, Shichrur" (Nazi camps—spring 1945: evacuation, last death marches, liberation), *Dappim Lecheker Tekufat Hashoah* 4 (1986): 179–180; Y. Bauer, "Mitz'adei Hamavet" (The death marches, January–May 1945), *Yahadut Zemanenu* 1 (1981): 199–200.

2. The statistical estimates for the number of inmates imprisoned in concentration camps in early 1945 range from 525,000 to 700,000. Some 250,000 of these were Jews. Bauer cites an exact figure of 524,286 camp inmates for 15 January 1945. See Bauer, "Mitz'adei Hamavet," 200. Krakowski speaks of some 700,000 prisoners, in "Machanot Hanazim," 180–189.

3. Bauer, "Mitz'adei Hamavet," 199.

4. Arthur Poznansky, interview by author, Yad Eliyahu, 29 November 1984.

5. Yechezkel Tydor, interview by author, Ramat Gan, 4 June 1984.

6. Eliyahu Gruenbaum, interview by author, Tel Aviv, 16 December 1984.

7. Avraham Ahuvia, personal diary (in possession of author), 5 February 1945. Originally written in Yiddish, the diary was later translated into Hebrew by its author.

8. Ahuvia diary, 11 February 1945.

9. Ahuvia diary, 23 March 1945.

10. Rabbi Herschel Schacter, interview by author, New York, 24 July 1985.

11. Tydor interview.

12. Ahuvia diary, 2 April 1945.

13. Tydor interview.

14. Schacter interview. On the liberation of the Buchenwald concentration camp, see Y. Eliach and B. Gurewitsch, *The Liberators: Eyewitness Accounts of the Liberation of Concentration Camps* (New York: Institute of Holocaust Research, 1981), 1: 16–25.

15. Baruch Merzel, interview with the author, Jerusalem, 27 August 1983.

16. Ahuvia diary, 21 April 1945.

17. Tydor interview.

18. D. Ofer, "From Survivors to New Immigrants: She'erit Hapletah and Aliyah," in *She'erit Hapletah, 1944–1948: Rehabilitation and Political Struggle*, ed. Y. Gutman and A. Saf (Jerusalem: Yad Vashem, 1990), 304–336; I. Wilner, "Foehrenwald—Machaneh Akurim Yehudi Acharon Begermaniah, 1951–1957" (Foehrenwald—the last DP camp in Germany, 1951–1957) (Master's thesis, Bar-Ilan University, Ramat Gan, 1988), 3. Other scholars claim that only 25,000 Jewish survivors resided in West Germany during that period. See Y. Gelber, "Partners and Adversaries: Jewish Survivors of World War II, the Jewish Agency, and Britain," in *Vision and Conflict in the Holy Land*, ed. R. I. Cohen (Jerusalem: Yad Ben-Zvi, 1985), 276. Apparently some 50,000 survivors remained in Germany after taking into account the high death rate immediately following liberation, as well as the first wave of repatriation. See Y. Gutman, "She'erit Hapletah—The Problems, Some Elucidation," in *She'erit Hapletah*, ed. Gutman and Saf, 510 n. 2. In the postwar years, the American zone attracted Jewish DPs; in August 1947, their numbers peaked at 157,000. See M. Proudfoot, *European Refugees, 1932–1952* (Evanston, Ill.: Northwestern University Press, 1956), 341.

19. Initially, DP affairs were handled by the Displaced Persons Section of the Supreme Headquarters Allied Expeditionary Forces (SHAEF), the Allied Supreme Command. When that body dissolved in mid-July 1945, jurisdiction over DP affairs passed into the hands of each of the Four Powers. From that date until October 1945, France, Britain and the United States (the USSR denied having a DP problem) acted in concert with UNRRA and the IGC (Intergovernmental Committee on Refugees) to address the DP problem, including that of tens of thousands of Jewish survivors. In October 1945, the DP "ball" was returned to the military's "court," when the Su-

preme Commander of each occupied zone was granted authority over the DPs in his area. Dinnerstein, *America and the Survivors*, 10–12.

20. Schacter interview.

21. The SHAEF memorandum is cited in A. Grobman, "American Jewish Chaplains and the Shearit Hapletah, April–June 1945," *Simon Wiesenthal Center Annual* 1 (1984): 91.

22. See Y. Weitz, "Hayishuv Veshe'erit Hapletah, 1944–1945" (The Yishuv and the survivors, 1944–1945) (Master's thesis, Hebrew University, Jerusalem, 1981), 88. Regarding conditions in the camps, see Dinnerstein, *America and the Survivors*, 39–71; Genizi, *Yo'etz Umekim*. Moreover, during this period in the DP camps almost no anti-Zionist ideologies were discernible that could have unbalanced the steadily gaining Zionist orientation. The ultraorthodox group in the camps was extremely small; the Communists and Bundists had returned to Poland as soon as the opportunity offered itself. The few Bundists remaining in the Feldafing camp, for example, joined the left wing of Po'alei Zion or groups with a Borochovian bias. See Z. Mankowitz, "Zionism and She'erit Hapletah" in *She'erit Hapletah*, ed. Gutman and Saf, 213.

23. B. Wasserstein, *Britain and the Jews of Europe, 1939–1945* (London: Institute of Jewish Affairs, 1979), 348–349.; R. Zweig, "Hamediniut Habritit Legabei Aliyah Leeretz Israel Betekufat Hashoah—Shelav Acharon" (British policy on immigration to Palestine during the Holocaust—the last stage), *Zionism* 8 (1983): 242; N. Katzburg, *Mediniut Bemavoch: Mediniut Britaniah Beeretz Israel, 1940–1945*) (Policy in a labyrinth: British policy on Palestine, 1940–1945) (Jerusalem: Yad Ben-Zvi, 1977), 71–72.

24. Two meetings of the Jewish Agency Executive, on 17 May 1945 and 21 May 1945, were almost entirely devoted to the question of entry permits. See meetings of the Jewish Agency Executive, the Central Zionist Archives (hereafter referred to as CZA).

25. Gelber, "Partners and Adversaries," 290.

26. D. Porat, "The Role of European Jewry in the Plans of the Zionist Movement During World War II and in Its Aftermath," in *She'erit Hapletah*, ed. Gutman and Saf, 286–287; Y. Weitz, "She'elat Haplitim Hayehudim Bemediniut Hatzionit" (The DP question in Zionist policy), *Cathedra* 55 (March 1990): 164–165.

27. Weitz, "Hayishuv Veshe'erit Hapletah," 113.

28. M. Avizohar, "Bikkur Ben-Gurion Bemachanot Ha'akurim Vetefisato Haleumit Betom Milchemet Ha'olam Hasheniah" (Ben-Gurion's visit to the DP camps and his national outlook in the aftermath of World War II), in *Yahadut Mizrach Eiropah bein Shoah Letekumah 1944–1948* (Eastern European Jewry from Holocaust to redemption 1944–1948), ed. B. Pinkus (Sde Boker: Ben-Gurion University, 1987), 265.

29. Aharon Hoter-Yishai 22 (4); Ze'ev Birger 32 (4), Yosef Lavi (Levkowitz) 37 (4), oral testimonies, Oral History Division, Institute of Contemporary Jewry, Hebrew University, Jerusalem.

CHAPTER TWO: FROM BUCHENWALD TO KIBBUTZ BUCHENWALD

1. Ahuvia diary, 22 April 1945.

2. Schacter interview.

3. Tydor interview.

4. Ahuvia diary, 25 April 1945.
5. Schacter interview.
6. Schacter interview.
7. Ahuvia diary, 9 May 1945.
8. Ahuvia diary, 26 May 1945.
9. Grobman, "American Jewish Chaplains and the Shearit Hapletah," 91–107.
10. Schacter interview.
11. Regarding the activity of other Jewish chaplains among the survivors, see Grobman, "American Jewish Chaplains and the Shearit Hapletah," 92–107.
12. Schacter interview.
13. Ahuvia diary, 2 June 1945.
14. A. Peck, "An Introduction to the Social History of the Jewish Displaced Persons' Camps: The Lost Legacy of the She'erith Hapletah," *Proceedings of the Eighth World Congress of Jewish Studies, Division B* (Jerusalem, 1982), 188.
15. Schacter interview.
16. This was also the case at Kibbutz Chafetz Chaim, which was established near the Zeilsheim DP camp in October 1945. Moshe Blumstein, interview by author, Bnei Brak, 23 February 1987.
17. Ahuvia diary, 9 June 1945.
18. F. M. Wilson, *Aftermath* (West Drayton, England: Penguin, 1947); Dinnerstein, *America and the Survivors*, 9–38; H. Yahil, "Pe'ulot Hamishlachat Haeretzisraelit Leshe'erit Hapletah, 1945–1949" (The Palestine delegation to the survivors: its activities, 1945–1949), *Yalkut Moreshet* 30 (November 1980): 7–40.
19. Tydor interview.
20. Blumstein interview.
21. From Tydor's remarks at a symposium held at Kibbutz Netzer Sereni, 8 May 1985.
22. Akiva Skidell, letter to his wife, Etty, 21 June 1945, Netzer Sereni Archives, K-4, 4a.
23. Dinnerstein, *America and the Survivors*, 13–15.
24. Schacter interview; M. Abramowitz, "DPs, GI's and CO's: Working Undercover in Post-war Europe," *Moment* (April 1982): 44–46.
25. Cited by Dinnerstein, *America and the Survivors*, 17.

Chapter Three: The Initial Period at Geringshof

1. Chaim-Meir Gottlieb, kibbutz diary, pt. 1, 24 June 1945. Diary entries were made in various languages (Yiddish, Polish, French, Hebrew), anonymously on occasion.
2. Avraham Ahuvia, remarks at a symposium held at Nezer Sereni, 8 May 1985.
3. Ibid.
4. Luba Lindenbaum, interview by author, Bnei Brak, 15 February 1987.
5. From the film *Nedudei She'erit Hapletah* (The journeys of the survivors) with Isaac Wilner, an Open University of Israel production for the course "The Holocaust" (Open University, 1983–1992). See also Wilson, *Aftermath*.
6. Chaim-Meir Gottlieb, kibbutz diary, pt. 1, 2 July 1945.
7. Ibid.

8. Tydor interview.

9. Yehudit (Itka Harash) Berkowitz, interview by author, Haifa, 22 July 1987.

10. Rita Wasserman questionnaire. All questionnaires are in the author's possession.

11. Esther (Landgarten) Forscher questionnaire.

12. Chava Yuskowitz questionnaire.

13. Lola (Sultanik) Ahuvia questionnaire.

14. Tydor interview.

15. Ibid.

16 Berkowitz interview.

17. Ahuvia diary, 10 July 1945.

18. Ibid.

19. Poznansky interview.

20. Gruenbaum interview.

21. Kibbutz diary, pt. 1, 12 July 1945.

22. Berkowitz interview.

23. Tydor interview.

24. Poznansky interview.

25. Ahuvia diary, 10 July 1945.

26. J. T. Baumel, "The Politics of Religious Rehabilitation in the DP Camps," *Simon Wiesenthal Center Annual* 6 (1990): 57–79.

27. Ahuvia diary, 10 July 1945.

28. The letter appeared in the kibbutz diary, 21 July 1945.

29. These certificates had been given to Aharon Choter-Yishai by Yehudah Arazi in Italy prior to Choter-Yishai's departure for Germany in May 1945, with instructions that if he found any survivors, they should be immediately granted certificates to enter Palestine. D. Porat, "The Role of European Jewry in the Plans of the Zionist Movement During World War II and in Its Aftermath" in *She'erit Hapletah*, ed. Gutman and Saf, 291.

30. R. S. Marcus, "Kibbutz Buchenwald," *Davar*, 19 July 1945, 2. Dobkin's letter to Marcus, Netzer Sereni Archives, K6–4.

31. See Y. Weitz, "She'erit Hapletah Bediuneihem Veshikuleihem shel Chavrei Hanhalat Hasochnut Mimai 1945 ve'ad November 1945" (She'erit hapletah in the deliberations of the Jewish Agency leadership, May 1945–November 1945), *Yalkut Moreshet* 29 (May 1980): 53–80; idem, "She'elat Haplitim Hayehudim Bemediniut Hatzionit" (The DP question in Zionist policy), *Cathedra* 55 (March 1990): 174. In opposition to this instrumental approach, Dina Porat argues that it was impossible to regard the survivors as "a tool for political gains" because of this group's size and nature. See D. Porat, "Role of European Jewry," 291.

32. Tydor interview.

33. Protokol der Geschaeftssitzung der Konferenz der befreiten (35 juedischen politischen Haeftlinge in Deutschland [americanische und englische Bestzungsone], St. Otilien Bei Landsberg a/Lech. den 25 July 1945. YIVO Archives, New York, DP collection, file 21. See also Y. Bauer, "The Initial Organization of the Holocaust Survivors in Bavaria," *Yad Vashem Studies* 8 (1970): 155.

34. Ahuvia diary, 8 August 1945.

35. Kibbutz diary, pt. 1, 10 August 1945.

36. Avraham Ahuvia, remarks at a symposium held at Netzer Sereni, 8 May 1985.

37. Kibbutz diary, pt. 1, 10 August 1945.

38. Ahuvia diary, 11 August 1945.

39. Kibbutz diary, pt. 1, 11 August 1945.

40. Tydor interview.

41. Azriel (Ernst/Pize) Simcha and others, interview by author, Kibbutz Netzer Sereni, 9 December 1987.

42. Ibid.

43. Rivka (England) Hoffman, interview by author, Bnei Brak, 25 October 1984.

44. Rachel (Shantzer) Teller, interview by author, Tel Aviv, 11 January 1987.

45. Ibid.

46. Simcha and others interview.

47. Akiva Skidell letter to his wife, Etty, 27 August 1945, Netzer Sereni Archives, K-4, 4a.

48. Tydor interview.

49. Ahuvia diary, 2 September 1945.

50. Kibbutz diary, pt. 1, 31 August 1945.

51. Kibbutz diary, pt. 1, 3 September 1945.

52. David Shealtiel, report to Mapai secretariat, 11 September 1945, Labor Party Archives, section 2, 45/24, Beit Berl.

53. Ibid.

54. Kibbutz diary, pt. 1, 3 September 1945.

55. Questionnaires: Lola (Sultanik) Ahuvia, Shmuel Yuskowitz, Avraham (Gottlieb) Ahuvia; Berkowitz interview.

56. Tydor interview.

57. I. Oppenheim, *Tenu'at Hechalutz Bepolin (1917–1929)* (The Hechalutz movement in Poland, [1917–1929]) (Jerusalem: Magnes, 1982), 648. See also Y. Weitz, "Hama'avak al Demut Ĥechalutz' Betenu'at Ha'avodah Beeretz Israel, 1943–1945" (Hechalutz's struggle for its identity within the Palestine Labor Party), *Dapim Lecheker Tekufat Hashoah* 7 (1989): 149–150.

58. Weitz, "Hayishuv Veshe'erit Hapletah," 48; D. Levin, *Bein Nitzoz Leshalhevet* (Caught between spark and flame) (Ramat Gan: Bar-Ilan University Press, 1987), 12–48; Mankowitz, "Idiologiah Upolitikah Beshe'erit Hapletah," 112–114; Bauer, *Flight and Rescue*, 43–44, 69–70.

59. Y. Weitz, "Emdot Vegishot Bemifleget Po'alei Eretz Israel Kelapei Shoat Yehudei Eiropah, 1939–1945" (The attitude of Mapai toward the destruction of European Jewry) (Ph.D. diss., Hebrew University, Jerusalem, 1987), 291–309; idem, "Hama'avak al Demut 'Hechalutz,' " 147–148.

60. H. Nir, *Hakibbutz Vehachevrah, 1923–1933* (Kibbutz and society, 1923–1933) (Jerusalem: Yad Ben-Zvi, 1984), 227.

61. This kibbutz is not cited in studies of the she'erit hapeletah in Germany. Generally Kibbutz Nili is cited as the second kibbutz to be founded, although this did not occur until November 1945.

62. H. Yahil, "Pe'ulot Hamishalachat Haeretz-israelit Leshe'erit Hapletah 1945–1949" (The Palestine delegation to the survivors, its activities, 1945–1949), *Yalkut Moreshet* 30 (Nov. 1980): 16.

63. Mankowitz, "Zionism and She'erit Hapletah," 206.

64. A Shapira, *Hahalichah al Kav Haofek* (Walking on the horizon) (Tel Aviv: Am Oved, 1989), 353.

CHAPTER FOUR: THE KIBBUTZ IN PALESTINE

1. Yedi'ot, Aliyah Chadashah, Spring 1945. CZA, S6-4246.
2. Naomi Applebaum questionnaire.
3. Avraham (Gottlieb) Ahuvia questionnaire.
4. Shmuel Yuskowitz questionnaire.
5. Lola (Sultanik) Ahuvia questionnaire.
6. Rita Wasserman questionnaire.
7. Weitz, "She'erit Hapletah Bediuneihem"; idem, "Hatenu'ah Hatzionit Nochach She'erit Hapletah Beshilhei Milchemet Ha'olam Hasheniah" (The Zionist movement facing the surviving remnants at the end of World War II), *Dapim Lecheker Tekufat Hashoah* 3 (1984): 139–158; idem, "Hayishuv Veshe'erit Hapletah"; H. Yablonka, *Achim Zarim: Nitzolei Hashoah Bemedinat Israel 1948–1952* (Foreign brethren: Holocaust survivors in the State of Israel 1948–1952), Jerusalem: Yad Itzchak Ben-Zvi Press and Ben-Gurion University of the Negev Press, 1994, 256–266. Plans to send emissaries to Europe were first discussed in the spring of 1945. See, for example, Mapai Secretariat Meeting, 15 May 1945, where the issue of sending emissaries to Western and Central Europe was raised. Labor Party Archive, Section 2 24/45; Hapo'el Hamizrahi Secretariat Meeting, April 1945, Yedi'ot Hamazkirut, 22 April 1945, 21 (24), Kibbutz Hadati Archive.
8. Avizohar, "Bikkur Ben-Gurion," 258.
9. Avizohar, "Bikkur Ben-Gurion," 265. For Ben-Gurion's attitude to Hashomer Hatza'ir activity among the she'erit hapletah, see E. Rabinovitz, *Bemaaei UNNRA im She'erit Hapletah, 1946–1948* (Emissary for UNNRA with Jewish Displaced Persons, 1946–1948) (Tel Aviv: Sifriyat Hapo'alim, 1990), 18.
10. A. Shapira, "The Yishuv's Encounter with the Survivors of the Holocaust", in *She'erit Hapletah*, ed. Gutman and Saf, 81.
11. I. Keynan, "The Yishuv's Mission to the Displaced Persons Camps in Germany: The Initial Steps, August 1945–May 1946", in *She'erit Hapletah*, ed. Gutman and Saf, 219. See also Y. Benkover's remarks about the intensive activity of Hashomer Hatza'ir members serving in the Jewish Brigade among the survivors in the summer of 1945. Benkover Report to the Kibbutz Hameuchad Secretariat, 11 September 1945, Kibbutz Hameuchad Archive, Section B1, Box 7, File 30.
12. Yahil, "Pe'ulot Hamishlachat Haeretz-israelit."
13. See letters dispatched from the Kibbutz Hameuchad to the Aliyah Desk at the Jewish Agency requesting exit permits for shlichim, as well as requests to foreign embassies for temporary visas. Kibbutz Hameuchad Archive, Section A1, Box 15, File 102. For a Kibbutz Hameuchad emissary who stowed away in order to reach Austria in 1946, see Ze'ev Utitz, interview by author, Tel Aviv, 24 May 1992.
14. I. Keynan, "Bein Tikvah Lecharadah: Tadmit She'erit Hapletah Be'einei Hashlichim Haeretz-israeliim Lemachanot Ha'akurim Begermaniah, 1945" (From hope to fear: The image of the survivors in the eyes of Palestinian emissaries to the German DP camps, 1945), in *Ha'apala: Studies in the History of Illegal Immigration into Palestine, 1934–1948*, ed. A. Shapira (Tel Aviv: Am Oved Press, 1990), 216.
15. Attempts by Hashomer Hatza'ir members serving in the Jewish Brigade to (in

the Hebrew idiom) "snatch souls" in Germany during the summer of 1945 are well substantiated. See, for example, Ben-Zion Yisraeli's remarks at a Mapai Secretariat Meeting, 10 August 1945, Labor Party Archive, Section 2 24/45.

16. Keynan, "Bein Tikvah Lecharadah," 218-219; Yablonka, *Achim Zarim*, 256-266.

17. See sample letters cited by Keynan, "Bein Tikvah Lecharadah," 222: "They have grown accustomed to death; they have trampled the living and the dead and the desire to help others has been almost uprooted from their hearts. . . . I believe that those who survived did so because they were egotistical and looked out primarily for themselves." David Shealtiel remarks at Mapai Secretariat Meeting, 11 September 1945, Labor Party Archive, Section 2, 24/45.

18. Avivah Halamish, interview by author, Tel Aviv, 5 December 1991. For a discussion of this phenomenon in historiographical and poetical works, see A. Halamish, "Illegal Immigration: Values, Myth and Reality," *Studies in Zionism* 9 (1988): 47-62.

19. The illegal immigrants sailed in sixty-four Mossad Le'aliyah Bet–sponsored ships and one Revisionist party–sponsored vessel.

20. N. Bogner, Iy Hagerush: Machanot Hama'apilim Bekafrisin, 1946-1948 (The deportation island: Jewish illegal immigrant camps on Cyprus, 1946-1948) (Tel Aviv: Am Oved, 1991), 13.

21. For objections to this matter see: Yedi'ot, Aliyah Chadashah, spring 1945, CZA, S6-4246. Even large settlement movements, like Hakibbutz Hameuchad, which endorsed recruiting at Atlit, battled for the right to meet directly with the new immigrants. See Hakibbutz Hameuchad Central Secretariat Meeting, 10 April 1945. Hakibbutz Hameuchad Archive, Section B1, Box 7, File 28.

22. Kibbutz diary, pt. 1, entry from Atlit period [no exact date], 64.

23. Yechezkel Tydor, interview by author, Jerusalem, 30 March 1983. Both Tydor and Gruenbaum concurred that the most effective party and/or institutional functionary at Atlit was Moshe Ya'ari, the Youth Aliyah representative, who worked at the camp from 1945 to 1946. He was then sent to work at the Cyprus detention camps. Moshe Ya'ari, telephone interview by author, 12 May 1992. Another party functionary at Atlit, Dov Goldstein, represented Hakibbutz Haartzi. Dov Goldstein, telephone interview by author, 12 May 1992.

24. Kibbutz diary, pt. 1, entry from Atlit period [n.d.], 37; Avraham Gottlieb letter from the kibbutz to Rachel Katznelson, 13 September 1945. Dobkin finally bowed to the unity concept, and communicated with Rabbi Marcus in October 1945: "The kibbutz members are presently at Afikim. We hope they will remain united in the future as they are bound by so much past suffering." Dobkin letter to Marcus, 18 September 1945, CZA, S6-834.

25. Yedi'ot Hamazkirut of Hakibbutz Hadati 27 (30), 2 October 1945. Hakibbutz Hadati Archive, Kevutzat Yavneh.

26. Ibid.

27. Kibbutz diary, pt. 1, 17 September 1945, 66-68.

28. Kibbutz Afikim was founded in the late 1920s by young members of Hashomer Hatza'ir–USSR. With the split in Hashomer Hatza'ir's world organization in 1930, this group joined the Netzach wing of Hashomer Hatza'ir from the Baltic countries, Czechoslovakia, and Austria. Thus an autonomous framework was created within Hakibbutz Hameuchad.

29. For the founding of Netzach, see M. Avizohar, *Berei Saduk: Idialim Chevratiim Uleumiim Vehishtakfutam Be'olamah shel Mapai* (National and social ideals as reflected in Mapai—1930–1942) (Tel Aviv: Am Oved, 1990), 221–223.

30. *Afikim* 392, 5 October 1945. The Afikim newsletters are housed in the Kibbutz Afikim Archive.

31. Ibid.

32. Kibbutz diary, pt. 1 [unsigned], 20 September 1945, 59–61.

33. Kibbutz diary, pt. 1, entry by A. Ahuvel [n.d.], p. 71.

34. Tydor interview, 30 March 1983.

35. Population movement of 1945, Kibbutz Afikim, Afikim archives, K\10.

36. Aliya (Gurevitsch) Levi, interview by author, Tel Aviv, 17 July 1991.

37. "Why Do We Eat Separately?" A. Gottlieb entry in kibbutz diary, pt. 1, 13 January 1946; "Why Do We Sit at Separate Tables?" *Afikim* 399, 18 January 1946.

38. "Besheelat Ha'aliyah [The question of aliyah]: Remarks at a Seminar for Counselors for Olim at Giv'at Hashloshah," 23–24 Jan. 1946. Hakibbutz Hameuchad Archive, Section A1, Box 11, File 2.

39. Some kibbutzim decided to add lectures on Knesset Israel The Community of Israel and the Haganah. The Hakibbutz Hameuchad absorption seminar program for new immigrants held at Giv'at Hashloshah in early February 1946 reflects the topics its leaders felt olim should be exposed to. Of the 123 hours of instruction, twenty were devoted to discussion of Zionism, twenty to the history of the workers' movement, eighteen to the history of the kibbutz, five to the geography, of Palestine, nine to world politics and concepts of socialism, four to poetry, eight to current events, three to a trip, twenty-six to training, and seven to a summary session. Only three hours were devoted to literature and none to Jewish history. Program for a seminar at Giv'at Hashloshah, 29 January 1946–13 February 1946, Hakibbutz Hameuchad Archive, Section A1, Box 2, File 7. For a comparison of Hakibbutz Haartzi's approach to study programs, see H. Yablonka, *Achim Zarin*, 146.

40. Levi interview.

41. Gruenbaum interview.

42. Lola (Sultanik) Ahuvia questionnaire.

43. Levi interview.

44. Rita Wasserman questionnaire.

45. This absorption differed intrinsically from individual absorption. It sought to preserve the group's identity as an autonomous collective and to guarantee its acceptance, as a group and not as individuals, within the host society.

46. Y. H. Yerushalmi, *Zakhor: Jewish History and Jewish Memory* (Philadelphia: Jewish Publication Society, 1982).

47. L. L. Langer, *Holocaust Testimonies: The Ruins of Memory* (New Haven and London: Yale University Press, 1991).

48. "Im Kibbutz Buchenwald" (With Kibbutz Buchenwald), *Afikim* 392, 5 October 1945.

49. Avraham (Gottlieb) Ahuvel, "Chanukkah . . . Sham Vepo" (Chanukkah . . . there and here), kibbutz diary, pt. 1 [n.d.].

50. "Yaldei Haifa Lekibbutz Buchenwald" (Haifa children visit Kibbutz Buchenwald), *Afikim* 398, 20 January 1946.

51. Dating from the arrival of Kibbutz Buchenwald, Afikim's holiday editions of

its newsletters focused upon descriptions of that holiday in the ghettos and camps. The Passover edition marks the return to a local orientation. The newsletter's subheading highlights this change "to our soldiers in foreign lands, to our members serving in the armed forces, to the Yishuv representatives, to the remnants battling angry waves to reach the homeland, to the imprisoned fighters for the Yishuv—greetings for success, freedom, and creativity." The survivors appear hear only within the coordinates of the Yishuv, within the context of the struggle for Aliyah Bet. "Im Ha'olim" (With the new immigrants), *Afikim* 404, 14 April 1946.

52. "Kinus Yotzei Buchenwald" (The Buchenwalders' convocation), *Afikim* 405, 28 April 1946.

53. A. Don-Yichya, "Mamlachtiyut Veshoah" (Statehood and the Holocaust), in *Bishvilei Hatechiyah* (On the roads to rebirth), ed. A Rubinstein (Ramat Gan: Bar-Ilan University Press, 1983), 167–188.

54. Yablonka, *Achim Zarim*, 216–224.

55. D. Porat, "Beselichah Ubechesed': Hamifgash bein Ruzka Korchak Levein Hayishuv Umanhigav" (With loving forgiveness: The meeting between Ruzka Korchak-Marle, the Yishuv, and its leaders), *Yalkut Moreshet* 52 (April 1992): 9–33. For the special treatment afforded partisans and ghetto fighters, see Ben-Zion Yisraeli, remarks at Mapai Secretariat Meeting, 10 August 1945. Regarding the she'erit hapletah, he commented, "Among these Jews there is an unestimably important core—the partisans and the ghetto fighters." Labor Party Archive, Section 2, 24/45.

56. Yablonka, *Achim Zarim*, 256.

57. In 1951, MP Rabbi Mordechai Nurock of the United Religious Front proposed a law recognizing the 27th day of Nisan as Holocaust and Uprising Remembrance Day. Despite the law's passage, in the fifties the government granted almost no official recognition to this date. The 1959 Holocaust and Heroism Remembrance Day Law established this date as the official national memorial day. The combination of "Holocaust and Uprising" and "Holocaust and Heroism" in the day's official titles is an excellent indicator of the victory of the approach that wished to emphasize heroism, equating it with the entire phenomenon of the Holocaust. See J. Tydor Baumel, *Kol Bechiyot: Hashoah Vehatefilah* (A voice of lament: the Holocaust and prayer) (Ramat Gan: Bar-Ilan University Press, 1992), 63–89.

58. For the attempt to establish memorial days for Holocaust victims, see Baumel, *Kol Bechiyot*, 63–89.

59. Weitz, "Sheelat Haplitim Hayehudim"; E. Friesel, "Churban Yehudei Eiropah—Gorem Behakamat Medinat Israel?" (The destruction of European Jewry—a factor in the creation of the State of Israel?), *Molad* 250 (1980): 21–31. For a governmental parallel to the attempts by survivors to downplay their distinctive characteristics, see Don-Yichya, "Mamalachtiut Veshoah," 180.

60. Tydor interview, 30 March 1983.

61. Gruenbaum interview.

62. Shlomo [?], "Acharei Azivato Shel Avraham Ziegler" (After Avraham Ziegler's departure), kibbutz diary, pt. 2 [n.d.], 63.

63. Kibbutz diary, pt. 2, 5 November 1946.

64. For a description of this metamorphosis in the kibbutzim, see A. Lieblich, *Kibbutz Makom* (Kibbutz anywhere) (Jerusalem, 1986), 288–299.

65. See entries in kibbutz diary, pt. 1 [in Yiddish, n.d.], 130–142.
66. Lola Ahuvia, telephone conversation with author, 19 April 1992.
67. For a description of Hapo'el Hamizrachi's state at that time, see M. Krona, *Morai Verabotai, Achai Vere'ai* (My teachers, my friends) (Tel Aviv: Moreshet, 1987), 226.
68. "Divrei Pereidah" (Parting words), *Afikim* 405, 3 May 1946.
69. *Yedi'ot Hamazkirut* of Hakibbutz Hadati, 35 (38), 2 May 1946. Hakibbutz Hadati Archive, Kevutzat Yavneh.
70. *Alonim* 21 (Iyar 1946), Hakibbutz Hadati Archive, Kevutzat Yavneh.
71. Berkowitz interview.
72. Avraham Ahuvia, "Ahavah," "Mikveh Israel," and "Kfar Hano'ar Hadati," kibbutz diary, pt. 1, 4 November 1945.
73. Berkowitz interview.
74. Naomi Applebaum questionnaire.
75. Kibbutz diary, pt. 2, 4 January 1947.
76. "Limlot Shnat Halimudim Lichevrah 'Havatikah' Shel K[ibbutz] B[uchenwald]" (A year of study for Kibbutz Buchenwald's veteran group), kibbutz diary, pt. 2 [n.d.], 17.
77. "Yesh Vayesh" (Enough and to spare), kibbutz diary, pt. 2, 22 January 1947.
78. "Im Bo Kibbutz Buchenwald Liafikim" (Upon Kibbutz Buchenwald's arrival at Afikim)—"A Letter from Benny," *Afikim* 397, 14 December 1945.
79. "Mikibbutz Buchenwald Bekafrisin Lekibbutz Buchenwald Beafikim" (From Kibbutz Buchenwald in Cyprus to Kibbutz Buchenwald in Afikim), *Afikim*, 20 December 1946.
80. The majority of the she'erit hapletah had but a hazy concept of life in the Yishuv when they arrived in Palestine. See Yablonka, *Achim Zarim*, 196–203.
81. Shmuel Yuskowitz questionnaire.
82. For evidence for this lack of contact, see Ophir Eliasi "Mibuchenwald Ve'ad Netzer Sereni" (From Buchenwald to Netzer Sereni), (Seminar paper, Y. H. Brenner Comprehensive High School, 1982).
83. Kibbutz diary, pt. 2, "Chronika" (Chronicle), 21 September 1946.
84. See, for example, B. Minkovsky's report on the new immigrants at Afikim dated 19 December 1946: "The merger between the two parties has been successful. The general atmosphere is one of comradeship based upon the days of shared suffering in the DP camps in Germany. The hachsharah period at Afikim has rallied them around the goal of founding a new kibbutz settlement for chalutzim from the she'erit hapletah. In anticipation of this goal, cultural and professional preparations are being undertaken. More than forty individuals are being trained in Afikim's agricultural branches and workshops. The Afikim members note the Buchenwalders' positive and responsible attitude toward work. They themselves feel that they are making progress. Four female members are working in the children's houses in preparation for infant care. One member is studying bookkeeping." Hakibbutz Hameuchad Archive, Section A1, Box 2, File 5.
85. See the protocols from the 13 October 1946 meeting. Hakibbutz Hameuchad Archive, Section B1, Box 1, File 31.
86. Protocols, Hashomer Hatza'ir Executive Committee Meeting, 21–22 Nov. 1945, Hashomer Hatza'ir Archive, 5.10.5. Cited by Yablonka, *Achim Zarim*, 256.

87. Yablonka, *Achim Zarim*, 196–199.
88. Ibid., 256.
89. Y. Talmon-Garber, *Yachid VecHevrah Bakibbutz: Mechkarim Sotziologiim* (Individual and society in the kibbutz: sociological studies) (Jerusalem: Magnes, 1970), 6, 37.
90. "Chronika," kibbutz diary, pt. 2, 14 February 1947, 14.
91. "Michtav Lagolah Me'et Shoshana S." (A letter to the Diaspora from Shoshana S.), kibbutz diary pt. 2, 13–14.

CHAPTER FIVE: THE KIBBUTZ IN THE DIASPORA

1. Group interview by author held at Kibbutz Netzer Sereni, 9 December 1987, with the participation of Ernst (Pize) and Hilda Simcha, Aharon Alfred Onhaus, Emanuel Shmuelevitsch, and Moshe Alter (hereafter referred to as Group interview, Netzer Sereni); Shlomo Schiff questionnaire; Manci Onhaus questionnaire; *Mi Hayah Ma'amin* (Who would have believed it?) (Netzer Sereni: Netzer Sereni Publications, 1985); Anna Adler Zweigenhaft, telephone interview by author, 4 July 1991.
2. Teller interview; Hoffman interview with author; Henia and Ya'akov Traube, interview by author, Bnei Brak, 25 February 1987.
3. Emanuel Shmuelevitsch, Alfred Aharon Onhaus, and Simcha Applebaum questionnaires.
4. Group interview, Netzer Sereni; Poznansky interview. After the founding of the State, Poznansky left for Israel, where he married and made a new life for himself.
5. Avraham Blattman, telephone interview by author, 29 December 1987.
6. K. S. Pinson, "Jewish Life in Liberated Germany," *Jewish Social Studies* 9 (1947): 101–126.
7. Bauer, Flight and Rescue, 75.
8. Genizi, *Yo'etz Umekim*, 15.
9. Brichah began in the fall of 1944 in the Vilna and Rovna areas, even prior to the arrival of Yishuv activists. For the history of the Brichah network, see Bauer, *Flight and Rescue*. Later, Brichah activists coordinated their activities with the Mossad Le'aliyah Bet. See articles about Aliyah Bet, 1934–1948, in *Idan* 1; Z. Tzahor, " 'Hamossad Le'aliyah Bet'—Mekor Hasamchut" (Mossad Le'aliya Bet—the source of its authority), *Cathedra* 39 (April 1986): 163–178.
10. Y. Gutman, *Hayehudim Bepolin Acharei Milchemet Ha'olam Hasheniah* (The Jews in Poland after World War II) (Jerusalem: Merkaz Zalman Shazar, 1985), 45–46.
11. For the influence of observant Jews on the nature of the she'erit hapletah, see J. Tydor Baumel, "The Politics of Spiritual Rehabilitation," 57–79.
12. Group interview by author at Kibbutz Shoval, 5 November 1987, with the participation of Yocheved (Schwimmer) Galil, Tovah Beinart (Gusta Ziegler), Bluma (Rosenstein) Rachaeilevitsch, Avraham (Romek) Mor, Chaim Meyers, Nomi Fried (Zosha Spokolna), and Bella (Shtaub) Meyers (hereafter referred to as Group interview, Kibbutz Shoval).
13. Ibid.
14. Traube interview.
15. Magda and Yitzchak Handler, conversation with author, 4 July 1991.
16. "They Returned from the Dead," *Cotton Baler*, 24 May 1946, 4, Netzer Sereni Archive, K4-5.

17. Rachel (Shantzer) Teller, telephone interview by author, 31 October 1990.
18. Luba Lindenbaum, interview by author, Bnei Brak, 15 February 1987.
19. Akiva Skidell, letter to his wife, Etty, 18 September 1945, Netzer Sereni Archive, K-4, 4a.
20. Group interview, Kibbutz Shoval.
21. See colloquium "Mishoah Letekumah" (From Holocaust to rebirth), *Cathedra* 55 (March 1990); Y. Weitz, "Sheelat Haplitim Hayehudim"; H. Lavsky, "She'erit Hapletah Vehakamat Hamedinah—Hizdamnut Asher Nutzlach" (The survivors of the Holocaust and the establishment of the State—an opportunity that succeeded), ibid., 175–181.
22. Rabinovitz, *Bemadei UNNRA*, 25.
23. Zweigenhaft interview.
24. Sarah (Hollander) Bar'am, interview by author, Kibbutz Na'an, 4 July 1991.
25. Pinson, "Jewish Life," 101–126.
26. D. Sha'ari, "She'erit Hapletah—its distinctive features), *Masuah* 7 (April 1979): 34.
27. Bar'am interview.
28. Geringshof diary, December 1945–July 1946, Netzer Sereni Archive, K-4-3a.
29. Ibid.
30. Blattman interview.
31. Bar'am interview.
32. These included Chativat Seridei Mizrach Eiropah (Division of Survivors from Eastern Europe), Haihud Hatzioni Hademokrati Bepolin (the Zionist-Democratic Union in Poland, which united Akiva and Hano'ar Hatzioni), and Haliga Leeretz Israel Ha'oevdet (The League for a Working Eretz Israel—Hashomer Hatza'ir and Dror).
33. Nocham was named by Jewish Brigade member Zvi Langsam (Shiloah). For the founding of Nocham and its ties to the Brigade, see Y. Ellinson, "Noham Vehabrigadah: Sugiyot Haachdut, Hareka Lamifgash Vehamifgash Beineihem Bebavariah, Mai–Detsember 1945" (Nocham and the Jewish Brigade: the question of unity and the background of their meeting in Bavaria, May–December 1945) (Seminar paper presented for the course "Hayishuv Vehashoah" [The Yishuv and the Holocaust], Tel Aviv University, June 1987), Netzer Sereni Archive, K12-3.
34. Mankowitz, "Idiologiah Upolitikah Beshe'erit Hapletah," 113–114.
35. On the unification of youth movements in Western Europe, see Mapai Secretariat Meeting, 15 May 1945, Labor Party Archive, Section 2, 24/45.
36. See C. Shatzker's remarks at the Sixth Yad Vashem International Historical Conference, in *She'erit Hapleath*, ed. Gutman and Saf 258–259. For Jewish youth movements in Germany, see idem, " 'Maccabi Hatza'ir'—Tenu'at Hano'ar Hayehudit Haacharonah Begermaniah" (Maccabi Hatza'ir—the last Jewish youth movement in Germany), in *Tenu'ot Hano'ar ba Hatzioniot Bashoah* (Zionist youth movements during the Holocaust) (Haifa: Haifa University Press and Lochamei Hagetaot, 1990), 81–103; idem, "Yichudah Shel Tenu'at Hano'ar," ibid., 7–11; idem, "The Jewish Youth Movement in Germany in the Holocaust Period," *Leo Baeck Institute Year Book* 22 (1987): 157–181, 23 (1988): 301–325.
37. Mankowitz, "Idiologiah Upolitikah," 119.
38. For the convention, see Mankowitz, ibid., 135. Statistics for Nocham

membership were cited by Y. Gelber at the Sixth Yad Vashem International Historical Conference, *She'erit Hapletah*, ed. Gutman and Saf 114–115. At that time, some 9,500 individuals belonged to chalutz movements in the American zone in Germany: 1,731 in Nocham kibbutzim and 1,643 non-kibbutz-affiliated members; 862 in Hashomer Hatza'ir kibbutzim; 446 in Betar kibbutzim; 947 in Dror kibbutzim; 327 in Po'alei Agudat Israel kibbutzim; 705 ordinary chalutzim; 853 in kibbutzim of former partisans, and 1,982 who belonged to the Zionist Organization of the DPs. See Gelber, ibid.

39. See Shapira, ibid., in *She'erit Hapletah*, ed. Gutman and Saf, 80–106.

40. Gutman, "She'erit Hapletah–The Problems, Some Elucidation," 520; Mankowitz, "Idiologiah Upolitikah," 139.

41. J. T. Baumel, "The Politics of Spiritual Rehabilitation," 57–79.

42. For the movement's founding, principles, and activity, see "Hukmah Tenu'at No'ar Chalutzit Begermaniah" (A Chalutz youth movement founded in Germany) *Basha'ar*, 2 November 1945, 2; Mankowitz, "Idiologiah Upolitikah," 144–178.

43. For the formation of the Beth Jacob movement after the war, see P. Benisch, *To Vanquish the Dragon* (Jerusalem and New York: Feldheim, 1991), 412–436; *Sefer Hayovel shel Beit Ya'akov Betel Aviv* (Tel Aviv Beth Jacob Jubilee Volume) (Tel Aviv, 1960).

44. Hoffman interview.

45. Ibid.

46. Akiva Skidell, letter to his wife, Etty, 22 September 1945, Netzer Sereni Archive, K-4, 4a.

47. Benisch, *To Vanquish the Dragon*, 430–431.

48. Group interview, Netzer Sereni.

49. Hoffman interview.

50. Akiva Skidell, letter to his wife, Etty, 24 September 1945, Netzer Sereni Archive, K-4, 4a.

51. Abramowitz, "DP's, GI's and CO's.

52. On the background to Aliyah Bet during that period and the creation of agents for ha'apalah, see M. Na'or, ed., *Idan* 1 ("Aliyah Bet: Mekorot, Sikumim, Parshiyot Nivcharot Vechomer Ezer") (Aliyah Bet: sources, summaries, episodes, and supplementary material) (Jerusalem: Yad Ben-Zvi, 1982); Tzahor, "Hamossad Le'aliyah Bet," 163–178.

53. Y. Gelber, *Sefer Hahitnadvut 3: Nosei Hadegel* (The book of volunteers 3: the standard-bearers) (Jerusalem: Yad Ben-Zvi, 1983), 641–642. See also I. Keynan, "She'erit Hapletah–Ollim o Mehagrim" (The DPs—olim or immigrants), *Iyunim Betekumat Israel* 1 (Sde Boker: Ben-Gurion University Press, 1991), 349–350.

54. Akiva Skidell, letter to his wife, Etty, 29 November 1945, Netzer Sereni Archive, K-4, 4a.

55. Geringshof diary, December 1945–July 1946, Netzer Sereni Archive, K4-3a.

56. Group interview, Netzer Sereni.

57. Group interview, Kibbutz Shoval.

58. Ibid.

59. Ibid.

60. Activity diary kept by House Two at Antwerp during preparatory period preceding embarkation on the *Tel Chai*, December 1945–March 1946, Netzer Sereni Archive, K4-3a.

61. Group interview, Kibbutz Shoval.

62. Ibid.
63. Ibid.
64. Ibid.
65. Ibid.
66. Gelber, *Sefer Hahitnadvut*, 644–645.
67. "Shorashim al Hamayim" (Roots on the water), Netzer Sereni Newsletter 1415, 4 April 1988, 4.
68. Ibid.
69. Ibid.
70. Group interview, Kibbutz Shoval.
71. Gelber, *Sefer Hahitnadvut*, 649.
72. Group interview, Netzer Sereni.
73. Group interview, Kibbutz Shoval.
74. Ibid.
75. Group interview, Netzer Sereni.
76. Group interview, Kibbutz Shoval.
77. Group interview, Netzer Sereni.
78. Bar'am interview.
79. Ibid.
80. Gavriel Rosenbaum, conversation with author, 4 July 1991.
81. Geringshof diary, December 1945–July 1946, Netzer Sereni Archive, K4-3a.
82. On the background of the arrival of emissaries from the Yishuv and the relationship that developed between them and the she'erit hapletah, see Yahil, "Pe'ulot Hamishlachat Haeretz-israelit," 7–40.
83. Geringshof diary, December 1945–July 1946, Netzer Sereni Archive, K4-3a.
84. Abramowitz, "DP's, GI's, and CO's," 45.
85. Bar'am interview.
86. *Besa'ar Beyom Sufah: Hamilchamah al Sha'arei Deganyah, Iyar Tashach, Mai 1948* (In a storm: the battle at the gates of Deganyah, May 1948) (Deganyah: Deganyah Press, 1949), 53.
87. Dolik Bergman, telephone interview by author, 31 December 1987.
88. Geringshof diary, December 1945–July 1946, Netzer Sereni Archive, K4-3a.
89. Shimon Fleishon, interview by author, Givataim, 31 December 1987.
90. Ibid.
91. Bergman interview.
92. "Bekibbutz 'Buchenwald' Begeringshof," *Nitzotz* 60 (15) (7 May 1946): 8.
93. Fleishon interview.
94. M. Na'or; ed., *Idan*, list of Aliyah Bet ships.
95. Bogner, *Iy Hagerush*, 236.
96. Gretel Tichauer, telephone interview by author, 14 December 1987.
97. Bogner, *Iy Hagerush*, 236.
98. M. Oren, *Lehatchil Acheret, Lichiot Acheret: Tenu'ot Hano'ar Bemachanot Hama'apilim Bekafrisin, 1946–1948* (To begin differently, to live differently: the youth movements at the illegal immigration camps in Cyprus, 1946–1948) (Efal: Yad Tabenkin, 1984), 124.
99. Blattman interview. For Jewish life in Germany during that period, see Genizi, *Yo'etz Umekim*, 35–104.

100. Bauer, *Flight and Rescue*, 284.
101. Bergman interview.
102. Bauer, *Flight and Rescue*, 286.
103. Author's correspondence with Gottfried Boerngraber, mayor of Neuhof (formerly Hattenof), 19 April 1988.
104. Mankowitz, "Idiologiah Upolitikah," 394.

Chapter Six: The Road to Independence

1. Resolutions adopted at general membership meeting, 31 May 1947, "Chronika" (Chronicle), Kibbutz Buchenwald diary kept at Afikim, 73.
2. Ibid.
3. Nachalat Yehudah diary, Netzer Sereni Archive, K-4, 18.
4. Kibbutz Buchenwald diary at Rishon Lezion, 7 September 1947.
5. Avraham Ahuvia, kibbutz diary at Afikim [n.d.].
6. "Shanim Rishonot Benetzer" (First years at Netzer), Netzer Sereni Newsletter 1467, 1 July 1988; Nachalat Yehudah diary, Netzer Sereni Archive, K-4, 18.
7. Nachalat Yehudah diary, Netzer Sereni Archive, K-4, 18; "Yamim Rishonim Benetzer" (First days at Netzer), Netzer Sereni Newsletter 1467, 1 July 1988.
8. Z. Tzur, *Hakibbutz Hameuchad Beyishuvah shel Haaretz* (The Kibbutz Hameuchad in the resettlement of the land), vol. 2 (1939–1945), (Efal: Yad Tabenkin, 1982), 287.
9. List of settlements founded in 1948, Netzer Sereni Archive, K-4, 14.
10. Letter from Kibbutz Buchenwald secretariat to Hakibbutz Hameuchad secretariat, Netzer Sereni Archive, K-4, 14.
11. The bodies were Kibbutz Lochamei Hagetaot, the nucleus named for Yosef Gardish, Kibbutz Buchenwald, Chatzerim, Hagar'in Habavli (Neveh Ur), Revivim, Beror Chayil, Ma'ayan Barukh, Bet Ha'emek, Malkiah, Palmach-Tzovah, Sharsheret (joined Nachsholim), and Kibbutz Efal. *Hakibbutz Hameuchad Beshnot 1947–1949* (Hakibbutz Hameuchad in the years 1947–1949) An accounting for the sixteenth convention (Efal: Yad Tabenkin, 1950), 58.
12. "Shanim Rishonot Benetzer" (see n. 6, above).
13. Ibid.
14. On this topic, see S. Maron, "Centrality of the Kibbutz Family," *Jerusalem Quarterly* 39 (1986): 73–81.
15. "Shanim Rishonot Benetzer."
16. For the background to the splits, see E. Tzur, "Bein Ichud Lepilug: Mapam Vechativoteha" (From unity to split: Mapam and its divisions) in *Hasmol Hameuchad: Darkah Hachevratit Shel Mapam Bereshit Hamedinah, 1948–1954, Kovetz Mechkarim 1* (The united Left of Israel: the social policies of Mapam during the formative years of the State, 1948–1954, Volume 1), ed. A. Margalit (Giv'at Havivah: Giv'at Haviva Publishing, 1991), 71–154; for what happened on an individual kibbutz, see Lieblich, *Kibbutz Makom.*
17. Letter from the secretary of the Public Committee for the Commemoration of Enzo Chaim Sereni to Chaim Ben-Menachem, director of the Postal Office, 5 October 1954, and Ben-Menachem's reply to the prime minister, 11 October 1954. State Archives, Box G/5436, File 1937.

18. See letter from Ben-Zion Eshel, National Names Committee, to S. Cahana, secretary to the prime minister, 31 October 1954. State Archives, G/5436, File 1437.

19. N. Alterman, "Shem Utzlilo" (A name and its ring), *Hatur Hashevi'i* (The seventh column) (Hakibbutz Hameuchad, 1972), vol. 2, 150.

20. "Netzer Sereni Law, 1954," 3 January 1955, *Divrei Haknesset*, leaflet 5, 474.

21. See Y. Weitz, "Yishuv, Golah, Shoah—Mitos Umetziut" (Yishuv, Holocaust and Diaspora—myth and reality), *Yahadut Zemanenu* 6 (1990): 133–150.

22. Announcement by the chairman of the Internal Affairs Committee on the Netzer Sereni Law, *Divrei Haknesset*, leaflet 9, 1872.

23. Kibbutz Buchenwald diary, 21 July 1945, pt. 1, 108.

24. Undated letter to members on Cyprus, Kibbutz Buchenwald diary, pt. 2, 19.

25. "Chronika," entry dated 10 March 1947, Kibbutz Buchenwald diary, pt. 2, 55.

26. "Dusiach" (Dialogue), Kibbutz Buchenwald diary, pt. 2 [n.d.], 96–97.

27. K. S. Pinson, "Jewish Life in Liberated Germany," *Jewish Social Studies* 9 (1947), 102.

CHAPTER SEVEN: KIBBUTZ BUCHENWALD IN HISTORICAL PERSPECTIVE

1. Avraham Ahuvia, Kibbutz Buchenwald diary, 21 Elul 1946 [14 September], p. 2, 1.

2. See Shlomo Drechsler (Derekh) as cited in D. Cana'ani, *Batei Midot: Masot al Chayei Shituf* (Mansions: essays on collectivism) (Merchavya: Sifriyat Hapo'alim, 1960), 22: "Every period of major social upheaval reawakens the idea of the commune as a solution for man and the world and the desire to achieve its realization."; E. Webber, *Escape to Utopia* (New York, 1959); M. Holloway, *Heavens on Earth* (New York: Dover, 1966); K. Kautsky, *Tenuot Komunistiot Biyemei Habeinaim* (Communist movements in medieval times) (Merchavia: Sifriyat Hapo'alim, 1949); H. A. Schubert, "Traditional Medieval Communities and Modern Intentional Communes—A Comparison," in *Communal Life: An International Perspective*, ed. Y. Gorni, Y. Oved, I. Paz (Efal: Yad Tabenkin, 1987), 154–158; S. Warm, *Komunot Ve'orchot Chayeyhem* (Communes and their way of life) (Tel Aviv: Aynot, 1968); Y. Oved, *Two Hundred Years of American Communes* (New Brunswick, N.J.: Transaction, 1988); B. Goodwin, *Social Science and Utopia* (Sussex: Harvester Press, 1978).

3. The role of the family within the commune is a subject of scholarly dispute. Whereas many scholars view the family as the commune's basic unit, sociologist and student of the collective phenomenon Rosebeth M. Kanter points out the unbridgeable tension between the two, arguing that in successful communes, loyalty to the nuclear family has been attenuated. Oved, *Two Hundred Years of Communes*, 22–23; R. M. Kanter, *Commitment and Community* (Cambridge, Mass.: Harvard University Press, 1972), 89–91.

4. Cana'ani, *Batei Midot*, 86–91. For a more detailed examination of the defining characteristics of the kibbutz, see J. Blassi, "Some Key Issues of Kibbutz History," in *Communal Life*, ed. Gorni et al., 232–242.

5. Among them we must note the studies of Yehudah Bauer, Nachum Bogner, Yisrael Gutman, Chaim Genizi, Leonard Dinnerstein, William Helmreich, Isaac

Wilner, Idit Zartal, Hagit Lavsky, Ze'ev Mankowitz, Abraham Peck, Irit Keynan, Leo Schwartz, and Anita Shapira. Full information appears in the Bibliography.

6. My thanks to Kenneth Stow for bringing this anthropological issue to my attention and for his help in developing this point.

7. Gruenbaum interview.

8. Yablonka, *Achim Zarim*, 181.

9. That is, they also included Romanians. After a short while, some of these settlements received reinforcements from local nucleii.

10. Yablonka, *Achim Zarim*, 184.

11. Letter from the nucleus to the Social and Cultural Department at Ma'anit, 12 April 1947, Hashomer Hatza'ir Archive, 4.20. Cited by Yablonka, *Achim Zarim*, 185.

12. Tzur, *Hakibbutz Hameuchad Beyishuvah shel Haaretz*, 322.

13. S. Knispel, "Lochamei Hagetaot: Sippur Hakibbutz" (Lochamei Hagetaot: the story of the kibbutz), seminar paper submitted to Dr. Hannah Yablonka, summer 1991. My thanks to the author for permission to read this paper. I also wish to thank Tzvika Dror, who informed me of the kibbutz's history and the struggle to choose a name. Tzvika Dror, telephone interview by author, 13 September 1992.

14. Letter from Ben-Zion Eshel, National Names Committee to the kibbutz secretariat, 5 February 1952, Kibbutz Lochamei Hagetaot Archive [unnumbered].

15. For the creation of this "elite," see W. B. Helmreich *Against All Odds: Holocaust Survivors and the Successful Lives They Made in America* (New York: Simon and Schuster, 1992).

16. See, for example, *Eidei Chayim* (Witnesses to life) (Moshav Nir Galim: Nir Galim Publishing, 1991); Z. Dror, ed., *Dapei Eidut* (Pages of Witness) (Kibbutz Lochamei Hagetaot: Ghetto Fighters House, 1991).

17. For an interesting discussion of the ways in which this decision was implemented and of the attitude of some kibbutz members toward their personal Holocaust experiences, see T. Segev, *The Seventh Million: The Israelis and the Holocaust* (New York: Hill and Wang, 1993).

18. Gruenbaum interview.

19. Poznansky interview.

20. Filmed interview with Yechezkel Tydor on the history of Kibbutz Buchenwald, from the Open University of Israel film series developed for the course "The Holocaust."

21. Berkowitz interview.

22. Traube interview.

23. Group interview, Netzer Sereni.

24. Ibid.

25. Teller interview.

26. Avraham Ahuvia, remarks at a symposium on Kibbutz Buchenwald, Kibbutz Netzer Sereni, 8 May 1985.

Bibliography

ARCHIVES

Central Zionist Archive (Jerusalem)

Aliyah Division Files. Atlit. S6-834
Aliyah Division Files. Yedi'ot. Aliyah Chadashah. S6-4246.
Meetings of the Jewish Agency Executive, 1945.

Hakibbutz Hadati Archive (Kevutzat Yavneh)

Newsletters.
Yedi'ot Hamazkirut.

Hakibbutz Hameuchad Archive (Efal)

Section 1A. Hakibbutz Hameuchad Secretariat. Correspondence.
Box 2, Files 5, 7.
Box 11, File 2.
Box 15, File 102.

Section 1B. Protocols of the Hakibbutz Hameuchad Secretariat.
Box 1, File 31.
Box 7, Files 28, 30.
Hakibbutz Hameuchad Beshnot 1947–1949. An Accounting for the Sixteenth
    Convention.

Hashomer Hatza'ir Archive (Giv'at Haviva)

Protocols. Hashomer Hatza'ir Executive Meetings.

Israel State Archives (Jerusalem)

Sharett, Moshe. Archives. Box 5436/G, File 1937.

Kibbutz Afikim Archive

Kibbutz newspaper, *Afikim*, 1945–1948.
Demographic changes in the course of 1945. Kibbutz Afikim. File K/10.

Kibbutz Lochamei Hagetaot Archive

Eshel, Ben-Zion. Letter from National Names Committee to the Kibbutz Secretariat, 5 February 1952. Unnumbered file.

Kibbutz Netzer Sereni Archive

Akiva Skidell Letters.
Activity diary. Kept by House Two at Antwerp during preparatory period preceding embarkation for Palestine on the *Tel Chai*, December 1945–March 1946. K-4, 4a.
Correspondence about Kibbutz Buchenwald, 1945. K6-4.
Kibbutz Buchenwald Diary. Parts 1, 2.
Ellinson, Y. "Nocham Vehabrigadah" (Nocham and the Jewish Brigade). Seminar paper presented for the course "Hayishuv Vehashoah." K-3, 12.
Geringshof Diary. December 1945–July 1946. K4-3a.
Nachalat Yehudah Diary. K4-18.
Netzer Sereni Newsletters. K4-2.
Correspondence. Kibbutz Netzer with Hakibbutz Hameuchad. K4-14.

Labor Party Archive (Beit Berl)

Section 2.
Protocols of Mapai Secretariat Meetings. 24/45.
Protocols of Mapai Center Meetings. 23/46.

YIVO Archive (New York)

She'erit Hapletah Collection.

INTERVIEWS

Oral History Division, Institute of Contemporary Jewry, Hebrew University, Jerusalem

Birger, Ze'ev. 34(4).
Hoter-Yishai, Aharon. 22(4)
Lavi, Yosef (Levkowitz). 37(4).

By author; transcripts in the author's possession

Ahuvia, Lola (Sultanik). Telephone interview, 19 April 1992.
Bar'am, Sarah (Hollander). Kibbutz Na'an, 4 July 1991.
Bergman, Dolik. Telephone interview, 31 December 1987.
Berkowitz, Yehudit (Itka Harash). Haifa, 22 July 1987.
Blattman, Avraham. Telephone interview, 29 December 1987.
Blumstein, Moshe. Bnei Brak, 23 February 1987.

Dror, Zvika. Telephone interview, 13 September 1992.
Fleishon, Shimon. Givataim, 31 December 1987. (Telephone interview, 14 December 1987).
Goldstein, Dov. Telephone interview, 12 May 1992.
Gruenbaum, Eliyahu. Tel Aviv, 16 December 1984.
Halamish, Aviva. Tel Aviv, 5 December 1991.
Handler, Magda and Yitzchak. Telephone interview, 4 July 1991.
Hoffman, Rivka (England). Bnei Brak, 25 October 1984.
Levi, Aliya (Evyasaf). Tel Aviv, 17 July 1991.
Lindenbaum, Luba (England). Bnei Brak, 15 February 1987.
Pozanansky, Arthur. Yad Eliyahu, 29 November 1984.
Rosenbaum, Gavriel. Telephone interview, 4 July 1991.
Schacter, Rabbi Herschel. New York, 24 July 1985.
Teller, Rachel (Shantzer). Tel Aviv, 11 January 1987.
Tichauer, Gretel. Telephone interview, 14 December 1987.
Traube, Henia and Yaakov. Bnei Brak, 25 February 1987.
Tydor, Yechezkel. Jerusalem, 30 March 1983; Ramat Gan, 4 June 1983.
Utitz, Ze'ev. Tel Aviv, 24 May 1992.
Ya'ari, Moshe. Telephone interview, 12 May 1992.
Zweigenhaft, Anna (Adler). Telephone interview, 4 July 1991.

GROUP INTERVIEWS

Kibbutz Shoval, 5 November 1987. Participants: Tova Beinart, Nomi Fried, Yocheved Galil, Bella Meyers, Chaim Meyers, Avraham Mor, Bluma Rachaeilevitsch.
Kibbutz Netzer Sereni, 9 December 1987. Participants: Moshe Alter, Oni Onhaus, Emanuel Shmuelevitsch, Azriel Simcha, Hilda Simach.

QUESTIONNAIRES

Ahuvia, Avraham	Netzer Sereni	Lerner Yisrael	Netzer Sereni
Ahuvia, Lola	Netzer Sereni	Ne'eman, Shlomo	Netzer Sereni
Alter, Moshe	Netzer Sereni	Offner, Eliyahu	Netzer Sereni
Alter, Yehudit	Netzer Sereni	Onhaus, Aharon Alfred	Netzer Sereni
Angel, Aryeh	Netzer Sereni	Onhaus, Manci	Netzer Sereni
Applebaum, Naomi	Netzer Sereni	Schiff, Shlomo	Netzer Sereni
Applebaum, Simcha	Netzer Sereni	Shmuelevitsch, Emanuel	Netzer Sereni
Forscher, Esther	Netzer Sereni	Sibersky, Nomi	Netzer Sereni
Ginzberg, Miriam	Netzer Sereni	Wasserman, Rita	Netzer Sereni
Ginzberg, Mordekhai	Netzer Sereni	Yuskowitz, Chava	Netzer Sereni
Glick, Alfred Yisrael	Herzliya	Yuskowitz, Shmuel	Netzer Sereni
Katzke, Aharon	Netzer Sereni	Zucker, Meir	Netzer Sereni
Landgarten, Zvi	Netzer Sereni		

NEWSPAPERS, 1945–1948

Davar
Ha'aretz
Hatzofeh

WORKS CITED

Abramowitz, M. "DPs, GI's and CO's: Working Undercover in Postwar Europe." *Moment* (April 1982): 44–48.

Ahuvia, Avraham. Personal Diary.

Avigur, S. "Lesikumo Shel Mifal Haha'apala" (Aliyah Bet—summation). In M. Naor, editor, *Idan* 1 (Aliyah Bet, 1934–1948): 170–181.

Avizohar, M. *Berei Saduk: Idialim Chevratiim Uleumiim Vehishtakfutam Be'olamah shel Mapai—1930–1942* (National and social ideals as reflected in Mapai—1930–1942). Tel Aviv: Am Oved, 1990.

Avizohar, M. "Bikkur Ben-Gurion Bemachanot Ha'akurim Vetefisato Haleumit Betom Milchemet Ha'olam Hasheniah" (Ben Gurion's visit to the DP camps and his national outlook in the aftermath of World War II). In *Yahadut Mizrach Eiropah Bein Shoah Letekuma 1944–1948* (Eastern European Jewry from Holocaust to redemption, 1944–1948), edited by B. Pinkus, 253–270. Sde Boker: Ben-Gurion University, 1987.

Bauer, Y. *Flight and Rescue: Brichah.* New York: Random House, 1970.

———. "The Initial Organization of the Holocaust Survivors in Bavaria." *Yad VaShem Studies* 8 (1970): 127–157.

———. "Mitz'adei Hamavet" (The death marches, January–May 1945). *Yahadut Zemanenu* 1 (1981): 199–221.

Baumel, J. Tydor. *Kol Bechiyot: Hashoah Vehatefilah* (A voice of lament: the Holocaust and prayer). Ramat Gan: Bar-Ilan University Press, 1992.

———. "The Politics of Spiritual Rehabilitation in the D.P. Camps." *Simon Wiesenthal Center Annual* 6 (1989): 57–80.

"Bekibbutz 'Buchenwald' Begeringshof." *Nitzotz* 60 (15), 7 May 1946.

Benisch, P. *To Vanquish the Dragon.* Jerusalem and New York: Feldheim, 1991.

Besa'ar Beyom Sufah: Hamilchamah al Sha'arei Deganyah, Iyar Tashach, Mai 1948 (In a storm: the battle at the gates of Deganyah, May 1948). Deganyah: Deganyah Press, 1949.

Blassi, J. "Some Key Issues of Kibbutz History." *Communal Life: An International Perspective,* edited by Y. Gorni, Y. Oved, and I. Paz, 232–242. Efal: Yad Tabenkin, 1987.

Bogner, N. *Iy Hagerush: Machanot Hama'apilim Bekafrisin, 1946–1948* (The deportation island: Jewish illegal immigrant camps on Cyprus, 1946–1948). Tel Aviv: Am Oved, 1991.

Cana'ani, D. *Batei Midot: Masot al Chayei Shituf* (Essays on collectivism). Merchavya: Sifriyat Hapo'alim, 1960.

Dinnerstein, L. *America and the Survivors of the Holocaust.* New York: Columbia University Press, 1982.

Don-Yichya, A. "Mamlachtiyut Veshoah" (Statehood and the Holocaust). In *Bishvilei Hatechiyah* (On the roads to rebirth), edited by A. Rubinstein, 167–188. Ramat Gan: Bar-Ilan University Press, 1983.

Dror, Zvika. *Dapei Eidut* (Pages of witness). Kibbutz Lochamei Hagetaot: Ghetto Fighters House, 1990.

Eidei Chayyim (Witnesses to life). Moshav Nir Galim: Nir Galim Publishing, 1991.

Eliach, Y., and B. Gurewitsch. *The Liberators: Eyewitness Accounts of the Liberation of Concentration Camps.* New York: Institute of Holocaust Research, 1981.

Eliasi, O. "Mibuchenwald Ve'ad Netzer Sereni" (From Buchenwald to Netzer Sereni). Seminar paper, Y. H. Brenner Comprehensive High School, 1982.

Friesel, E. "Churban Yehudei Eiropah—Gorem Behakamat Medinat Israel?" (The destruction of European Jewry—a factor in the creation of the State of Israel?). *Molad* 250 (1980): 21–31.

Gelber, Y. "Partners and Adversaries: Jewish Survivors of World War II the Jewish Agency, and Britain." In *Vision and Conflict in the Holy Land*, edited by R. I. Cohen, 274–308. Jerusalem: Yad Ben-Zvi, 1985.

Gelber, Y. *Sefer Hahitnadvut 3: Nosei Hadegel* (The book of volunteers 3: the standard bearers). Jerusalem: Yad Ben-Zvi, 1973.

Genizi, H. *Yo'etz Umekim: Hayo'etz Latzava Haamerikani Veleshe'erit Hapletah, 1945–1949* (The advisor on Jewish affairs to the American army and the Displaced Persons, 1945–1949). Tel Aviv: Sifriyat Hapo'alim, 1987.

Goodwin, B. *Social Science and Utopia.* Sussex: Harvester Press, 1978.

Grobman, A. "The American Jewish Chaplains and the Remnants of European Jewry, 1944–1948." Ph.D. diss., Hebrew University, Jerusalem, 1981.

Grobman, A. "American Jewish Chaplains and the Shearit Hapletah, April–June 1945." *Simon Wiesenthal Center Annual* 1 (1984): 89–111.

Gutman, Y. *Hayehudim Bepolin Acharei Milchemet Ha'olam Hasheniah* (The Jews in Poland after World War II). Jerusalem: Mercaz Zalman Shazar, 1985.

Gutman, Y., and A. Saf. *She'erit Hapletah 1944–1948: Rehabilitation and Political Struggle.* Jerusalem: Yad Vashem, 1990.

Gutman, Y. "She'erit Hapletah—The Problems, Some Elucidation." In *She'erit Hapletah, 1944–1948: Rehabilitation and Political Struggle*, edited by Y. Gutman and A. Saf, 509–530. Jerusalem: Yad Vashem, 1990.

Halamish, A. "Illegal Immigration: Values, Myth and Reality." *Studies in Zionism* 9 (1988): 47–62.

Heller, J. *Bema'avak Limedinah: Hamediniut Hazionit, 1936–1948* (The struggle for the Jewish State: Zionist politics, 1936–1948). Jerusalem: Mercaz Zalman Shazar, 1984.

Helmreich, W. B. *Against All Odds: Holocaust Survivors and the Successful Lives They Made in America.* New York: Simon and Schuster, 1992.

Holloway, M. *Heavens on Earth.* New York: Dover Publications, 1966.

Kanter, R. M. *Committment and Community.* Cambridge, Mass.: Harvard University Press, 1972.

Katzburg, N. *Mediniut Bemavoch: Mediniut Britaniah Beeretz Israel, 1940–1945* (Policy in a labyrinth: British policy in Palestine, 1940–1945). Jerusalem: Yad Ben-Zvi, 1977.

Kautsky, K. *Tenu'ot Komunistiot Beyemei Habeinaim* (Communist movements in medieval times). Merchavya: Sifriyat Hapo'alim, 1949.

Keynan, I. "Bein Tikvah Lecharadah: Tadmit She'erit Hapletah Be'einei Hashlichim Haeretz-israeliim Lemachanot Ha'akurim Begermaniah, 1945" (From hope to fear: the image of the survivors in the eyes of Palestinian emissaries to the German DP camps, 1945). In *Ha'apala: Studies in the History of Illegal Immigration into Palestine, 1934–1948*, edited by A. Shapira, 221–229. Tel Aviv: Am Oved University Press, 1990.

———. "The Yishuv's Mission to the Displaced Persons Camps in Germany: The Initial Steps, August 1945–May 1946." In *She'erit Hapletah, 1944–1948: Rehabilitation and Political Struggle*, edited by Y. Gutman and A. Saf, 231–248. Jerusalem: Yad Vashem, 1990.

————. "She'erit Hapletah: Olim o Mehagrim" (The DPs—olim or immigrants). *Iyunim Betekumat Yisrael* 1, 343–358. Sde Boker: Ben-Gurion University Press, 1991.

Knispel, S. "Lochamei Hagetaot: Sippur Hakibbutz" (Lochamei Hagetaot: the story of the kibbutz). Seminar paper submitted to Dr. Hannah Yablonka, Ben-Gurion University, summer 1991.

Krakowski, S. "Machanot Hanatzim Beaviv 1945—Pinui, Tza'adot Hamavet Haachronot, Shichrur" (Nazi camps—spring 1945: evacuation, last death marches, liberation). *Dappim Lecheker Tekufat Hashoah* 4 (1986): 179–192.

Krona, M. *Morai Verabotai, Achai Vere'ai* (My teachers, My friends). Tel Aviv: Moreshet, 1987.

Langer, L. L. *Holocaust Testimonies: The Ruins of Memory*. New Haven and London: Yale University Press, 1991.

Lavsky, H. "She'erit Hapletah Vehakamat Hamedinah—Hizdamnut Asher Nutzlah" (The survivors of the Holocaust and the establishment of the state of Israel). *Cathedra* 55 (March 1990): 175–181.

Levin, D. *Bein Nitzotz Leshalhevet* (Caught between spark and flame). Ramat Gan: Bar-Ilan University Press, 1987.

Lieblich, A. *Kibbutz Makom* (Kibbutz Anywhere). Jerusalem: Schocken, 1986.

Mankowitz, Z. "Idiologiah Upolitikah Beshe'erit Hapletah Beezor Hakibbush Haamerikai Begermaniah, 1945–1946" (The politics and ideology of survivors of the Holocaust in the American zone of Occupied Germany, 1945–1946). Ph.D. diss., Hebrew University, Jerusalem, 1987.

Mankowitz, Z. "Zionism and She'erit Hapletah." In *She'erit Hapletah, 1944–1948: Rehabilitation and Political Struggle*, edited by Y. Gutman and A. Saf, 211–230. Jerusalem: Yad Vashem, 1990.

Maron, S. "Centrality of the Kibbutz Family." *The Jerusalem Quarterly* 39 (1986): 73–81.

Mi Hayah Ma'amin? (Who would have believed it?). Netzer Sereni: Netzer Sereni Publications, 1985.

Naor, M., ed. *Idan* 1 ("Aliyah Bet: Mekorot, Sikumim, Parshiot Nivcharot Vechomer Ezer") (Aliyah Bet: sources, episodes, and supplementary material). Jerusalem: Yad Ben-Zvi, 1982.

Nir, H. *Hakibbutz Vehachevrah, 1923–1933* (Kibbutz and society, 1923–1933). Jerusalem: Yad Ben-Zvi, 1984.

Ofer, D. "From Survivors to New Immigrants: She'erit Hapletah and Aliyah." *She'erit Hapletah, 1944–1948: Rehabilitation and Political Struggle*, edited by Y. Gutman and A. Saf, 304–336. Jerusalem: Yad Vashem, 1990.

Oppenheim, I. *Tenu'at Hechalutz Bepolin (1917–1929)* (The Hechalutz movement in Poland [1917–1929]). Jerusalem: Magnes, 1982.

Oren, M. *Lehatchil Acheret, Lichiot Acheret: Tenu'ot Hano'ar Bemachanot Hama'apilim Bekafrisin, 1946–1948* (To begin differently, to live differently: the youth movements at the illegal immigration camps in Cyprus, 1946–1948). Efal: Yad Tabenkin, 1984.

Oved, Y. *Two Hundred Years of American Communes*. New Brunswick, N.J.: Transaction Publishers, 1988.

Peck, A. "An Introduction to the Social History of the Jewish Displaced Persons' Camps: The Lost Legacy of the She'erith Hapletah." *Proceedings of the Eighth World Congress of Jewish Studies, Division B*, 187–196. Jerusalem, 1982.

Pinson, K. S. "Jewish Life in Liberated Germany." *Jewish Social Studies* 9 (1947): 101–126.

Porat, D. "The Role of European Jewry in the Plans of the Zionist Movement During World War II and in Its Aftermath." *She'erit Hapletah, 1944–1948: Rehabilitation and Political Struggle*, edited by Y. Gutman and A. Saf, 286–303. Jerusalem: Yad Vashem, 1990.

———" 'Beslichah Ubechesed': Hamifgash bein Ruzka Korchak Levein Hayishuv Umanhigav" (With loving forgiveness: the meeting between Ruzka Korchak-Marla, the Yishuv, and its leaders). *Yalkut Moreshet* 52 (April 1992): 9–33.

Proudfoot, M. *European Refugees, 1932–1952*. Evanston, Ill.: Northwestern University Press, 1956.

Rabinovitz, E. *Bemadei UNNRA im She'erit Hapletah, 1946–1948* (Emissary for UNNRA with Jewish Displaced Persons). Tel Aviv: Sifriyat Hapo'alim, 1990.

Schubert, H. A. "Traditional Medieval Communites and Modern Intentional Communes—A Comparison." In *Communal Life: An International Perspective*, edited by Y. Gorni, Y. Oved, I. Paz, 154–158. Efal and New Brunswick, N. J.: Yad Tabenkin and Rutgers University Press, 1987.

Sefer Hayovel Shel Beit Ya'akov Betel Aviv (Tel Aviv Beth Jacob Jubilee Volume). Tel Aviv, 1960.

Segev, T. *The Seventh Million: The Israelis and the Holocaust*. New York: Hill and Wang, 1993.

Sha'ari, D. "She'erit Hapletah—Kavei Yichud" (She'erit Hapletah—its distinctive features). *Masuah* 7 (April 1979): 20–44.

Shapira, A. *Hahalichah al Kav Haofek* (Walking on the horizon). Tel Aviv: Am Oved, 1989.

Shapira, A. "The Yishuv's Encounter with the Survivors of the Holocaust." In *She'erit Hapletah, 1944–1948: Rehabilitation and Political Struggle*, edited by Y. Gutman and A. Saf, 80–106. Jerusalem: Yad Vashem, 1990.

Shatzker, C. "The Jewish Youth Movement in Germany in the Holocaust Period." *Leo Baeck Institute Year Book* 22 (1987): 157–181; 23 (1988): 301–325.

———. "Yichuda shel Tenu'at Hano'ar" (The uniqueness of the youth movements). In *Tenu'ot Hano'ar Hazioniot Bashoah*) (Zionist youth movements during the Holocaust), 5–11. Haifa: Haifa University Press and Ghetto Fighters' House, 1989.

———. " 'Maccabi Hatza'ir'—Tenu'at Hano'ar Hayehudit Haachronah Begermaniah" (Maccabi Hatza'ir—the last Jewish youth movement in Germany). In *Tenu'ot Hano'ar Hatzioniot Bashoah*, 81–103. Haifa: Haifa University Press and Ghetto Fighters' House, 1989.

"Shorashim al Hamayim" (Roots on the water). *Alon Netzer Sereni* 1415, April 1988, 4.

Skidell, A. "Im Hatzava Ha'amerikani Begermaniah Hakvushah" (With the American army in occupied Germany). *Yalkut Moreshet* 30 (November 1980): 157–169).

Talmon-Garber, Y. *Yachid Vechevrah Bakibbutz: Mechkarim Sotziologiim* (Individual and society in the kibbutz: sociological studies). Jerusalem: Magnes, 1970.

Tzahor, Z. " 'Hamossad Le'aliyah Bet'—Mekor Hasamchut" ("Mossad Le'aliyah Bet"—the source of its authority). *Cathedra* 39 (April 1986): 163–178.

Tzur, E. "Bein Ichud Lepilug: Mapam Vechativoteha" (From unity to split: Mapam and its divisions). In *Hasmol Hameuchad: Darkah Hachevratit Shel Mapam Bereshit Hamedinah, 1948–1954, Kovetz Mechkarim* 1 (The united Left: the societal direction of Mapam at the beginning of the State, 1948–1954, vol. 1) edited by A. Margalit, 71–154. Giv'at Haviva: Giv'at Haviva Publishing, 1991.

Tzur, Z. *Hakibbutz Hameuchad Beyishuvah shel Haaretz* (The Kibbutz Hameuchad in the settlement of Eretz Israel), vol. 2, 1939–1945. Efal: Yad Tabenkin, 1982.

Warm, S. *Komunot Veorchot Chayeyhem* (Communes and ways of life). Tel Aviv: Aynot, 1968.

Wasserstein, B. *Britain and the Jews of Europe, 1939–1945*. London: Institute of Jewish Affairs, 1979.

Webber, E. *Escape to Utopia*. New York, 1959.

Weitz, Y. "Emdot Vegishot Bemifleget Po'alei Eretz Israel Kelapei Shoat Yehudei Eiropah, 1939–1945" (The attitude of Mapai toward the destruction of European Jewry). Ph.D. diss., Hebrew University, Jerusalem, 1987.

———. "Hama'avak al Demut 'Hechalutz' Betenu'at Ha'avodah Beretz Israel, 1933–1945" (Hechalutz's struggle for its identity within the Palestine Labor Party). *Dappim Lecheker Tekufat Hashoah* 7 (1989): 149–150.

———. "Hatenu'ah Hatzionit Nochach She'erit Hapletah Beshilhei Milchemet Ha'olam Hasheniah" (The Zionist movement facing the she'erit hapletah at the end of World War II). *Dappim Lecheker Tekufat Hashoah* 3 (1984): 139–158.

———. "Hayishuv Veshe'erit Hapletah, 1944–1945" (The Yishuv and the she'erit hapletah, 1944–1945). Master's thesis, Hebrew University, Jerusalem, 1981.

———. "Reshit Hakesher Bein Chayalei Habrigadah Levein She'erit Hapletah" (First contacts between the soldiers of the Jewish Brigade and the Jewish survivors). *Yahadut Zemanenu* 3 (1986): 227–247.

———. "She'elat Haplitim Hayehudim Bemediniut Hatzionit"(The DP question in Zionist policy). *Cathedra* 55 (March 1990): 162–174.

———. "She'erit Hapletah Bediuneihem Veshikuleihem shel Chavrei Hanhalat Hasochnut Mimai 1945 ve'ad November 1945" (She'erit hapletah in the deliberations of the Jewish Agency leadership, May 1945–November 1945). *Yalkut Moreshet* 29 (May 1980): 53–80.

———. "Yishuv, Golah, Shoah—Mitos Umetziut" (Yishuv, Diaspora, and Holocaust—myth and reality). *Yahadut Zemanenu* 6 (1990): 133–150.

Wilner, I. "Foehrenwald—Machaneh Akurim Yehudi Acharon Begermaniah, 1951–1957" (Foehrenwald—the last DP camp in Germany, 1951–1957). Master's thesis, Bar-Ilan University, Ramat Gan, 1988.

Wilson, F. M. *Aftermath*. West Drayton, England: Penguin, 1947.

Yablonka, H. *Achim Zarim: Nitzolei Hashoah Bemedinat Israel 1948–1952* (Foreign brethren: Holocaust survivors in the State of Israel 1948–1952). Jerusalem: Yad Izhak Ben-Zvi Press and Ben-Gurion University of the Negev Press, 1994.

Yahil, H. "Pe'ulot Hamishlachat Haeretz-israelit Leshe'erit Hapletah, 1945–1949" (The Palestine delegation to the she'erit hapletah: its activities, 1945–1949). *Yalkut Moreshet* 30 (November 1980): 7–40; 31 (April 1981): 133–176.

Yerushalmi, Y. H. *Zakhor: Jewish History and Jewish Memory*. Philadelphia: Jewish Publication Society, 1982.

Zweig, R. "Hamediniut Habritit Legabei Aliyah Leeretz Israel Betekufat Hashoah—

Shelav Acharon" (British policy on immigration to Palestine during the Holocaust—the last stage). *Zionism* 8 (1983): 195–243.

MISCELLANEOUS

Correspondence between the author and Yisrael Chofesh, director of the Kibbutz Afikim Archive.

Correspondence between the author and Gottfried Boerngraber, mayor of Neuhof (formerly Hattenhof), 19 April 1988. Divrei Haknesset (Official record of Israeli parliament).

Nedudei She'erit Hapletah. A film with Isaac Wilner. An Open University of Israel production for the course "The Holocaust." Open University, 1983–1992.

Symposium held at Netzer Sereni on 8 May 1985 to mark the fortieth anniversary of the liberation of the Buchenwald Camp and Kibbutz Buchenwald's founding. Participants: Avraham Ahuvia, Eliyahu Gruenbaum, Yechezkel Tydor.

Filmed interview with Yechezkel Tydor on the the history of Kibbutz Buchenwald. From a film series developed by the Open University of Israel for the course "The Holocaust." Open University 1983–1992.

Index

About the Author

Judith Tydor Baumel is a lecturer at the Department of Jewish History at the University of Haifa and specializes in twentieth-century Jewish history with special emphasis on Holocaust, women's studies, and historical memory. She is the author of numerous articles on these subjects and has written several books on the Holocaust. *Unfulfilled Promise* examined the rescue and resettlement of Jewish refugee children in the United States during the Holocaust; *A Voice of Lament: The Holocaust and Prayer* (in Hebrew) explored the connection between Holocaust and liturgy. She is now working on a study of the historical roots of the militant Jewish Right in the United States through an examination of the history of the Bergson Group during the 1940s.

Born in New York in 1959, Dr. Baumel moved with her family in 1974 to Israel, where she completed her studies. She is married and the mother of two daughters.